ROMAN ART IN THE PRIVATE SPHERE

ROMAN ART IN THE PRIVATE SPHERE

New Perspectives on the Architecture
and Decor of the
Domus, Villa, and Insula

Edited by Elaine K. Gazda

Assisted by Anne E. Haeckl

Ann Arbor
THE UNIVERSITY OF MICHIGAN PRESS

10-27-92

1994   1993   1992   1991   4   3   2   1

Library of Congress Cataloging-in-Publication Data

Roman art in the private sphere : new perspectives on the architecture
and decor of the domus, villa, and insula / edited by Elaine K.
Gazda ; assisted by Anne E. Haeckl.
    p.   cm.
    Substantially enlarged and revised papers originally presented at
the meeting of the College Art Association of American in Boston in
Feb. 1987.
    Includes bibliographical references and index.
    Contents: Introduction / Elaine K. Gazda — The Pompeian atrium
house in theory and in practice / by Eugene Dwyer — Painted
perspectives of a villa visit : landscape as status and metaphor /
by Bettina Bergmann — Sculptural collecting and display in the
private realm / by Elizabeth Bartman — The decor of the house of
Jupiter and Ganymede at Ostia Antica : private residence turned gay
hotel? / by John R. Clarke — Signs of privilege and pleasure :
Roman domestic mosaics / by Christine Kondoleon — Power,
architecture, and decor : how the late Roman aristocrat appeared to
his guests / by Simon P. Ellis.
    ISBN 0-472-10196-X (alk. paper)
    1. Art, Roman. 2. Interior architecture—Rome. 3. Interior
decoration—Rome. 4. Dwellings—Rome. I. Gazda, Elaine K., 1943– .
II. Haeckl, Anne E.
N5760.R66   1991
747.2937—dc20   90-20766
                                                          CIP

In memory of Kathleen J. Shelton

Acknowledgments

This book is based on a conference session by the same title that I chaired at the annual meeting of the College Art Association of America in Boston in February 1987. All the essays have been substantially enlarged and revised, and some have been completely rewritten to embrace the broader issues addressed by the book. I am very grateful to Jeffrey Muller of Brown University for asking me to organize the session and to all of the participants for agreeing to publish their work in this form.

I am also grateful to John D'Arms, Miranda Marvin, and John Humphrey for reading various parts of the manuscript and providing much helpful advice and bibliography. Any omissions or errors are, of course, my own responsibility. I also want to thank Colin Day, director of the University of Michigan Press, for inviting me to submit the manuscript, and my husband, James McIntosh, for lending moral support and encouragement.

In attempting to view the subject from the perspective of past and current developments in Roman art, I was aided greatly by research assistants at the University of Michigan. Anne Haeckl, Karen Ros, Molly Lindner, and Andrew Kosak helped me track down bibliography and sift through it for relevant work. Diane Atnally Conlin prepared the final text of the bibliography. During the course of editing the essays and writing the introduction, Anne Haeckl was an invaluable collaborator without whose help this book could not have been completed.

Contents

Introduction

Elaine K. Gazda

In his essay of 1969, "Roman Art in Modern Perspective," Otto Brendel urged that the future direction of research on Roman art take greater note of art made for private contexts:

> Obviously the task now before us will be, in a critique of Roman art as a whole, to restore the balance which must have once existed between the public and the private sector.[1]

Behind Brendel's statement lies a basic fact of the study of Roman art—that the official art and architecture of the Roman state dominates our perception of Roman artistic achievement.[2] Twenty years later, though much progress has been made in understanding the diversity and range of Roman works, that fact remains essentially unaltered. Emphasis on the study of public monuments understandably continues, given that they express the collective ideas and achievements of the Roman people through the commemoration of major historic events, public religious rites, and imperial policies and personages. Moreover, many of the great state monuments were designed by the best artists in the realm. Often datable and better documented than private works, Roman public monuments will continue to provide a chronological armature for the field of Roman art history as a whole. But when it comes to the world of the private citizen and other private individuals, these monuments are limited in what they reveal.

It is to works of the private sphere that we must turn for forms and images that express the personal beliefs, tastes, and self-perceptions of the Romans. These are the works that help to define the individual Roman's place in the world. A vast number of Roman artistic and architectural remains were fabricated for funerary, votive, domestic, and commercial purposes by artists and craftsmen working all over the Empire in a wide range of styles and techniques. According to Brendel, "Not only is the private sector of Roman art the more numerous by far; it also is the one more varied. For its spread and, indeed, for its very existence it must be held an essential—not merely marginal—factor of the cultural life in ancient Rome."[3] Clearly, works of this kind must take their proper place in a balanced assessment of the development and meaning of Roman art.

In taking up this challenge, one finds that many problems inherent in the study of Roman art as a whole are intensified for Roman art of the private sphere. One problem is posed by the scant documentation available to the student of art created outside the purview of official Rome. Official art can be studied in relation to the historical record and can be associated with specific imperial patrons and their policies. Works made for private settings can only rarely be connected with persons or patrons about whom something more than a name is known. This is even true of the majority of works from as well-preserved a site as Pompeii, and of works that have no comparable archaeological contexts or records even less can be said about the original circumstances for which they were made. Partly as a result of these difficulties, the question of what this art meant to its Roman patrons and viewers is not easily addressed.

The pattern of scholarship presents another difficulty. Research has centered on questions of chronology, typology, style, technique, and iconography, often without a thorough consideration of the original location or social context. Moreover, media and monument or object types tend to be studied separately and are seldom discussed in relation to one another as part of a larger whole.[4] For example, monuments of private art such as sarcophagi, wall paintings, and mosaics have been investigated largely for their utility in sorting out stylistic developments and chronological sequences. Such studies, though fundamental to all archaeological and art historical research, often fail to address questions about the meaning of private art to its Roman patrons and the function of private art in its specific settings. To address such questions it is necessary to take a more integrated approach that associates the works with their social (and, when possible, archaeological) context.

A third significant impediment to the study of Roman private art as a product of its own time and place is a stubborn prejudice that informs the scholarly tradition in Roman art in general. There is a persistent tendency to assume that Roman art lacked originality, that it was largely derivative of Greek art. According to this view, all or most Roman art—including building types and architectural decoration, sculptural ornament on sarcophagi, funerary altars and urns, votive bronzes, ideal sculpture for gardens, floor mosaics, wall paintings, and *Kleinkunst*—is based on masterful monuments of the Greeks that the Romans profusely admired and diligently copied. Roman art seen from the Helleno-centric point of view supplies a mine of evidence, however imperfect, for reconstructing lost Greek masterpieces that the Roman works are presumed to imitate.[5] Certainly it is true that much Roman art draws heavily upon Greek models. But by insisting that the relationship between Roman art and Greek models was one of slavish dependence on the part of the Roman artist, scholars for many years stifled inquiry into how the Romans actually perceived Greek art and how they integrated what they borrowed—or were inspired by—into their own cultural context in a meaningful, even original, way. In the realm of private art the problem has been compounded by the perception that Roman works are of lower quality than their Greek counterparts. This view both fails to take into account the many Roman works of art that are of excellent quality and ignores the fact that different artistic traditions, not all of them Hellenic, contributed to developments of style and technique during the Roman period.[6]

It is an assumption underlying this volume of essays that a specifically Roman purpose and meaning can be discovered in the private art produced and enjoyed by the Romans. This assumption is fundamental to all studies of Roman state monuments, but it has been slow to penetrate research on the art of the private sphere. There is, however, a growing body of literature that sees Roman private art as a valid and unique expression of Roman cultural and social values. Art historians, supported by the work of social historians, have begun to interpret works of the private realm in light of their patrons' requirements and social circumstances.[7]

Among the monuments and objects made for private settings, those we identify as funerary lend themselves most readily to such contextual interpretation. They are clearly associated with specifically Roman beliefs, burial practices, and commemorative conventions and often are inscribed with the names of their owners along with indications of the owners' social status. Scholars have increasingly taken this information into account in assessing the significance that these private works originally possessed.[8] Works of votive art that were commissioned, created, and dedicated in the private sphere represent another class of objects ripe for study from this perspective. The traditionally held view that Roman art is merely decorative and derivative is more deeply ingrained in what we identify as domestic art. Though recent scholarship has made progress here as well, in relation to Roman private art as a whole, the domestic sphere would seem to be in greatest need of reassessment.[9]

In the past decade or two many new insights have been gained in understanding funerary, votive, and domestic works as products of their own Roman contexts. Unfortunately, these insights have for the most part escaped the notice of all but a small number of specialists. Publications are scattered in various scholarly journals and are difficult to integrate into a coherent picture. Partly for that reason they have not yet been incorporated into a more balanced overall assessment of Roman art. While it is premature to attempt such a reevaluation of the field as a whole, this is an opportune moment to focus more sharply on recent and current research on works of the private domain.

The recently published volume *A History of Private Life: I. From Rome to Byzantium*, edited by P. Veyne, provides a tangible sign of the current high level of interest in the private sphere in Roman studies in general. Its treatment of art in the context of Roman private life, however, is disappointing. References to works of art are largely relegated to illustrations whose captions too often reveal only a superficial acquaintance with the objects and the issues they raise. Although a valuable chapter by Yvon Thébert deals substantively with the Roman house, its specialized focus is limited to one province in one period, North Africa in the imperial era.[10] The relative lack of attention to art in a book that purports to present the topic of private life in Roman antiquity to a broad audience underscores the need for a discussion such as the one offered collectively by the essays in the present volume.

In response to the need to reassess the art of the domestic realm, the essays in this volume focus on the architecture and decor associated with wealthy Roman residences and related private establishments. They range temporally from the late Republic to the late Empire and geographically from Italy to the provinces, and they encompass the major architectural forms (*domus*, villa, and *insula*) and modes of decoration (wall painting, sculpture, and mosaic). Though each essay addresses a specific topic, they are mutually complementary and, as a group, convey a clear sense of the common concerns of patrons and artists in creating appropriate settings for the private lives of the affluent.[11]

In a discussion of the world of the well-to-do Roman residence, the term *private* needs to be understood with a different nuance from our customary sense of its meaning. It is important to remind ourselves that the modern conception of private life would have been foreign to the ancients. Indeed, some historians claim that private life as we know it did not exist for the Romans before the advent of Christianity.[12] The *familia* included not only immediate family members and other blood relations, but many persons who had no such connection at all, such as slaves, freedmen, philosophers, and teachers.[13] Moreover, the responsibilities of men of high station were such that their private homes provided for many functions that today we would consider to be decidedly public.[14] Perhaps in viewing the realm of private art as a whole, it is possible to make a clear distinction between private and public. Brendel, for example, believed "that in Roman art, as in Roman juridical thought, a fundamental division existed between a *res publica* and a *res privata.*"[15] But in relation to the wealthy Roman residence and its household such a distinction is less clear-cut. The degree of distinction between private and public depends to some extent on the kind of residence in question—for example, urban town house and apartment or suburban villa. The social obligations an owner had in each place differed considerably, and the nature of the distinction between public and private differed correspondingly.[16] In the case of transient residences, such as hotels, we must account for yet another set of factors in defining the term *private.*

For the relationship between private and public in the town house setting we can rely on the ancient authority of Vitruvius, who is perhaps the most clearly prescriptive of Roman authors on how houses must accommodate the wide range of social requirements of their owners. What he claims for the Romans of Italy in the Augustan Age apparently held true throughout the Empire until late antiquity.[17] Thébert, mindful of Vitruvius, recently characterized the design and decoration of well-to-do town houses of Roman Africa in words that might be applied to all such Roman establishments:

> The design of individual rooms and the overall organization of a building, taken together, emphasized the power of its owner and provided a prestigious background against which he played his assigned social role. Not until the Renaissance do we find in Western cities such a large number of private homes so clearly designed to allow their owners to live luxuriously while meeting the obligations incumbent upon men of high rank.
>
> The significance of the surroundings is emphasized by the decor. . . . Vitruvius emphasizes that a room's decor must be adapted to its purpose; he might well have added that its sumptuousness must be strictly in keeping with the importance of the room.[18]

The point is simply this: From what we know of such establishments, we cannot assume that Roman domestic art and architecture were things entirely removed from the public arena and therefore devoid of significance to an audience beyond the immediate *familia.* A passage from Cicero's *De oratore* (3.33.133) illustrates that Roman men of influence were traditionally treated as public figures whether they were at home or in the forum:

> . . . We have actually seen Manius Manilius walking across the forum, and the remarkable thing was that in doing this he was putting his wisdom at the service of all his fellow-citizens; and in the old

days persons resorted to these men both when they were going for
a walk as described and when seated in their chairs of state at home,
not only to consult them on points of law but also about marrying off
a daughter, buying a farm, tilling their estates, and in short every
sort of liability or business.[19]

In order to grasp the meaning that the Romans attached to art made for private
residences it is essential to understand the societal role those residences played
in the lives of their owners.

The essays in this volume take this principle for granted. The foundation
of social history underlies each essay, and works of art and architecture are
regarded—explicitly or implicitly—as social documents. The authors share a
respect for the integrity of Roman art and architecture of the private realm as
an expression of the Roman social situation. They see this art as addressing an
interlocking set of patronal concerns having to do with decorum, status, wealth,
social privilege, and obligation. Patrons are portrayed as actively interested in
the character of their surroundings as expressions of their own power, influence, and interests, and artists as responsive to their patrons' desires. Many of
these artistic responses are seen as original Roman statements, some drawing
on an older classical vocabulary and others on fresh sources of inspiration. Thus
the authors acknowledge that Roman domestic art, like all other forms of Roman
art, must be understood in terms of its own cultural context.

This shared outlook, however, does not mean that the authors approach
Roman architecture and decor exclusively from a sociohistorical perspective.
They follow different avenues in assessing the significance of the buildings and
their artistic contents to their Roman patrons and "public." They raise a variety
of issues (ranging from social function and meaning to design and style), and
they employ different methods of analysis (including historiographic, iconographic, stratigraphic, stylistic, literary, and contextual). Although diverse in approach and method, the essays are nonetheless closely interrelated. Certain
common themes are taken up in relation to different patrons, places, and periods—for example, several of the authors deal with the patron's appreciation of
stylistic and iconographic nuance, his role in the creation of original subject
matter, and his interest in the articulation of social, political, and philosophical
concepts. Thus, as a collection, the essays reinforce one another in creating an
overall impression of the circumstances and conditions that shaped art and
architecture in the domestic sphere.

Discussion focuses first on the Bay of Naples, where the private lives of
the wealthy elite of the late Republic and early Empire are documented more
amply than anywhere else in the Roman world. Literary accounts and archae-

ological remains of town houses and villas attest to the extraordinary luxury of life for prosperous Romans in the city, in the country, and along the seacoast.[20] Pompeii alone preserves the greatest abundance of evidence anywhere for one of these two main types of well-to-do private residence in Roman Italy—the atrium town house, or *domus*.[21] The atrium house, as Vitruvius relates, contained not only the private living quarters of the owner but also public rooms and gardens that served as the center of the owner's life of *negotium*, his civic and political activity.[22] Both the architecture and decor of the town house were orchestrated to create appropriate settings in which the owner, his dependents, and his adherents acted out their socially ordained roles.

Despite the obvious importance of the atrium house as a fundamental living unit in Italy of this era, in recent years surprisingly little has been written about its architectural form in relation to the social function it fulfilled.[23] Most commentary on this subject has been presented by students of domestic decor—painting, mosaic, and sculpture—who nowadays take into account the distinction between the public and private portions of the house when assessing the character of the decoration found in different spaces and its appropriateness to the purposes that those spaces served.[24] A few have even considered how the decoration affects movement through the spaces and how the decorative schemes correspond to the actual use of the room.[25] Yet the atrium house itself merits our close attention here, both as an original, highly characteristic Roman architectural form and as a vital center of activity associated with private life. Its form and function are fundamental to our perception of art in the private sphere.

The tendency to neglect the central role of the atrium house in Roman social life may result unconsciously from the fact that reconstructions of its history have been based on an underlying assumption of decline. This simplistic view charts a steady decay of the ideal republican form described by Vitruvius, to an adulterated form in the early Empire when Vitruvian proportional and decorative standards were abandoned or ignored, to ultimate extinction when the house was replaced by the multifamily dwelling during the later first and second centuries A.C. In the first essay in this volume, Eugene Dwyer undertakes to expose the effect that a deeply entrenched nineteenth-century tradition of moralizing criticism has had in perpetuating this assumption down to the present day.

This tradition, itself rooted in the commentary of Roman authors who were critical of developments in their own day, associates the beginning of the decline of the architectural form of the atrium house with the immense wealth that flowed into Italy during the late Republic as a result of conquests in the East. When newly rich grandees added Eastern peristyles and other luxuries to their homes, they were attacked for their excesses by their more conservative peers, self-appointed guardians of austere Roman virtues. As time went on this opulent life-style—or, as the tradition would hold, a somewhat tawdry semblance of it—became available to the *novi homines* who lacked an aristocratic heritage. While conservative republican critics mourned the loss of old Roman values and morals, later generations scorned the imitation of aristocratic *luxus* by a newly rich class of freedmen. Nineteenth-century scholarship followed suit.

Dwyer argues that such views do not accurately reflect the situation of the early imperial atrium house in Pompeii and, by extension, in similar Italian cities. He holds that despite changes in the social standing of the owners, the traditional forms and functions of atrium houses remained essentially unaltered at least down to 79 A.C. In reassessing the status of the atrium house in the early Empire, he first challenges the validity of basing our conception of the ideal atrium house, as nineteenth-century scholars did, on a set of proportions and decorative conventions prescribed by Vitruvius. Instead, Dwyer defines the ideal in terms of the kinds of spaces and their functions—e.g., the *fauces*, atrium, *tablinum*, and *triclinium* where traditional religious and social rituals were performed and enacted. As long as these remained constant, the ideal (or standard) remained intact. The addition of peristyles and variations in proportional relationships and decorative schemes had little real effect on life in the *domus*.

Dwyer points out another difficulty with the commonly held view that the single-family atrium house was supplanted by the multifamily *insula*, a process that we identify today as beginning in Neronian Rome and culminating in second-century A.C. Ostia. He believes that this notion, fostered by twentieth-century students of Roman architecture predisposed to thinking in terms of the decline of the *domus*, is misleading because it is based on a false comparison of the housing situation in smaller Italian cities with that in the capital and its cosmopolitan port.[26] In addition, Dwyer contends that contemporary scholars who challenge the viability of the atrium house either as an architectural form or as a social and economic entity ignore the abundance of Pompeian evidence that points in the opposite direction.[27]

Dwyer thus challenges us to rethink time-honored assumptions about the atrium house and its architectural and artistic development. He asserts that our reconstruction of that development must now go beyond a simple evolutionary conception and account for the fact that choices of architectural forms and decorative modes introduced during different periods remained simultaneously available to patrons during the early Empire.[28] Dwyer argues for the survival of the atrium house, whose adaptation to the changing social structure allowed it to serve the complex needs of prominent Romans well into the Flavian era.

His conclusions, along with his descriptions of the traditions, rituals, and practical functions associated with the atrium house, provide an essential backdrop against which to view the other essays, several of which deal with the *domus* in later manifestations at other locations throughout the Empire.[29]

If the *domus* fulfilled in large part the needs of the owner's life of *negotium*, the villa provided a retreat from the affairs of the town, a place where the proprietor could enjoy periods of *otium*, or leisure, engaging in activities that nourish the mind, body, and spirit.[30] The sprawling villa of the late Republic and early Empire provided an even larger arena than the town house for display of opulent architecture and decor. These villas became visible testimony of Rome's newfound wealth and power and of its leaders' cultivation and learning. The taste for extravagant building afforded architects a fertile terrain for bold innovation, funded by new wealth from the Eastern conquests and made structurally feasible by the new concrete technology.[31]

Roman villas in Italy and the provinces are currently the subject of much sociohistorical, cultural, and archaeological investigation. This research has explored not only the architecture and way of life associated with luxurious seaside pleasure domes, which even in their own day attracted much public notice, but also working country estates supported by the slave economy. The recent excavation and monumental publication of the Villa of Settefinestre at Cosa exemplifies a trend toward socioeconomic analysis of such establishments.[32] In social and cultural investigations the villas along the coast of the Bay of Naples have justly claimed a large share of attention.[33] Much of our evidence for villa life derives from literary sources, but archaeological discoveries of recent decades at well-preserved sites like the Villa of San Marco at Stabiae and the so-called Villa of Poppea at Oplontis, coupled with the growing interest in social and cultural history, has spurred art historical research into questions concerning the taste of the villa owners and the originality, function, and significance of the decorations of their homes. Wall paintings, mosaic pavements, and sculptural ornaments have been the subject of much study from a patron-oriented perspective. Students of Roman art have also been concerned with the influence the palatial villas of Campania may have exerted on homeowners of lesser means.[34]

In chapter 2, Bettina Bergmann focuses on the luxurious environment of the coastal villa through the eyes of a contemporary witness, the poet Statius, whose evocative account of a visit to the villa of his patron, Pollius Felix, on the Sorrentine peninsula provides a rare opportunity to observe how such opulent homes were justified and how the villa mentality might have given rise to new modes of artistic expression. Bergmann's main subject is a recently invented genre of painting—the topographical landscape—which, she argues, emerged in connection with this environment.[35] Statius's description of his patron's villa corresponds closely to the archaeological remains and physical setting of an excavated villa on the Punta della Calcarella that has been plausibly attributed to Pollius. By comparing the poetic description to the architectural remains and to the typical features of topographical landscape paintings, Bergmann shows that all three—the poem, the architecture, and the paintings—draw upon the same repertory of Hellenistic *topoi* to celebrate the patron's prowess, even virtue, as a builder and master of the environment. The painted topographical views, like their poetic and architectural counterparts, further celebrate the villa owner's appreciation of Greek literary and artistic culture, which was so marked a feature of the regional *milieu*. The sophisticated patron, his client-poet, his architect-decorator, and their audiences obviously delighted in the interplay of these literary, architectural, and painted allusions. Moreover, it is clear that both poet and architect catered to their patron's desire for self-glorification and gave expression to his specifically Roman worldview.

Bergmann's interpretation also makes clear the enthusiastic embrace of private *luxus* by villa owners even in the era when moralist critics pointed to it as a sign of social decay and used it as a symbol of anti-imperial propaganda. In the villa, *luxus* celebrates the great builders, tamers of the universe, imposers of order; and the owner is portrayed as a heroic figure in this mold. The stark contrast between the attitudes expressed by villa owners and those of their moralizing critics exposes a mixture of attitudes of a society in flux.[36]

For the art of mural painting, Bergmann's study offers a new model for future interpretative inquiry. She expands on directions of recent scholarship, which attempt to comprehend Roman paintings in light of their patrons' wishes and needs and in relation to their physical contexts.[37] By including the evidence of architecture and topography in addition to that of painting and poetry, Bergmann shows how the new genre of topographical landscape painting can only have grown out of the Roman villa mentality, which was obsessed with man-controlled nature shaped into perfect views.

Recent scholarship on sculpture has also opened new paths to understanding the intent behind the decor of wealthy Roman homes. Much has been written of late about the sculptural ensembles found in houses and villas of the Bay of Naples and elsewhere in Italy. As in studies of major public sculptural displays, a primary concern has been to reconstruct the original arrangements and discover their thematic programs.[38] In chapter 3, Elizabeth Bartman shifts our focus away from the early Empire and the Bay of Naples to address the subject of collections of sculpture as an element of Roman domestic decor. Bartman demonstrates that throughout the history and geographical expanse of the Empire, wealthy Romans collected sculpture for display in their homes.

She questions whether an exclusively programmatic approach can adequately reveal the motives behind the formation of private collections and the meaning such assemblages held for their owners.

To explain the eclectic character of extant Roman collections of sculpture, scholars have tended to assume that the Roman principle of *decor*, or appropriateness, guided patrons in their selection. Bartman points out, however, that the art historical definition of *decor* is often too narrow, admitting only appropriateness of subject, where the Roman concept embraced aesthetic and formal factors as well. Rather than seeking a unity of theme in collections of sculpture, Bartman finds that eclecticism was a desirable characteristic in itself, with prestigious roots in the famous public collections of works of art plundered by triumphant generals during Rome's rise to world dominance. When choosing subjects appropriate to certain types of spaces, Roman patrons were demonstrably conscious of thematic concerns. However, literary and, occasionally, archaeological evidence reveals that patrons also valued works for their antiquity, their pedigree, their capacity to evoke historical and other associations, and their formal and technical qualities. Neither the originality of a work nor its association with the name of a famous artist seems to have played a paramount role in the patron's decision. Replicas of well-known prototypes, which account for a large proportion of the sculptures collected by Roman connoisseurs, evidently commanded admiration equal to that accorded the original models.

Originality was, however, apparently appreciated in the display of sculpture. While the limited series of replicas resulted in a certain monotony of statuary types, Bartman argues that by coordinating the decor of rooms (including paintings, mosaics, and sculptures) and by employing certain thematic or formal patterns, such as pendants, in arranging sculptures in a given space, patrons were able to impart personal nuances of form and meaning to their collections of otherwise familiar types. Like Pollius and the poet and architect he patronized, the owners of sculptural collections emerge as visually astute observers, delighting in complex optical interplays of form and space. Patrons and visitors of refined sensibility might, as in the case of a Hadrianic *domus* on the Via Cavour in Rome, appreciate the subtleties inherent in the juxtaposition of old and new versions of the same statuary type.[39] Private homes provided the ideal settings for the close observation required. Bartman's analysis should encourage students of Roman sculpture to pay more attention to formal and aesthetic factors in sculptural arrangements and to acknowledge the patron's ability to make informed choices (whether in formal or thematic matters) that satisfied his personal tastes and needs.

The patron's choice has lately emerged as an important factor in studies that focus on the meaning of Roman wall painting,[40] and, as Dwyer points out, it is bound to have important bearing on future attempts to determine the chronology of Roman private art and architecture. In chapter 4, John Clarke's essay on the House of Jupiter and Ganymede in Ostia Antica, the interests of the patron are shown to be key to understanding both the function of the building and the meaning of the central painting of its decorative program. Contrary to most studies of programmatic painting, which neglect the details of the archaeological context, Clarke's study takes them fully into account.[41]

Clarke introduces the third major form of Roman private residence, the *insula* apartment. Apartments and shops routinely stood side by side in Roman *insulae*. The building about which Clarke writes apparently served first as a residence and then as a commercial establishment in two successive periods of occupation. Clarke reviews and revives an earlier theory that the apartment was remodeled in the late second century A.C. to serve as a hotel for homosexual men. As such, the building would have stood at the interface between the public and private spheres, its erotic purpose essentially private in nature even if money did change hands. The architecture and decor of the hotel find their closest parallels in the realm of the Roman house, no doubt in part because the original form of the private residence was not drastically altered in the remodeling. Clarke argues, further, that the character of the decor deliberately evoked the ambience of the type of wealthy private home that would have suited the social station of the hotel's clientele. In the context of Clarke's essay we must understand *patrons* to mean the well-to-do men to whose sexual preferences the hotel catered.

Clarke has discovered previously unknown details of iconography in the wall paintings of the House of Jupiter and Ganymede and has integrated them into an exciting new reconstruction. A figure of Leda can now be added to the picture of Jupiter and Ganymede that forms the centerpiece of the decorative scheme of the main reception room of the hotel. Clarke interprets Leda as an intercessor between the audience and the mythological male lovers, one who encourages the viewer to contemplate the female as well as male loves of Jupiter and the choice he has made between them in this instance. Clarke argues that this painting, which is unique among the extant representations of the three immortals, was created to suit the sexual orientation of the patrons of the hotel.

Clarke's multivalent interpretation has social implications as well. As an erotic scene in the mythological mode, the painting of Jupiter and Ganymede finds its closest parallels in well-appointed Roman homes where such paintings appear in public spaces like the *tablinum*. Interestingly, what had been the *tablinum* of the original private apartment continued to serve as a reception room in the hotel. The similarity of the architecture to a private residence as well as the cultural allusions and quality of the decor combine to support Clarke's theory that the hotel was intended for affluent men of the upper and commercial classes who frequented Ostia on business. Such surroundings would have been similar to what these men had in their own homes. Clarke's conclusions once again confirm the importance of considering the role of the patron as well as the physical and social context when interpreting the significance of works of art.

Mosaics have received much attention in recent scholarship, but too few studies seek to interpret themes as emanating from the patron's interests and from his desire to glorify his role within his own social *milieu*. Some deny any role whatever for the patron.[42] Christine Kondoleon's discussion in chapter 5 of mosaics in domestic decoration illuminates the effects of assimilation of Roman culture by provincial aristocrats from the middle to the late Empire. The patron's role in developing new iconographic imagery is central to Kondoleon's argument for the importance of domestic mosaics in the Roman provinces. Drawing on established Roman decorative traditions, many mosaics found in well-to-do (atrium-peristyle) homes illustrate the progress of Romanization. Kondoleon reconstitutes the cultural context of certain mosaics with the aid of literary sources, and is able to determine that these mosaics often reflect contemporary social institutions and public events paid for by wealthy patrons.

Kondoleon's study focuses on the events of the amphitheater, games, and spectacles that permit her to interpret the dialogue between reality and fiction and to explore the relationship between popular culture and the culture of the ruling class. As the owner of Clarke's Ostian hotel chose to appeal to the tastes of his guests through mythological allusions, so also the *domini* of Kondoleon's provincial houses couched their references to their public benefactions in mythological terms. Kondoleon also implies that the mythological mode of representation might not be restricted to the aristocracy to quite the extent that we have hitherto presumed. Public spectacles designed to please commoners often enacted episodes from myth. The distinction between myth and reality became blurred when such performances involved the execution of a prisoner who was cast in the role of an unfortunate character in the story.

Kondoleon reinforces points raised by Dwyer, Bergmann, and Ellis (chap. 6) concerning the patron's wish to portray himself as the central character in the drama.[43] While Dwyer portrays the owner, who controlled the social, economic, and religious life of the household, conducting his affairs set off in his *tablinum* as if upon a stage, Bergmann focuses on the patron in retirement from most of these daily rituals and at leisure to indulge in intellectual pursuits. His virtues (and pretentions) are celebrated in terms of literary *topoi* and allusions to his role as a great builder, tamer of the natural environment, and worthy citizen of the new Roman world order. In Kondoleon's essay, the patron's role as benefactor to his personal clients, his city, and the Empire at large emerges forcefully, despite social changes that continued to take place during the high and late Empire—changes that saw a growing concentration of power in the hands of a few aristocrats who served the imperial government. Private pleasures and public status were still the principal concerns of the patrons Kondoleon discusses, as they were for the patrons of Dwyer, Bergmann, and Clarke.

In chapter 6, Simon Ellis, like Kondoleon, treats the self-heroizing interests of the late imperial aristocrat who, in the centralized bureaucratic organization of the period, held greater political power than his earlier and more numerous counterparts. Ellis examines some of the social and political changes in late antiquity and their effects on architecture and art. The use of triconch (three-apsed) dining halls and other special forms of reception room reflects both the more specialized functions of the late Roman house and the aristocrat's desire to present himself in an impressive setting. The dining halls of four late imperial residences, decorated with iconographically assertive mosaics, support Ellis's case. His view that the mosaic scenes in some cases were tailored to the specific activities of the owner accords with Kondoleon's. Ellis, however, extends the line of interpretation to include marble-columned halls and sculpture collections orchestrated to articulate the owner's powerful political position and heroic status.[44] Architecture and decor work in harmony to proclaim the fundamental message.

The emphasis on the patron's *negotium*—his public *auctoritas* and *imperium*—contrasts markedly with the emphasis on the cultivated *otium*—the patron's aesthetic discernment and sophistication—which informs earlier displays of sculpture like the one from the Via Cavour *domus* discussed by Bartman and the ambience of early imperial seaside villas like that described by Statius and Bergmann. In the late Empire the life of *otium* was more fiction than reality. The villa was no longer a retreat from the cares of the active life as it had been during the late Republic and early Empire; it had gradually become one of the centers of *negotium*.

In summarizing the contents of the essays in this volume I have attempted to draw out their common themes and approaches. It is important, however, to remember that despite many striking continuities in the purpose and meaning of domestic architecture and decor throughout Roman history, social and political life in the Roman Empire underwent constant change. A full account of Roman art in the domestic sphere must recognize both the continuities and the changes.

This book does not purport to present a comprehensive view of the art and architecture of the Roman residence. In concentrating on wealthy town houses and country estates, we pass over the dwellings of the urban and rural poor. Archaeology tells us little about the lower class, though some concerted attempts have been made to unearth traces of its material life,[45] and current anthropologically oriented research is beginning to shed light on settlement patterns and the infrastructure of the Roman economy.[46] Even from the households of the elite, however, much is missing here. Furnishings, objects of daily use, clothing, and other personal items belonging not only to the owner and his immediate family but also to the members of the extended household would have to be included to complete the picture of art in the private sphere.[47] The purpose of the present volume is to draw attention to current approaches to the more traditional areas of research on domestic art and architecture in the hope that new perspectives will be more rapidly integrated into a balanced reevaluation of the history of Roman art as a whole. The next step will be to expand the definition and the field to include the full range of artistic expression through all strata of Roman society.

NOTES

All English translations of German and French texts are by A. E. Haeckl.

1. O. Brendel, "Roman Art in Modern Perspective," in *Prolegomena to the Study of Roman Art* (New Haven and London 1979) 153.

2. The term *art* in this discussion is meant to include architecture unless the context indicates otherwise.

3. Brendel (supra n. 1) 168. The misprint *every* has been corrected here to read *very*.

4. In research on private art and architecture (as well as on public or official monuments), certain kinds of studies have come to dominate the scholar's approach to the material and to influence the kinds of questions asked. Chief among these are catalogs and *corpora* whose main function is to sort and classify the physical remains according to a workable typology. Because the emphasis in such studies is on discerning particular relationships—e.g., chronological, technical, stylistic, iconographic—within a group of typologically related objects or buildings, they tend to isolate the works from the contexts in which they were found. Even excavation reports typically publish finds according to type rather than context. Interpretation of the finds in context is normally the final step in the process. Thus building types, wall paintings, mosaics, sculptures, and other objects are published in discrete catalogs and *corpora*, seldom in relation to one another. See B. S. Ridgway, "The State of Research on Ancient Art," *AB* 68 (1986) 7–23, for discussion of trends in recent scholarship on Greek and Roman art.

5. Even iconographical studies such as those of programmatic wall painting emphasize the Roman artist's dependence on Greek models. K. Schefold, "Der zweite Stil als Zeugnis alexandrinischer Architektur," in B. Andreae and H. Kyrieleis eds., *Neue Forschungen in Pompeji* (Recklinghausen 1975), expresses this viewpoint succinctly when he says, "On Roman walls Greek motifs were placed in a nonspecific spatial environment for the first time. As always in Roman art, the motifs are Greek in origin; only the synthesis is Roman" (p. 53). In "Römische Visionen und griechische Motive am Fuss des Vesuvs," *La regione sotterrata dal Vesuvio* (Naples 1982), Schefold again approaches Roman

wall painting as a new synthesis based in all its details on Greek art: "It is astonishing how all these Roman visions harken back exclusively to Greek models, how the contemporary is excluded from the house and reserved for public monuments" (p. 13).

On the other hand, H. Eristov, "Peinture romaine et textes antiques: Informations et ambiguités. À propos du *Recueil Milliet*," *RA* 1987, 109–23, emphasizes that the Roman penchant for decorating private houses with copies of famous Greek paintings ultimately tells us more about Roman aesthetics than about Greek art. In the houses of Roman Campania, Greek-inspired paintings are "subordinated to decorative exigencies: in order to organize pendants on opposite walls and to direct the gaze of the viewer, painters modified or inverted scenes. . . . The individual painting loses its autonomy to become only one element in a pictorial discourse or cycle" (p. 111). When copies of Greek paintings are integrated into Roman domestic decor, they "acquire a new meaning" and pose a series of new questions about "the conditions of their production, their relationship to the rooms they adorn, and the taste and culture of their patrons" (p. 110).

Other sources on the question of Roman copying include (on painting) Brendel (supra n. 1), especially pp. 179–82; and (on sculpture) B. S. Ridgway, *Roman Copies of Greek Sculpture: The Problem of the Originals* (Ann Arbor 1984); C. C. Vermeule, *Greek Sculpture and Roman Taste* (Ann Arbor 1977); M. Bieber, *Ancient Copies* (New York 1977); and M. Marvin, "Copying in Roman Sculpture: The Replica Series," *Retaining the Original: Multiple Originals, Copies, and Reproductions* (*Studies in the History of Art* 20, Washington, D.C. 1989) 29–45. See also the comments of Ridgway (supra n. 4) 10.

D. Michel, "Bermerkungen über Zuschauerfiguren in pompejanischen sogenannten Tafelbildern," *La regione sotterrata dal Vesuvio* (Naples 1982) 537–98, offers a provocative Romano-centric sociological and psychological study of one aspect of the Roman interpretation of Greek models in wall painting. Michel turns her attention to the subsidiary observer figures that frequently appear in Pompeian paintings of Greek mythological subjects and notes that scholarly interest in the figures has previously been confined to "the search for a Greek model, the characteristics of a specific Pompeian stylistic phase, or a mythological identification for the figures. In this regard, the observer figures have usually been evaluated negatively as compositional flaws. No one has investigated these figures for their own expressive value" (p. 539). Michel proceeds to do so, and emerges with a positive interpretation of the Roman "extras." According to Michel, the observer figures may have functioned in a variety of ways to help the patron comprehend: as intermediaries between Greek mythology and a Roman audience; as contemporary "stand-ins," intended to make a remote mythological episode more immediate, relevant, and involving for the Roman viewer; as compositional markers inserted by the artist to focus attention on crucial action; even as voyeurs meant to enhance the viewer's response to erotic scenes. In the houses of Pompeii, Michel finds persuasive evidence for creative interaction of patron, artist, and audience; a phenomenon with broader implications for the dynamics of Roman reception of Greek art and culture.

6. B. M. Felletti Maj, *La tradizione italica nell'arte romana* (*Archaeologica* 3, Rome 1977), is among the most important of the recent studies of the role of the Italic tradition in the art of the late Republic and early Empire.

7. E. Panofsky's theory of iconological interpretation is an example of a well-established model that encourages collaboration among humanistic disciplines. See his essay, "Iconography and Iconology: An Introduction to the Study of Renaissance Art," in E.

Panofsky, *Meaning in the Visual Arts* (Garden City, N.Y. 1955) 26–54, esp. 39. Studies by M. Foucault, such as his book *The Archaeology of Knowledge* (New York 1972), have been very influential in encouraging a broadly contextual approach. For example, Foucault stresses the importance of treating every object, whether of aesthetic interest or not, as a document in its own right, the informative product of its own culture and people. The trend in recent scholarship toward patronage studies is exemplified by B. Gold ed., *Literary and Artistic Patronage in Ancient Rome* (Austin 1982); and A. Wallace-Hadrill ed., *Patronage in Ancient Society* (*Leicester-Nottingham Studies in Ancient Society* 1, London and New York 1989).

Interest in the social history of Roman art has been greatly stimulated by the Marxist-oriented work of R. Bianchi Bandinelli, including his widely known *Rome: The Centre of Power. Roman Art to A.D. 200* (London 1970).

8. See D. E. E. Kleiner, "Roman Funerary Art and Architecture: Observations on the Significance of Recent Studies," *JRA* 1 (1988) 115–19; and N. B. Kampen, *Image and Status: Roman Working Women in Ostia* (Berlin 1981). Sarcophagi are still treated typologically and iconographically, though newer, more socially oriented studies affect this area too.

9. In the context of this volume the term *domestic* refers to private Roman dwellings and their decoration. Imperial palaces, though arguably private in the sections in which the imperial family actually resided, are considered here for comparative purposes but are not the focus of discussion.

10. P. Veyne ed., *A History of Private Life: I. From Pagan Rome to Byzantium* (Cambridge, Mass. and London 1987). From the perspective of the present volume, Y. Thébert's chapter, "Private Life and Domestic Architecture in Roman Africa" (pp. 313–410), holds the greatest interest. The theoretical assumption that underlies Thébert's treatment of the urban mansions of a provincial Roman elite—"that the organization of domestic space is not determined by autonomous private needs, but is, rather, a social product" (pp. 320–21)—is shared by the authors whose work is collected here. Although Thébert's primary concern is "the message of the architecture" of the houses of North African notables, he recognizes that "the significance of the surroundings was emphasized by the decor" (p. 392) and cites well-chosen and thoughtfully analyzed examples thereof.

Thébert's synthesis offers a welcome introduction in English, copiously illustrated with plans and photographs of important houses, to the extensive body of French archaeological work on the Roman *domus* in the cities of North African provinces. The level of scholarship apparent in the text, however, is unfortunately not matched by the rather cursory documentation, which tends to limit the reader's access to wider research on the subject.

11. This introduction will summarize and discuss the contents of the essays.

12. Veyne (supra n. 10) 1–3.

13. See Dwyer, chapter 1 in this volume. See also R. P. Saller, "*Familia, Domus,* and the Roman Conception of the Family," *Phoenix* 38 (1984) 336–55; Veyne (supra n. 10) 71–93; B. Rawson, "The Roman Family," chap. 1 in B. Rawson ed., *The Family in Ancient Rome* (Ithaca 1986) 1–57; P. Garnsey and R. P. Saller, "Family and Household," chap. 7 in *The Roman Empire: Economy, Society, and Culture* (Berkeley and Los Angeles 1987) 126–47; and B. D. Shaw, "The Family in Late Antiquity: The Experience of Augustine," *Past and Present* 115 (May 1987) 3–51.

14. J. Marquardt, *Das Privatleben der Römer* 2d ed., A. Mau ed. (*Handbuch der römischen*

Alterthumer 7, 1, Leipzig 1886), remains useful. On the implicitly "public" functions of certain sections of the Roman house, see especially pp. 218–24; on the *salutatio* in the atrium and *tablinum* and on the uses of *triclinia*, pp. 302–9. For a more up-to-date viewpoint, see Thébert (supra n. 10) 353–82. For further discussion of the Roman institution of *clientela* and domestic architecture, see Dwyer and Ellis, chapters 1 and 6, respectively, in this volume.

15. Brendel (supra n. 1) 155. The Romans themselves could draw sharp distinctions between private and public life. For example, H. Drerup, *Zum Ausstattungsluxus in der römischen Architektur* (*Orbis Antiquus* 12, Münster 1957), quotes Cicero's aphorism (*Mur.* 76), which is elegantly phrased in chiastic word order to underscore the contrast between *res privata* and *res publica*, on the diametrically opposed popular attitudes toward personal versus official ostentation: *Odit populus Romanus privatam luxuriam, publicam magnificentiam diligit* ("The Roman people abhor private luxury; public magnificence they prize") (p. 6).

16. Roman sources on the life led in the Roman villa include the letters of Cicero and Pliny the Younger; on Statius and the villa, see Bergmann, chapter 2 in this volume. On the strong associations between the Roman villa and the private sphere of *otium* in contrast to public *negotium* and life in the urban *domus*, see H. Mielsch, *Die römische Villa: Architektur und Lebensform* (Munich 1987) 37–39 and 45–49. Mielsch asserts that:

> The expression of ambition for power was not allowed to play a major role in the special forms of Roman villa architecture. The aesthetic enjoyment of the landscape seems more important, as attested by the popularity of maritime villas which did not possess large estates. Political pretension, as in the palaces of Eastern (Persepolis) and perhaps also Hellenistic rulers, was foreign to the nature of the villa. Already in the earliest testimony of the Scipionic Circle, it is clear that owners loved to visit their villas because there they were liberated from the pressures of official duties and political activity. Any overt manifestation of ambition for power would have been grossly out of place. Naturally, this does not mean that the *imperium* and political influence of the owner could not find indirect expression through the splendor of the villa and its decoration. However, the essence of the villa lay in its separation from the political and military sphere from which its owner sprang. (p. 46)

See also X. Lafon, "À propos des *villae* républicaines: Quelques notes sur les programmes décoratifs et les commanditaires," *L'Art décoratif à Rome à la fin de la république et au début du principat. Table ronde, Rome, 1979* (Collection de l'École Française de Rome 55, Rome 1981) 151–72.

17. See Dwyer (chap. 1 in this volume) for a quotation of Vitruvius's well-known remarks on the subject of "private" vs. "public" areas of the Roman house.

18. Thébert (supra n. 10) 392–93. See also P. Zanker, "Die Villa als Vorbild des späten pompejanischen Wohngeschmacks," *JdI* 94 (1979) 465–66, in which the author interprets the rapidly standardized decorative programs of luxurious private villas and town houses as an expression of the same fiercely competitive ethos that directed the public lives of Rome's late republican elite.

19. Translation from H. Rackham, *Cicero: De Oratore* 2 (Cambridge, Mass. and London 1960) 103. I am grateful to John D'Arms for this reference.

A. Wallace-Hadrill, "The Social Structure of the Roman House," *BSR* 56 (1988) 43–97, has recently added a further dimension to our understanding of what he terms the "language of public and private" in the Roman house. He sees a polarity between public and private as only one of two "axes of differentiation" that inform the social structure of the *domus*, the other being a contrast between grand and humble. By creating a grid of the two interlocking axes, Wallace-Hadrill captures the full spectrum of social distinctions possible in Roman domestic architecture, from "public and grand" atriums and *tablina* to "private and humble" slave quarters. This schema has obvious implications for interpreting decor in Roman houses. As Wallace-Hadrill demonstrates in regard to Fourth Style wall painting, art was a crucial element in expressing the subtle spatial and social differentiations within the Roman house.

20. For literary and epigraphical evidence, see J. D'Arms, *Romans on the Bay of Naples: A Social and Cultural Study of the Villas and Their Owners from 150 B.C. to A.D. 400* (Cambridge, Mass. 1970), "Ville rustiche e ville di *otium*" in F. Zevi ed., *Pompei 79* (Naples 1984) 65–86, and *Commerce and Social Standing in Ancient Rome* (Cambridge, Mass. 1981). In addition, see Mielsch (supra n. 16) and the sources cited therein for a survey of the archaeological remains of villas.

21. See Saller (supra n. 13) on the meaning of *domus* as house and household and as a symbol of status and honor.

22. See Vitruvius's passage as quoted by Dwyer (chap. 1 of this volume), and Dwyer's discussion of religious life in the Roman house, where the role of paterfamilias as head of the family cult seems to have been more private than public in character.

23. The most notable exception is Wallace-Hadrill (supra n. 19). For recent studies of the Roman house at Pompeii that treat architecture apart from its social significance, see L. Richardson, Jr., *Pompeii: An Architectural History* (Baltimore and London 1988); S. F. Weiskittel, "Vitruvius and Domestic Architecture at Pompeii," *Pompeii and the Vesuvian Landscape* (Washington, D.C. 1979) 25–38; A. Hoffmann, "L'Architettura," in F. Zevi ed., *Pompei 79* (Naples 1984) 97–118; and H. Eschebach, "Zur Entwicklung des pompejanischen Hauses," *Wohnungsbau im Altertum* (*Diskussionen zur archäologischen Bauforschung* 3, Berlin 1978) 152–61. Zanker (supra n. 18) approaches the development of domestic architecture and decor in Pompeii as one aspect of a larger social process, the hellenization of Roman culture as a whole. Thébert (supra n. 10) 319–23, on the other hand, declares outright his sociological perspective on the peristyle houses of Roman North Africa in asking, "What can we learn about private life from the study of domestic architecture?" (p. 319).

24. For painting, see A. Laidlaw, *The First Style in Pompeii: Painting and Architecture* (*Archaeologica* 57, Rome 1985); A. Barbet, *La peinture murale romaine: Les styles décoratifs pompéiens* (Paris 1985); D. Corlàita Scagliarini, "Spazio e decorazione nella pittura pompeiana," *Palladio* n.s. 23–25 (1974–76) 3–44; E. Leach, "Patrons, Painters, and Patterns: The Anonymity of Romano-Campanian Painting and the Transition from the Second to the Third Style," in B. Gold ed. (supra n. 7) 135–73; V. M. Strocka and H. Vetters, *Die Wandmalerei der Hanghäuser in Ephesos* (*Forschungen in Ephesos* 8, 1, Vienna 1977); V. M. Strocka, "Pompejanische Nebenzimmer," B. Andreae and H. Kyrieleis eds., *Neue Forschungen in Pompeji* (Recklinghausen 1975) 101–14; and V. M. Strocka ed., *Casa del Principe di Napoli* (*VI 15, 7.8*) (*Deutsches archäologisches Institut, Häuser in Pompeji* 1, Tübingen 1984–85), the first volume in an ambitious projected series of publications of individual Pompeian houses. Each volume will attempt to give as complete a picture as possible of the subject house: accurate plans, drawings, and photos; its architectural and occupa-

tional history; its phases of decoration; and a catalog of paintings, mosaics, sculpture, stucco, furniture, small finds, etc. For a similar study of a house in Herculaneum, see Tran Tam Tinh, *La Casa dei Cervi a Herculaneum* (*Archaeologica* 74, Rome 1989). A database for Pompeian houses and their contents has recently been established by the Neapolis Project; see *Rediscovering Pompeii* (Rome 1990), the catalogue of an exhibition sponsored by IBM-ITALIA, New York City, IBM Gallery of Science and Art, 12 July–15 September, 1990.

For sculpture, see E. Dwyer, *Pompeian Domestic Sculpture: A Study of Five Pompeian Houses and Their Contents* (*Archaeologica* 28, Rome 1982), and "Sculpture and Its Display in Private Houses of Pompeii," *Pompeii and the Vesuvian Landscape* (Washington, D.C. 1979) 59–77; W. Jashemski, *The Gardens of Pompeii, Herculaneum, and the Villas Destroyed by Vesuvius* (New Rochelle, N.Y. 1979); D. K. Hill, "Some Sculpture from Roman Domestic Gardens," in E. MacDougall and W. Jashemski eds., *Ancient Roman Gardens* (Washington, D.C. 1981) 81–94; S. de Caro, "The Sculptures of the Villa of Poppaea at Oplontis: A Preliminary Report," in E. MacDougall ed., *Ancient Roman Villa Gardens* (Washington, D.C. 1987) 77–133; and R. Neudecker, *Die Skulpturenausstattung römischer Villen in Italien* (*Beiträge zur Erschliessung hellenisticher und kaiserzeitlicher Skulptur und Architektur* 9, Mainz 1988).

For mosaics, see A. Barbet, "Quelques rapports entre mosaïques et peintures murales à l'époque romaine," *Mosaïque: Recueil d'hommages à Henri Stern* (Paris 1983) 43–53, pls. 26–35; and J. Clarke, "Relationships between Floor, Wall, and Ceiling Decoration at Rome and Ostia Antica: Some Case Studies," *Bulletin d'information de l'Association internationale pour l'étude de la mosaïque antique* 10 (1985) 93–103.

25. Clarke, supra n. 24 and in "Kinesthetic Address and the Influence of Architecture on Mosaic Composition in Three Hadrianic Bath Complexes at Ostia," *Architectura* 5 (1975) 1–17; B. Wesenberg, "Zur asymmetrischen Perspektive in der Wanddekoration des zweiten pompejanischen Stils," *MarbWPr* (1968) 102–9; and Barbet, *La peinture murale* (supra n. 24). See also Wallace-Hadrill (supra n. 19) 69–77 for an analysis of the "social function of decoration" in respect to the Four Styles of Pompeian wall painting.

26. E. Bartman, "*Decor et Duplicatio*: Pendants in Roman Sculptural Display," *AJA* 92 (1988) 211–25, and chapter 3 in this volume, discusses one of the few known and partially excavated town houses in the city of Rome. The house on the Via Cavour is dated to the Hadrianic period and is therefore contemporary with Ostian *insulae*. Given the limits of our evidence for the development of housing in cosmopolitan centers, Dwyer's cautionary remarks seem all the more apt. See also R. Meiggs, "The Houses," chap. 12 in *Roman Ostia* 2d ed. (Oxford 1973) 235–62.

27. Among the scholars cited in this context by Dwyer (chap. 1 of this volume) are P. Zanker (supra n. 18) and P. Veyne (supra n. 10).

28. See, for example, the work of A. Laidlaw (supra n. 24) as discussed by Dwyer (chap. 1 of this volume).

29. Especially Bartman, chapter 3, Kondoleon, chapter 5, and Ellis, chapter 6 in this volume.

30. As Mielsch (supra n. 16) 130–33 notes, the distinction between the villa as the seat of *otium* and the *domus* as the arena of *negotium* was never sharp or absolute. Business could be conducted at one's villa. Pliny the Younger describes certain of his villas as being more relaxing than others where he often had to put on his toga to receive dignitar-

ies. See also p. 147 on the fact that during the imperial period the villa as a place of *otium* increasingly became a fiction; for example, the imperial court and governmental responsibilities accompanied emperors to their country estates (as at Hadrian's Villa). Mielsch further contends that the villa fulfilled a different function in the provinces, where it was not dedicated to *otium* (p. 163). D'Arms, "Ville rustiche" (supra n. 20), makes the point that owners valued their villas not only as restful retreats, but also as real estate investments and productive properties whose earning potential was crucial. With respect to architectural forms (such as fountains, gardens, *euripi*, exedrae, and other rooms oriented toward a chosen view) and decorative schemes, Zanker (supra n. 18) contends that the villa exerted a reciprocal influence on the town house.

31. See discussion in Mielsch (supra n. 16) 32–35 of the enthusiastic embrace of agricultural as well as architectural innovation in the second century B.C. On hydraulic concrete, see E. K. Gazda and J. P. Oleson, *Cosa, Caesarea, and Vitruvius: Contributions to the History of Roman Concrete*, in preparation.

32. A. Carandini et al., *Settefinestre: Una villa schiavistica nell'Etruria romana* 3 vols. (Modena 1985); see also N. Brockmeyer, "Die *villa rustica* als Wirtschaftsform und die Ideologisierung der Landwirtschaft," *Ancient Society* 6 (1975) 213–28, on the *villa rustica* and the ideology of the Roman agricultural writers. The late antique villa at Piazza Armerina has inspired several publications that treat socioeconomic issues, including G. Manganaro, "Die Villa von Piazza Armerina, Residenz der kaiserlichen Prokurators, und ein mit ihr verbundenes Emporium von Henna," in D. Papenfuss and V. M. Strocka eds., *Palast und Hütte* (*Alexander von Humboldt-Stiftung. Symposium* 6, Mainz 1982) 493–513; and A. Carandini et al., *Filosofiana: La villa di Piazza Armerina* (Palermo 1982). Recent archaeological studies of villas in Italy include those at Buccino, Francolise, La Befa, Minori, Monte Romano, Pagliaro Murato, Pigno presso Ceri, Russi, San Vicenzo al Volturno (Molise), and Sperlonga, and the Villa of the Volusii at Lucus Feroniae. In the provinces several might be cited: Clantwort Major, Barnsley Park, and Castle Copse in England; Ivajlorgrad in Bulgaria; and Nea Paphos on Cyprus. In a number of cases remains of painted, mosaic, and sculptural adornments have survived. Selected publications of these villas are cited in the bibliography at the end of this volume. For the origin and development of seaside villas in the late Republic see X. Lafon, "À propos des villas de la zone de Sperlonga: Les origines et le développement de la *villa maritima* sur le littoral tyrrhénin à l'époque républicaine," *MEFRA* 93 (1981) 297–353. For remarks on the number of villa sites known, see J. D'Arms, *Commerce and Social Standing* (supra n. 20) 76–77.

33. The study of the villa owners by D'Arms, *Romans* (supra n. 20), has stimulated much interest in this subject and remains basic to the work of current investigators. More recently, in "Ville rustiche" (supra n. 20) and especially in chapter 4 of *Commerce and Social Standing* (supra n. 20), D'Arms has written about the owners of the Campanian villas.

34. On literary sources, see E. Lefèvre, "Plinius-Studien, I. Römische Baugesinnung und Landschaftsauffassung in den Villenbriefen (2,17; 5,6)," *Gymnasium* 84 (1977) 519–41; and G. Tosi, "La villa romana nelle epistulae ad Lucilium di L. Anneo Seneca," *Aquileia nostra* 45–46 (1974–75) 217–26. Mielsch (supra n. 16) includes much of the literary documentation in his comprehensive study of the architecture and life-style of the Roman villa. Though much of Mielsch's study is concerned with architectural development of the villa types from Republic to late Empire, he includes discussion of elements of villa

decor and aspects of social ritual. See also P. Zanker, *The Power of Images in the Age of Augustus* (Ann Arbor 1988), chap. 1, pp. 5–31; Zanker (supra n. 18); and Leach (supra n. 24). Studies of mural painting that provide insight into the function and meaning of the decoration of Roman villas include Leach (supra n. 24); A. Allroggen-Bedel, "Die Wanddekorationen der Villen am Golf von Neapel," *La regione sotterrata dal Vesuvio* (Naples 1982) 519–30; and Barbet, *La peinture murale* (supra n. 24), among others.

Other studies focus on the sculptural ornamentation of specific villas. See H. Döhl and P. Zanker, "La scultura," in F. Zevi ed., *Pompei 79* (Naples 1984) 177–210; D. Pandermalis, "Zum Programm der Statuenausstattung in der Villa dei Papiri," *AM* 86 (1971) 173–209; M. Wojcik, *La Villa dei Papiri ad Ercolano: Contributo alla riconstruzione dell'ideologia della nobilitas tardorepubblicana* (Rome 1986); G. Sauron, "Templa serena. À propos de la 'Villa dei Papyri' d'Herculanum: contribution à l'étude des comportements aristocratiques romains à la fin de la république," *MEFRA* 92 (1980) 277–301; and S. de Caro (supra n. 24).

Mosaics from wealthy villas tend to be from a later period of the Empire. See Kondoleon (chap. 5) and Ellis (chap. 6) in this volume.

35. See also Mielsch (supra n. 16) 52, 70, and 137–40 on the importance of views to the villa owner in contrast to the more programmatic and political concerns of the owner of a town house; and Zanker (supra n. 18) 468–75 on the attempts of householders in Pompeii to approximate in an urban environment the types of vistas coveted by villa owners.

36. Zanker (supra n. 18) 460–67 asserts that the late republican villa was the very embodiment of wealth and hellenized luxury to contemporary Romans and, as such, became the occasional focus of social and political tensions and conflicts. See Dwyer (chap. 1 in this volume) esp. n. 27, on contemporary Roman criticism of extravagance in private architecture. Ellis (chap. 6 in this volume) takes up later implications of the *luxus* mentality.

37. See, for example, Barbet, *La peinture murale* (supra n. 24); Strocka, *Casa del Principe di Napoli* (supra n. 24); Jashemski (supra n. 24); and Allroggen-Bedel (supra n. 34). Bergmann, chapter 2 in this volume, demonstrates that Roman authors besides the oft-quoted Vitruvius, Cicero, and Pliny can, when analyzed from an art historical perspective, shed fresh light on otherwise ill-attested aspects of Roman domestic interiors, such as patronage and the interpretation of decor. In this, Bergmann's sensitive reading of Statius reinforces points brought forward in Leach's study (supra n. 24) of mid-first-century A.C. wall painting. A. Borbein, "Zur Deutung von Scherwand und Durchblick auf den Wandgemälden des zweiten pompejanischen Stils," in B. Andreae and H. Kyrieleis eds., *Neue Forschungen in Pompeji* (Recklinghausen 1975) 61–70, mines the same vein when he compares passages from Lucretius's great Epicurean poem *De Rerum Natura* to the compositional organization and devices of Second Style wall painting. Borbein thereby adds a transcendent new dimension to the content and meaning of the illusionistic architectural and garden vistas painted in the houses of Rome's philosophically educated, late republican elite.

38. In addition to the sources cited supra n. 33, see Dwyer (supra n. 24); Hill (supra n. 24); and M. Torelli, "Una 'galleria' della villa: Qualche nota sulla decorazione del complesso," *I Volusii Saturnini: Una famiglia romana della prima età imperiale* (Archeologia. Materiali e problemi 6, Bari 1982) 97–104; Neudecker (supra n. 24); and Mielsch (supra n.

16). Among studies of public sculptural ensembles, see M. Marvin, "Freestanding Sculptures from the Baths of Caracalla," *AJA* 87 (1983) 347–84; R. Bol et al., *Das Statuenprogramm des Herodes-Atticus-Nymphäums* (*Deutsches archäologisches Institut. Olympische Forschungen* 15, Berlin 1984); M. Fuchs, *Untersuchungen zur Ausstattung römischer Theater in Italien und die Westprovinzen des Imperium Romanum* (Mainz 1987); and H. Manderscheid, *Die Skulpturenausstattung der kaiserzeitlichen Termenanlagen* (*Monumenta Artis Romanae* 15, Berlin 1981).

39. Bartman (supra n. 26).

40. Leach (supra n. 24); Laidlaw (supra n. 24); and Michel (supra n. 5).

41. The traditional approach is exemplified by the works of Schefold (supra n. 5). Among studies that attempt to take into account the physical and/or intellectual environment of Roman domestic wall paintings are M. L. Thompson, "The Monumental and Literary Evidence for Programmatic Painting in Antiquity," *Marsyas* 9 (1961) 36–77; Michel (supra n. 5); and Borbein (supra n. 37).

42. See Thébert (supra n. 10) 392–405 for a discussion of the differences of opinion on the role of the patron in mosaic decoration. Among studies that acknowledge the importance of the patron and his cultural context are a monograph by T. Sarnowski, *Les représentations de villas sur les mosaïques africaines tardives* (*Archiwum filologiczne* 37, Wroclaw 1978), on the ideology of *latifundia* in relation to the depictions of villas on North African mosaics; an article by P. A. Février, "Images, imaginaire et symbolisme. À propos de deux maisons du Maghreb antique," *Mosaïque: Recueil d'hommages à H. Stern* (Paris 1983) 159–62, which considers certain images commonly found in the provincial mosaics of wealthy pagan and Christian houses of the third and fourth centuries A.C. as symbols of the traditional Roman cultural ideal of *otium*; S. Settis, "Neue Forschungen und Untersuchungen zur *villa* von Piazza Armerina," in D. Papenfuss and V. M. Strocka eds., *Palast und Hütte* (*Alexander von Humboldt-Stiftung. Symposium* 6, Mainz 1982) 515–34; and Carandini et al. (supra n. 32), in which new interpretations of the famous hunt mosaic are offered. See also S. Ellis (chap. 6 in this volume) on mosaics from Piazza Armerina. Barbet, "Quelques rapports" (supra n. 24) studies the physical contexts and the rapport of mosaics with paintings, factors that have important implications for our understanding of how interiors were orchestrated and how we can interpret them. K. Dunbabin, *The Mosaics of Roman North Africa* (Oxford 1978) 24, takes as one of the premises of her important book the claim that "a major influence on the development of the African mosaics was exercised by the patrons who commissioned them"; see pp. 24–26 for discussion of "the patrons who determine the innovations in commissioning works for their own private houses." See also P. Veyne, "Les cadeaux des colons à leur propriétaire," *RA* 1981, 245–52. D. Parrish, "The Mosaic of Xenophon and the Seasons from Sbeitla (Tunisia)," *Mosaïque: Recueil d'hommages à Henri Stern* (Paris 1983) 297–306, asserts a possible meaning that a mosaic portrait of Xenophon may have held for its owner; and G.-C. Picard, "La villa du Taureau à Silin (Tripolitaine)," *CRAI* 1985, 227–41, proposes that the owner of the Villa of the Bulls at Silin made references to imperial propaganda and demonstrated his devotion to the emperor Caracalla in the mosaic decoration of his sumptuous residence.

For the importance of taking contemporary context into account when interpreting mosaic decoration in Roman houses as an expression of the owner's attitudes and viewpoint, see M. H. Quet, "De l'iconographie à l'iconologie: Approche methodologique. La symbolisme du décor des pavements de la 'Maison des Nymphes' de Nabeul," *RA* 1984, 79–104. In this review article, Quet's primary criticism of J. P. Darmon, *Nymfarum Domus: Les pavements de la Maison des Nymphes à Neapolis (Nabeul, Tunisie) et leur lecture (EPRO* 75, Leiden 1980) is that the author has largely based his iconographic analysis of the mosaics in a splendid North African *domus* of the fourth century A.C. on sources drawn from classical Greece and especially from Athens in the fifth century B.C. Quet demonstrates that the mosaic pavements of the House of the Nymphs are firmly embedded in the pagan intellectual culture of late antique Roman Africa and that "the symbolism of the decoration supports a pagan philosophical reading as rich and even more complex than Darmon's" (p. 99).

43. The example of Orpheus, discussed in this volume by Bergmann (chap. 2) and Kondoleon (chap. 5), is a telling instance.

44. Paintings must have contributed to the ensemble, but few traces of them have survived. Eristov (supra n. 5) 118 points out that the letters of Symmachus describe a patron of the late fourth century A.C. who was acutely interested in the decoration of his residences and who wrote fulsome letters of recommendation for a favorite painter, Lucillus. Eristov also cites the late antique aristocrat Cassiodorus, who instructed the master of the house to keep a tight rein on any painters, sculptors, and stuccoists he employed and not to defer to their judgments.

45. One of the earliest attempts was at Karanis in the Egyptian Fayoum. With the Karanis excavation F. W. Kelsey pioneered an approach to archaeological research whose objective was, in his words, "the reconstruction of the environment of life in the Graeco-Roman period." See E. K. Gazda ed., *Karanis: An Egyptian Town in Roman Times* (Kelsey Museum of Archaeology, Ann Arbor 1983) 4, and the select bibliography in that volume, pp. 46–49.

46. See, for example, S. Dyson, "The Villas of Buccino and the Consumer Model of Roman Rural Development," in C. Malone and S. Stoddart eds., *Papers in Italian Archaeology* 4, 4: *Classical and Medieval Archaeology* (*BAR International Series* 246, Oxford 1985).

47. In the 1987 conference session that inspired this volume, Kathleen Shelton addressed this matter in her response to the papers.

CHAPTER 1

The Pompeian Atrium House in Theory and in Practice

Eugene Dwyer

When destroyed in 79 A.C., Pompeii was a town of atrium houses. The significance of this fact is not always given its due in modern scholarship on the Roman atrium house (*domus*), even though the subject is essentially defined by the more than two hundred houses accidentally preserved at Pompeii. Contrary to archaeological evidence that the atrium house, at least at Pompeii, was a viable and fully functioning institution in 79 A.C., a majority of modern studies have concluded that it was in decline in the first century A.C.[1] By analyzing the atrium house in terms of theory and practice, or form and function, this essay will explore the reasons behind the paradox, whose genesis appears to lie in a tradition of examining the architecture and decor of the atrium house primarily from a formal perspective. This essay will attempt to trace the tradition, which still influences modern students to overvalue formal considerations at the expense of practical function, from Roman writers of the Republic to great scholars of the nineteenth century. As a corrective, this essay will offer an alternative viewpoint, also based on Roman sources, that emphasizes the importance of the social functions of the atrium house and the significance of the range of choices in design and decor available to patrons in the first century A.C.

A reassessment of the status of the atrium house in the early Empire must begin by addressing three questions: What were the essential forms and traditional functions of the Pompeian atrium house? How did they respond to changes in Roman society during an era of social transformation? And how have the form and function of the atrium house been interpreted from antiquity to the present?

Connected with the question of form and function is the common assumption that there was an ideal atrium house. The Pompeian atrium house is normally defined as a large rectangular hall, longer than it is wide, onto which a series of symmetrically arranged rooms opens (fig. 1-1). On each flank of the hall two or three doors conceal small rooms (*cubicula*) used for sleeping or storage. At the far end of each lateral wall, the hall space opens up on either side into a pair of open areas (*alae*). At the back of the hall, terminating its longitudinal axis, lies the *tablinum*, the sanctuary of the master. Most students of Roman architecture conceive of this ideal primarily as an architectural one based on the proportional standards set forth by Vitruvius in his *De Architectura* (6.3). This conception, however, would exclude a majority of the atrium houses in Pompeii that exhibit many non-Vitruvian variations in proportional relationships among the essential parts of the house. The ideal, if it existed, must be conceived in terms of the basic requirements that the house fulfilled, in particular those of religion, civic life, and domestic security.

At the time of Pompeii's destruction, the "idea" of an atrium house certainly existed. Religion and social convention taught the Pompeians how to interpret the real spaces that opened up to them when they passed in from the street. The fact that it is comparatively easy to identify the essential features—*fauces*, atrium, *tablinum*, *cubicula*—in several hundred Pompeian buildings offers dramatic empirical evidence of the existence of a standard house type.[2] Builders must have more or less fulfilled the expectations of their patrons. Desirable and suitable properties must have been reoccupied and undesirable ones pulled down. The perpetuation of this standard—or ideal—plan must, accordingly, reflect the continuity of the purposes it served. In this context, the social and practical functions of the traditional spaces of the atrium house merit a brief review.

The atrium house seems to epitomize the patriarchal structure that we associate with Roman culture. Ancient literary sources make it clear that down to the end of the Republic the atrium was that part of the house most associated with the *mos maiorum*, or ancestral tradition. Originally the place of the hearth, the atrium was the center of household life and the site of the shrine (*lararium*) of the ancestors and tutelary gods of the family. Roman religion defined the family by its descent through the male line. According to Polybius and Pliny, wax images of the male ancestors were prominently displayed in the atrium and worn by members of the family at the funeral of the paterfamilias.[3] As such funerals took place only once in a generation, it may be that the masks and related images owed their position in the atrium to some more atavistic purpose, perhaps as surrogates for house burials of Neolithic times.[4] Although the right of keeping ancestral images properly belonged only to heads of patrician families, it became a normative custom, subject to usurpation by inferior members of society.[5] Under the late Republic and early Empire it was the undisguised ambition of *novi homines,* or men elevated to patrician status, to have such images. In Pompeii, there is no proof that the marble and bronze portraits of distinguished ancestors that were prominently displayed in numerous atriums (fig. 1-2) all belonged to members of the patrician class.

In addition to being (together with the family sepulchers) the prescribed place of family worship, the atrium also played an important part in occasional ceremonies such as marriage, being the place where the bride was received into the family of her husband and his ancestors.[6] Roman religion, therefore, gives clear reason why the atrium would have been considered as the visible symbol of the lineage and the patrimony of the house owner (*dominus*).[7]

It was in the *tablinum* that men of importance customarily received daily courtesy calls (*salutationes*)[8] from their adherents (*clientes*)[9] and others who were in one way or another indebted to them. In the early Republic, the client was a member of the family of his master (*patronus*), often by a special ceremony of adoption. Thus, the institution had its origins in the private sphere of family religion. In the late Republic and early Empire, the relationship and its rite of *salutatio* became more of a simple demonstration of political and economic loyalty and dependence.[10] The political messages emblazoned on the exterior walls of many Pompeian houses have given us a good idea of the significance of patrons and clients in political life.[11] The *tablinum* adjoins the atrium much as a modern proscenium stage, though it is usually elevated by only a few inches. The *tablinum* could be closed off from the atrium by means of curtains or folding doors. The spectacle of a fatherly patron established in his *tablinum,* receiving the obligatory morning visit from his clients, led Frank Brown to call the atrium the "matrix of the authority of the father."[12] The phrase not only conveys the familial and social importance of the paterfamilias, but also gives us a vivid picture of the architectural setting and its importance in enhancing ritual. It is not accidental that domestic atriums, in their capacity for ritual, inspired such diverse architectural forms as the Forum of Augustus[13] and the Christian church.[14] The same spatial arrangement finds parallels in Roman palace basilicas, meant for imperial audiences, and in Christian basilicas of later times. Though the similarities that exist in plan and elevation between the republican *domus* and these later buildings may be "pseudomorphic" from a strictly architectural point of view, the dependence of rituals associated with both later institutions on the family ritual makes the connection more plausible.

The atrium and adjoining *tablinum* thus functioned as a numinous locus for the owner with respect to his role in religious and other social rituals. In this environment, the *dominus* was set off as a static presence on a stage, not unlike the image of a god in his sanctuary. Moreover, the centralized position of the atrium complex made it the ideal setting for another of the owner's important roles. As defender of the household, he used the stage, or *tablinum*, as a command post from which he assured himself of the security of his world. Within the house the security of the *dominus* concerned dependent members of his family and his possessions, and, extending from the house into the city, it concerned his clients, his peers, and those to whom he was obliged: it was by means of these complex relationships that the *dominus* defined his place in the life of city and Empire. Within the house, the central strategic location of the *tablinum* has long been noted by architectural historians. As Engelmann pointed out, the *tablinum* observes not only the atrium before it, but also the peristyle or garden behind it.[15] Access to the peristyle and to the inner parts of the house is usually by means of a narrow passage alongside the *tablinum*. Hence the *tablinum* is well placed to observe all who enter and leave the inner parts of the house. Whether the *dominus* himself or his servant was present in it, the *tablinum* was the place from which the security of the household was controlled.

The entire structure of the atrium house was designed to insure the security of family members, a fact not ordinarily emphasized in discussions of Roman domestic architecture. This was achieved by making the house inaccessible from the outside during the night and by limiting access to certain areas during the day. As represented in Pompeii, the *domus* had few outside doors—one or two at most—and few, if any, windows on the ground floor. What windows there were, were narrow, covered with stone or ceramic grills, and located high in the wall. (Some houses had balconies for lighting and for increasing floor space on the second story.)[16] Doors were strong and fastened with locks. They were locked from the inside as well as from the outside, and passage was impossible without the knowledge of the *ianitor*.[17]

Precautions taken to insure the security of family members also served to protect movable property, but additional measures were necessary, and these focused on the area of the atrium. Objects not required on a daily basis might be locked into rooms such as *cubicula*, the keys being retained by a trusted servant or by the *dominus* himself. Objects more likely to be used might be kept in wooden cabinets located in the atrium. Money, required for the daily allowance given by the *patronus* to his client (i.e., the *sportula*), was kept in large stationary chests, also located in the atrium.[18] The number of locks and keys used to secure the property of the household must have been sizable even in smaller establishments. (Anyone who has read the old excavation reports from Pompeii will have been impressed with the extraordinary number of lock parts that were found in the excavation of a typical house.) The control of the keys was a matter requiring trust and conferring power. As the great majority of locks were to be found in the vicinity of the atrium, we can conclude that this was the most secured part of the house, hence the most secure.[19]

The concern of the *dominus* with security also manifested itself in relations with his clients and friends. From earliest Roman times well into the Empire, these adherents had customarily gathered in the atrium, which insured a degree of privacy necessary for planning, plotting, or doing business that could not be done in public. A ritualized daily gathering of "friends" brought together for their *salutationes* or for evening dinner provided the opportunity for discussions of a political nature that might, under other circumstances, arouse suspicion among other factions in the public life of the city. Strong doors were in position and ready to be closed if necessary. Backdoor exits were also a possibility. In every respect, the atrium house was a place ideally suited for doing private business. Ideal as a theater in which the *dominus* might be viewed, the atrium along with the *tablinum* was also an ideal theater for the *dominus* to keep watch over his adherents, his family, and his possessions.

As an ideal form shaped by the ensemble of family rituals—social, religious, political, and economic—and by the need for household security, the atrium house at Pompeii exhibited extraordinary tenacity throughout the period of the late Republic and early Empire. Not only did the atrium house remain the dominant form of housing in 79 A.C., but objects excavated in atriums destroyed by Vesuvius testify to the continuity of its function.[20] Given the evidence for functional continuity, proportional relationships within the house seem largely irrelevant to the history of the atrium house form. Yet deviations from the Vitruvian canon of proportions have been one of the most influential factors in leading modern scholars to conclude that by 79 A.C. the atrium house was in an irreversible decline. A second factor has been the modern conviction that the social changes wrought by Rome's transition from Republic to Empire must necessarily be reflected by changes in Roman family housing.

We turn, therefore, to the second question posed by this paper: How were the form and function of the atrium house affected by a period of profound social transformation? Modern critics have often linked the purported decline of the atrium house in the first century A.C. to the weakening of the powers of the late republican aristocracy. The changes in Roman civilization brought about by the movement away from the aristocracy of the Republic toward the more centralized and bureaucratic government of the Empire had certain residual effects on the institution of marriage, the authority of a father over his children, the right of property, and the patron/client relationship. Many students of Roman architecture have thought it reasonable to expect that, as powers once vested in the *dominus* fell increasingly to the state, the *domus* would evolve accordingly. If political power had indeed been dissipated and liberty lost, as Tacitus said they were, then the atrium house, which once served as a kind of political center for a powerful man and his adherents, must have given way to another, less autonomous unit: apartment housing analogous to the modular type designed in the early twentieth century by Bauhaus architects for workers in a uniform and centralized society.

We can detect a kind of typological inevitability (in the Marxian sense of the word) in the familiar efforts of many social and architectural historians to demonstrate a progression from the atrium house architecture of Pompeii to the apartment blocks (*insulae*) found first in Neronian Rome after the fire of 64 A.C. and then in Ostia of the second century A.C. According to this scholarly tradition, the developmental history of Roman domestic architecture progressed in several key stages. In late republican and early imperial Pompeii came the *vicus*, or neighborhood block, with its cult under the direction of the *vici magistri,* a creation of Augustus that ostensibly improved civic life, but in reality must have been an intrusion into otherwise private matters of the neighborhood. (It is not difficult to imagine resistance to this idea from reactionary quarters.) The changes brought about in the rebuilding of Nero's *nova urbs*, the new city center built in Rome after the fire of 64 A.C., were, in fact, the consequences of centralized authority coupled with opportunity. In the case of Nero's city, the atrium house was thought by modern scholars to have been extinguished as a species and replaced by the modular apartment block. By the following century—the time period represented by the Ostian *insulae*, with their plurality of family residences—the effects of this continued assault on the organic integrity of families were seen to have left their stamp on a new ideal housing type (fig. 1-3).

The developmental scenario favored by most students of Roman architecture—a general trend away from the atrium houses of aristocratic Pompeii and toward the *insulae* of bureaucratic Rome and Ostia—is based on the hypothesis of typological evolution in a uniform society. Social changes, however, may not have occurred uniformly and consistently throughout the Roman Empire, or even within the Italian peninsula. Moreover, we would need more data about the ownership of individual houses than are now available in order to prove a causal relationship between a decline in Rome's republican aristocracy and the ostensible disappearance of the atrium house. Even at a site as well preserved and documented as Pompeii, little can be said with certainty concerning the ownership of houses in 79 A.C. Despite the worthy efforts of G. Fiorelli and M. Della Corte,[21] there is insufficient evidence to justify the kind of statistical study that would permit generalizations about the sort of houses preferred by members of Pompeii's identifiable social classes.[22] Furthermore, the houses of Flavian Pompeii simply do not conform to the predictions of the developmental model as currently formulated. If the model were accurate, by 79 A.C. one would expect Pompeii to show in its buildings the presumed effects of a bureaucratized imperial government, viz., an increase of smaller, isolated dwellings (precursors of apartments), in consequence of the breakdown of extended families that had been characteristic of the old patronage system. In fact, not only is it difficult to demonstrate the existence of any remote ancestors of the Ostian *insulae* in the Pompeii of 79 A.C., but, moreover, we find that Pompeii offers a surprising number of large and elegant residential units compared with its humbler houses.[23] J. Packer's recent study of middle- and lower-class housing in Pompeii has focused attention on the less prosperous inhabitants of the town, but does not change the fact that large atrium houses still dominated in 79 A.C.[24] Faced with empirical evidence that the atrium house retained its preeminence throughout the history of Pompeii, some modern critics have pointed to deviations from the Vitruvian ideal plan as evidence of its demise.[25] As we have demonstrated, however, more than architectural form was involved in the Roman experience of the ideal *domus*. Defined in terms of the social function it fulfilled, the atrium house, supposedly a relic of the aristocratic past, was apparently thriving in a city of the Empire as late as 79 A.C.

There is yet another argument against the developmental model that sees the dissolution of the Pompeian atrium house in the apartment blocks of Rome and Ostia. Conclusions drawn from the capital city of Rome and the cosmopolitan emporium of Ostia may not apply to a Campanian town such as Pompeii. We must admit that we know very little about the general condition of the *domus* in Rome during the first and second centuries A.C. Although Neronian Rome is usually envisioned as a city of *insulae,* this reconstruction is based largely on the remains of Ostia in the following century. Moreover, as a provincial town, Pompeii might not have been comparable to contemporary Rome or Ostia. Building materials and traditions would have been different for each, as would economic conditions. It is entirely possible, however, that Pompeii in 79 A.C. was more representative of norms in Roman private housing than were Rome or Ostia. The atrium house may have been much in evidence in Italian towns of the period. For municipalities other than Rome, there seems to be no logical reason to prefer Antonine Ostia over Flavian Pompeii as a model for trends in Roman domestic architecture during the first century A.C. Our knowledge of the *insulae* of second-century Ostia has introduced a persistent anachronistic bias into analyses of the status of the atrium house in the early imperial period. This bias represents a serious impediment to objective assessment of the evidence available from the first century A.C.

Belief in the hypothetical change from the *domus* to the *insula* as the primary form of housing under the Empire has been partly responsible for the prominent tendency in modern studies of the Pompeian atrium house to trace its development from a supposed high point in the late Republic through a decline in the early Empire. Another, equally prominent tendency is to associate this decline with society's moral decay, a notion deeply rooted in the criticism of the ancients themselves. A review of literary testimony from the first centuries B.C. and A.C. provides a partial answer to the third question raised in this essay: How have ancient and modern opinion evaluated the theory and reality of the Pompeian atrium house? We shall see that Roman critics of the *domus*, who tended to focus on aspects of form (i.e., the degree of *luxus* involved in the decor of a house), have influenced modern interpretations more profoundly than have Roman apologists, who spoke to the importance of function (i.e., the social necessity for grandeur in private houses). For example, in a 1973 study of the Roman atrium house, B. Tamm noted that some scholars have characterized certain changes in the form of the republican *domus*—"the building in of a second floor in discarded patrician houses, the disappearance of *tablina*, the peristyles becoming more luxurious and transformed into new family centra of the house"—as signs of deterioration, "some sort of degeneration."[26] With a nod to Cato and his confreres, many scholars have associated these changes with a picture of increased luxury bringing about or accompanying the enervation of public life and the *mos maiorum* of the family.

Latin literature gives much support to the theory of moral decline. For all Roman writers (even Vitruvius), formal and aesthetic principles could not be divorced from moral ones. The best life was the simple one. Rome's success in pacifying her neighbors, however, became her own downfall. In the second century B.C., formerly austere values began to falter with the introduction into central Italy of hellenized tastes for such forms of expression as theater and rhetoric. In architecture, the influence from the East appears to take the form of a mania for adding peristyles to the backs of atrium houses, enclosing the gardens that had been there. As the Hellenistic mimetic modes were criticized by conservative Romans, so were peristyles and ornamented architecture in general.[27] Columns, especially those made of exotic imported stone like those in Scaurus's atrium, became favorite targets.[28] Motives such as political ambition or, even worse, sensual abandon and moral decadence might be imputed by critics of grand houses. Public sumptuary laws might be used to control the height of a man's house, or his appearance in public, but they were not very effective against his purported luxurious way of life within his own home. A culture that could not distinguish between aesthetics and morals was bound to suspect new forms of decoration and those, like Q. Metellus, who introduced them.[29]

But there was another side to the ancient story. There were apologists for classical art, and Cicero and Vitruvius were among those who spoke up in defense of grandiose architecture, even in the private sphere. It is significant that Cicero, an upwardly mobile *novus homo* in Rome's socially stratified society, and Vitruvius, an "objective" architectural theorist, both based their justifications on the social function of the *domus*. Theory and practice agreed that some men must have larger houses in order to fulfill their social obligations. Cicero writes that such a man builds

> not for himself alone but for others also, so in the home of a distinguished man, in which numerous guests must be entertained and crowds of every sort of people received, care must be taken to have it spacious.[30]

Apparently sensitive to the concerns of moralizing critics, Cicero adds, admittedly somewhat hopefully,

> The truth is, a man's dignity may be enhanced by the house he lives in, but not wholly secured by it; the owner should bring honor to his home, not the house to its owner.[31]

Vitruvius, although conservative and a moralist in many respects, found social justification for the spacious peristyles and marble columns of his day.[32] In an important passage from his *De Architectura* (6.5), Vitruvius gives his rationale for the *domus:*

> After setting the positions of the rooms with regard to the quarters of the sky, we must next consider the principles on which should be constructed those apartments in private houses which are meant for the householders themselves, and those which are to be shared in common with outsiders. The private rooms are those into which nobody has the right to enter without an invitation, such as bedrooms, dining rooms, bathrooms, and all others used for the like purposes. The common are those which any of the people have a perfect right to enter, even without an invitation: that is, entrance courts, *cavaedia*, peristyles, and all intended for the like purpose. Hence, men of everyday fortune do not need entrance courts, *tablina*, or atriums built in the grand style, because such men are more apt to discharge their social obligations by going round to others than to have others come to them. . . . For men of rank who, from holding offices and magistracies, have social obligations to their fellow-citizens, lofty entrance courts in regal style, and most spacious atriums and peristyles, with plantations and walks to some extent in them, [must be constructed] appropriate to their dignity. They need also libraries, picture galler-

ies, and basilicas, finished in a style similar to that of great public buildings, since public councils as well as private law suits and hearings before arbitrators are very often held in the house of such men.[33]

Thus, Vitruvius, like Cicero, cites the traditional needs of the family and the obligations of some distinguished men to accommodate the public in their houses as the only legitimate reasons for building on a grand scale. Classical refinements in plan and decoration, unjustified on the grounds of utility alone, serve as no more than suitable expressions of the worth (*dignitas*), credibility (*auctoritas*), and power (*potestas*) of the *dominus*.[34]

The arguments of Cicero and Vitruvius did not put an end to complaints about grand houses. When, under the Empire, men of anti-imperial sentiment attempted to revive the values of the Republic, moralizing criticism was their most effective weapon. Juvenal and Petronius were particularly savage in their attacks on imperial freedmen and their new wealth. Skeptics were unlikely to believe that concerns other than expressing their own self-importance had motivated these great builders. Petronius's literary creation, Trimalchio, stands for a well-defined and much-despised class of men.[35]

The emotionally charged idea of "decline" has unfortunately worked to obscure the actual significance of late republican and early imperial critics of the atrium house. Ironically, the very Roman writers who denounce changes to the traditional (or ideal) atrium house serve to confirm archaeological evidence for its vitality. "Change" may have meant "decline" to certain conservative Romans and, as we discuss below, to certain nineteenth-century scholars, but it need not do so for modern architectural historians. The fact that the atrium house remained a subject controversial enough to provoke debate in the Augustan period argues strongly in favor of its continued viability, whether or not the latest forms of the *domus* were universally admired by contemporaries in the first century A.C.

The impact of moralizing Roman criticism on academic thought in the nineteenth century is readily apparent. In the case of the atrium house, the fact that the taste of men like Trimalchio seemed to coincide with the flashy—some would say meretricious—style of decoration prevalent in the last years of Pompeii led nineteenth-century authorities to side with the moralists. Moreover, filtered through the compendia of August Mau and his contemporaries, the influence of jaundiced Roman views on new developments in domestic decor can still be discerned in recent scholarship on the atrium house.[36] It is noteworthy that even Vitruvius, who accepted the social need for palatial houses, was among the most virulent critics of the taste with which Roman patrons of the early years of the Empire decorated such houses.

No one can write about Pompeii without citing the fundamental work of August Mau, but the aesthetic theory that underlies his chronology of Pompeian wall decoration should not be accepted as fact. Building on a few passages in which Vitruvius describes a sequence of three styles, Mau developed an elaborate chronology of four styles for republican and imperial Pompeian masonry and painted walls that, in its broad outline, has held firm to the present day.[37] In this well-known construct, however, Mau's aesthetic bias colors his judgment. Following the lead of Vitruvius, who objected to Third Style "fresco paintings of monstrosities, rather than truthful representations of definite things" as found on Second Style walls,[38] Mau characterized the Fourth Style wall decoration of atrium houses built or remodeled in the years between the damaging earthquake of 62 A.C. and the final destruction of 79 A.C. as gaudily colored and lacking the substance of houses decorated in the Republic.

In Mau's chronology, the decoration typical of each successive stage displays an evolution from substance to superficies or, in the aesthetic terminology current in Mau's late nineteenth-century circles, from tactile form to optical form. Where the Romans had subordinated aesthetic concerns to moral ones, Mau proposed an aesthetic system that was tainted with moralizing. In both traditions, societal decadence was seen as the result of a departure from an earlier standard of integrity. Moreover, both the Roman moralists and Mau tended to divorce the decor of the *domus* from the social functions it fulfilled. Vitruvius deplored the folly of contemporary taste in wall painting, but acknowledged the necessity of large houses for important personages. The social significance of Pompeian wall decoration lay largely beyond the scope of Mau's monumental work of classification.

A comparison of two Pompeian houses, the House of the Faun and the House of Marcus Lucretius, provides an instructive focus for a reassessment of the status of the atrium house and its decor in the early Empire. The houses have been selected for what they have in common—both are atrium houses, luxuriously appointed and proudly inhabited at the moment of Pompeii's destruction—and what they do not—dimensions, style of decor, occupational and architectural history, and, possibly, social class of the owner. By comparing these points of similarity and difference, one can further discuss the issues raised by this essay: the relationship of form to function in the atrium house, the impact of social change on that relationship, and the attitudes of ancient and modern observers to any perceived change therein.

The House of the Faun (VI xii 2) stands out in discussions of the Roman *domus*. It has been considered by modern students as the typical aristocratic Pompeian house of the republican era (figs. 1-4 and 1-5).[39] It is so typical, in fact, that it seems to have been built to specifications given by Vitruvius in several places in his discussion of the *domus*. Mau thought the house possessed such an extraordinary unity of plan that it had descended nearly intact from its origins in the third or second century B.C.[40] For Mau this period represented the acme of Pompeian building, in the years before the city had surrendered its independence and become a colony of Rome. Under the colony and until the destruction of the city, the house clearly maintained its position of civic prominence, with virtually the entire ground floor being opened to the public.[41]

Built of noble tufa blocks coated with plaster and decorated in the First Style of Pompeian wall painting, it presented an aspect comparable to the most dignified public buildings in the city. The entrance way was grand, in keeping with the large number of visitors who might be expected to congregate there awaiting the morning *salutatio*. An effort was made to give the house noble proportions, evident in plan. The Tuscan atrium, one of the largest in Pompeii, must also have been one of the grandest (see fig. 1-5).[42] This part of the house is distinguished for its fine floor mosaics and its pavements in polychrome intarsia (*opus sectile*). The *tablinum* had a fine pavement in the latter, which was a new and costly art. An opening in the north wall of the *tablinum* afforded a view of the first peristyle, built in the Ionic order. Ornamenting the floor of a monumental room opening onto the north portico of this peristyle was the famous Alexander mosaic.[43] A second, Corinthian tetrastyle, atrium is thought to have served the needs of the family, though it was also monumental in aspect. Beyond the Ionic peristyle lay a larger peristyle in the Doric order completing the sequence of orders within the house.[44]

Because of its antiquity (i.e., second century B.C. or earlier in date of construction) and close conformity to the Vitruvian ideal, the House of the Faun has often been held up as a model of *republican* form and taste.[45] By comparison, a number of houses built or remodeled during the later years of the city, when measured by the same standards, have fared poorly in modern estimation. One such house, intended to accommodate a much smaller group of visitors, was the House of Marcus Lucretius (IX iii 5).[46] It derives its traditional name from a painting inscribed with the name and title "Marcus Lucretius, Priest of Mars (*flamen Martis*)," perhaps the owner of the house or, what is more likely, a distinguished ancestor or patron.[47]

The House of Marcus Lucretius appears to have been thoroughly remodeled, or even rebuilt, in the period following the earthquake of 62 A.C. (figs. 1-6 and 1-7).[48] The rebuilt house combines parts of earlier, smaller rubble concrete structures of a common design, resulting in an irregular L-shaped plan. The main block of the house, however, preserves the essential features of a traditional atrium house—*fauces*, atrium with flanking *cubicula* and *alae*, *tablinum*, and a garden (*hortus*), which in this case lacks a peristyle (see fig. 1-6). Fresh and well preserved in the decades immediately following its excavation (in the years 1845–50), the house undoubtedly made a strong impression on Mau and his contemporaries—Helbig, Overbeck, and others—who were beginning to look at Pompeian decor from a historical (i.e., developmental) perspective. Together with the House of Siricus (VII i 25/47), located just across the Via Stabiana and excavated at about the same time, it offered nineteenth-century students a choice example of that type of house whose ornate decoration was considered extreme by comparison with more sober republican standards (fig. 1-8). To students under the influence of the harmonious beauties of the House of the Faun, the House of Marcus Lucretius seemed to overcompensate in "superficial" decor what it lacked in "substance": the optical sense prevailed over the tactile sense. Compared with the House of the Faun, whose First Style walls conveyed an impression of dignity and solidity, the fantastic illusionistic paintings and gilded stucco decoration in the Fourth Style seemed garish and meretricious if only because of their excellent preservation at the time.[49] (At the time of the initial comparison, the House of the Faun had been uncovered for twenty-five years, time enough for its own more garish effects to have faded.)

Nineteenth-century criticism of the House of Marcus Lucretius was also directed at its architectural form. Unlike the House of the Faun, the House of Marcus Lucretius did not conform to Vitruvian specifications. The proportions of the *tablinum* with respect to those of the atrium are a case in point. Concerning the design of the *tablinum*, Vitruvius writes:

> The *tablinum* or alcove, if the breadth of the atrium is 20 feet, must be two-thirds in width. If the breadth of the atrium is 30 to 40 feet, half is to be given to the alcove. When the breadth is from 40 to 60, two fifths are to be assigned to the alcove. For the smaller atria cannot have the same kind of symmetry as the larger. For if we use the symmetry of the larger atria in the smaller, it cannot be useful for the alcove or the wing. But if we use the symmetry of the smaller in the larger, the details will be huge and monstrous.[50]

At five meters, or approximately twenty Roman feet, in width, the *tablinum* of the House of Marcus Lucretius is "huge and monstrous" by Vitruvian standards, according to which it should only be about fifteen feet wide.[51]

The nearly square *triclinium* that adjoined the *tablinum* of the House of Marcus Lucretius was also judged to be awkward and un-Vitruvian. According to Vitruvius, "dining rooms ought to be twice as long as they are wide."[52] Both the *tablinum* and the *triclinium* looked out over a postage-stamp-size garden populated with small gilded marble statuettes of satyrs and animals (see fig.

1-7).[53] Here, too, nineteenth-century scholars found an unflattering comparison with the House of the Faun, whose Ionic peristyle seemed to have been decorated with exquisite bronze statuettes like the well-known dancing faun.[54]

The comparison of the House of the Faun and the House of Marcus Lucretius, the former a prototypically aristocratic house built in the second century B.C. and still maintained with a traditional decor and the latter a common house remodeled or rebuilt in the latest style of decoration, may be thought to illustrate different social classes and the requirements of two distinctly different *patroni*. I submit, however, that even if such a social distinction could be proven, it would not mean that the atrium of the House of Marcus Lucretius served its owner any less well. The owner of the House of Marcus Lucretius put considerable effort into creating a sumptuous setting for himself, albeit on a smaller scale and in a different style than did the owner of the House of the Faun. Within the atrium area, for example, the *tablinum* was given the greatest attention. It is very large in proportion to the atrium, as we have seen, and lavishly appointed. Even E. Falkener, who in the 1840s witnessed the excavation of this part of the house, described with rare (if somewhat horrified) admiration an elaborate gilded and patterned ceiling that he took great pains to reassemble and restore.[55] Another unusual feature about this room was the fact, also observed by Falkener, that wooden panel paintings had been set into the lateral walls.[56] Moreover, the garden with its elaborate sculptural decorations was clearly visible from the atrium as an opulent backdrop to the *tablinum*. As for the *triclinium*, awkward as it may seem according to the Vitruvian canon, it was, nevertheless, the site of one of the finest paintings found in Pompeii, the Drunken Hercules.[57]

Despite variations in scale, design, and decor, the comparison of the two houses reveals a remarkable similarity in their basic function and structure. Both conform to the atrium house ideal as we have attempted to define it. That is to say, both houses have all the requirements—*fauces*, atrium, *tablinum*, *triclinium*, etc.—for the same social rituals: the family cult, the *salutationes* of "friends," the formal dinners next to the garden in the evening. To a great extent the requirements of these two owners must have been quite similar. That their houses were of a different scale, conformed to different proportional standards, and were decorated in different styles does not alter this fact. What is *not* clear from the comparison is any change in the essentials of the standard house plan. In fact, it can be said that the ideal house changed surprisingly little in its essentials over the two-hundred-year period represented by these two houses.[58] At the end, the House of the Faun was still as well suited to Roman life as it had been when it was built. Moreover, the atrium remained important. In the House of Marcus Lucretius the atrium and adjacent *tablinum* were still the center of the house about which were performed all of the social and familial rites.[59]

In light of this fact, it is necessary to rethink our notion of the development of the atrium house and its decor. Some students of painting have already begun to do so. For example, Anne Laidlaw has determined that walls continued to be decorated in Mau's First Style, with all its conservative associations, until the very last days of Pompeii. Not only does such a fact play havoc with the relative chronology established for the sequence of styles, but, even more significantly, it obliges us to consider the appropriateness of the context and the meaning of a style to the person who chose it. Laidlaw's discovery reminds us of the contemporaneity of all Pompeian houses: allowing for damage, we see them all as they were in 79 A.C.[60] Whether or not an "early" house like the House of the Faun represents an earlier stage of evolution, it was undoubtedly one of the most desirable houses in the city in 79 A.C. Just like prospective home buyers today, the inhabitants of Pompeii had houses of more than one historical period and more than one architectural style available to them. So too the painters and patrons had more than one style of decoration available to them.[61] Mau's progressive linear sequence obscures this simple fact. The evolution (if it can be called that) of styles in architecture and in painting must have been very complex.

Despite this movement in the direction of pluralism, one form remains surprisingly consistent: the atrium. Though it may have existed in many variations of scale and decoration in 79 A.C., we cannot overlook or discount the fact that an ideal still existed and that it held meaning for Roman *patroni*. Drawing on Vitruvius's proportional standards, modern scholars have attempted to codify this ideal in terms of architectural theory. But the ideal quality of the atrium house cannot be understood solely as a set of proportions or designs transmitted by a single author, even one of such authority as Vitruvius. We must bear in mind that Vitruvius also admits a social ideal. As outlined above, the ideal embodied a matrix of deeply held social values and requirements ranging from matters of practical security to the correct performance of religious and social ritual. Owners and architects in early imperial Pompeii were obliged to adapt architectural form to the quotidian rituals of wealthy Roman patrons: theory aside, practice prevailed.

NOTES

I would like to express my gratitude to Kenyon College for a grant to help with the cost of illustrations for this chapter.

1. The subject of this paper, viz., the viability of the atrium house at Pompeii in 79 A.C., is taken up by J. B. Ward-Perkins in chapter 14 of *Etruscan and Roman Architecture* (Harmondsworth 1970), who gives the most concise presentation of the evolutionary theory:

The most conspicuous casualty of the new planning was the atrium. Once the physical and social centre of the Italic house, it had already begun to lose its predominant role during the later Republic, as more and more aspects of daily life moved to the lighter, more secluded setting of the peristyle. Now, with the addition of increasingly substantial upper storeys and galleries, it became in many cases little more than a passageway and a light-well, finally disappearing altogether. (p. 313)

A. G. McKay, *Houses, Villas, and Palaces of the Roman World* (Ithaca 1975) 41, writes of the second century B.C., "The atrium, once the heart of the house, no longer seemed adequate to the changing times." (The survival of the atrium and its evolution under the influence of the new peristyle form are discussed on p. 46.)

A. Boethius, *The Golden House of Nero* (Ann Arbor 1960) 137, was more inclined to see the evolution from the "aristocratic" atrium house to the popular apartment house (of independent formal origin) in terms of societal change. Attempting to find a beginning for the apartment house form among the most basic forms of popular architecture, Boethius even suggests its evolutionary priority to, or at least coexistence with, the *domus* in early Pompeii (p. 146). On the popular houses of Pompeii, see infra n. 24.

The conclusion that the atrium house was a classical form in decline is implicit in A. Mau's typological chronology of building materials that corresponds to his better known typology of wall decoration (see A. Mau, *Pompeii: Its Life and Art*, English trans. by F. W. Kelsey [New York 1907] 35–44, and infra n. 39) and has been assumed by nearly every historian of Roman architecture since. B. Tamm, "Some Notes on Roman Houses," *OpRom* 9:9 (1973) 53–60, summarizes trends in scholarship on the atrium house. The idea that the atrium has been replaced as the social center of the house is also implicit in P. Zanker's important study of Pompeian houses with interior gardens, "Die Villa als Vorbild des späten pompejanischen Wohngeschmacks," *JdI* 94 (1979) 460–523.

A. Wallace-Hadrill, "The Social Structure of the Roman House," *BSR* 56 (1988) 43–97, includes a discussion of the history of the atrium house that is refreshingly free of the language of "decline." As does the present author, Wallace-Hadrill views the atrium as an architectural form deeply embedded in the patterns of Roman social life, particularly the *patronus/cliens* relationship. He recognizes that "the atrium-peristyle matrix was a heritage of the late republic which left its characteristic stamp on the Vesuvian houses of 79 A.D." (p. 88) and seeks a structural explanation for its gradual disappearance from the post-Pompeian *domus*. He connects the transformation of reception and entertaining spaces in houses of the second century A.C. with changing tastes and styles of self-presentation among the Roman imperial elite: "The development of magnificent 'audience rooms' which replace the function of the tablinum and atrium, allowing for the eventual abandonment of the atrium as an architectural feature . . . suggests an attempt to impose greater control on the exposure of the master to the public" (p. 90). According to Wallace-Hadrill, the substance of the social institution of patronage did not change in the imperial period, but its style did. The architectural response was a slow process of experimentation with alternative domestic settings for the patronal ritual; Wallace-Hadrill points to changes in the traditional atrium/*tablinum* unit in the House of the Vettii at Pompeii and the House of the Mosaic Atrium at Herculaneum.

2. H. Knell, "Vitruvs Entwurfvorschriften zum Profanbau," *MdI* 92 (1985) 169–200, demonstrates that, at least in terms of the model of architectural design recommended by Vitruvius, the "ideal atrium house" was a commodious concept, a "unitized system

which could conform to a variety of needs" (p. 194). According to Knell's calculations, the Vitruvian model for the atrium house offered "dozens of possible variations, from which the owner and architect could pick and choose according to their desires" (p. 192).

3. These passages (Polyb. *Hist.* 6.53, and Pliny *HN* 35.6) are discussed by nearly every student of Roman portraiture. See, e.g., J. M. C. Toynbee, *Roman Historical Portraits* (London 1978) 10.

4. See Dragoslav Srejović, *Europe's First Monumental Sculpture: New Discoveries at Lepenski Vir* (New York 1972). In historical times burial within the limits of the city was expressly forbidden by law. Nevertheless (if we can assume a cultural memory of greater antiquity), the atrium (i.e., the hearth) retained its importance as the place where the body of the deceased was exposed for formal mourning for a period of up to a week following death. For the Roman funerary ritual, see J. M. C. Toynbee, *Death and Burial in the Roman World* (Ithaca 1971) 43–45.

5. In this context, C. Marius's purported speech to the effect that his vigorous virtue is more important than the possession of ancestor busts tells more about Roman society than Marius would have liked to believe. See Sallust *Iug.* 4, 85.

6. See J. Marquardt, *Das Privatleben der Römer* 2d ed., ed. A. Mau (*Handbüch der römischen Alterthumer* 7, 1, Leipzig 1886) 55–58.

7. This is not to say that the *domina,* or wife of the *dominus,* played an insignificant role either in the family cult or in the administration of the *domus.* A monument that illustrates the legal and religious relationship of the *domina* to her husband is the well-known altar from Cerveteri, now convincingly interpreted by M. Torelli, *Typology and Structure of Roman Historical Reliefs* (Ann Arbor 1982) 16–20. The owner and head of the family may be called *dominus, patronus,* or paterfamilias, depending on the context.

8. On the *salutatio,* see Marquardt (supra n. 6) 259–63.

9. On the *clientes* and *clientela* in general, see the bibliography in R. P. Saller, *Personal Patronage under the Early Empire* (Cambridge 1982) 209–16.

10. In my discussion of patronage I follow Saller (supra n. 9). For further discussion of the rite of *salutatio* under the late Empire, see S. Ellis, chapter 6 in this volume.

11. See James L. Franklin, *Pompeii: The Electoral Programmata, Campaigns and Politics,* A.D. *71–79* (Rome 1980).

12. Frank E. Brown, *Roman Architecture* (New York 1971) 14.

13. This point was first made by B. Götze, *Das Rundgrab in Falerii* (Stuttgart 1939) 52, and is too summarily dismissed by P. Zanker, *Forum Augustum* (Tübingen 1968) 35 n. 159.

14. I.e., as *domus Dei.* See, e.g., J. F. Niermeyer, *Mediae Latinitatis Lexicon Minus* (Leiden 1976) s.v. "*domus* (7.-12.)." Wallace-Hadrill (supra n. 1) emphasizes the power of allusion in the interplay of public and private forms that characterizes the architecture and decoration of many wealthy Pompeian houses: "It is by borrowing the language of actual public spaces in the domestic context that architect and decorator can evoke in the visitor the 'feel' of something more than a private house" (p. 59).

15. McKay (supra n. 1) 34 and 241 n. 40 notes that this point was made by G. Patroni, "Tablino e cella triplice nell'architettura etrusca," *RendLinc* ser. 6, vol. 12 (1936) 808–18, who emphasized the key relation of the *tablinum* to the garden (*hortus*) at the back of the house. McKay also cites P. Grimal, *Les jardins romains* 2d ed. (Paris 1969), who follows Patroni on the centrality of the *tablinum.* The point had been made in Guhl and Koner in R. Engelmann ed., *Leben der Griechen und Römer* 6th ed. (Berlin 1893):

Zwischen beiden [i.e., atrium and peristyle] liegt ein offener Saal, der den Mittel-oder Hauptpunkt des Hauses ausmacht, das Tablinum. . . . Hier war der Aufenthalt des Hausherrn, der den vorderen und hinteren Teil des Hauses von hier gleichmässig übersehen konnte; hier wurden Dokumente und Geld statt, sodass das Tablinum als des Comptoirzimmer des Herrn, wenn er sich mit Schreiberei beschäftigte, bezeichnet, werden konnte. (pp. 561–62)

One is reminded, not inappropriately, of the phenomenon of "Panopticism" so ingeniously described by M. Foucault, *Discipline and Punish* (New York 1977).

16. A number of houses with balconies were discovered in G. Fiorelli's excavations carried out in the 1860s. See, for example, the "Casa del Balcone Pensile" (VII xii 28), G. Fiorelli, *Descrizione di Pompei* (Naples 1875) 291–92.

17. Marquardt (supra n. 6) 228–36, with relevant sources.

18. For chests (*arcae*), see E. Pernice, *Hellenistische Tische, Zisternmündungen, Beckenuntersätze, Altäre und Truhen (Die hellenistische Kunst in Pompeji* 5, Berlin/Leipzig 1932) 76–94, with provenances. For the *sportula*, in origin a meal (the name deriving from the basket in which the meal was carried), but frequently a gift of money, see Marquardt (supra n. 6) 207–12.

19. The rooms of the atrium, viz., the *cubicula*, in the House of Marcus Lucretius (which will be discussed at length in this essay) do not, judging by the objects found in them, seem to have served as functional bedrooms. More likely, they served as storerooms for goods of the household. For a partial list of their contents, see E. Dwyer, *Pompeian Domestic Sculpture: A Study of Five Pompeian Houses and Their Contents (Archaeologica* 28, Rome 1982) 25–31.

20. See supra nn. 18 and 19 for the connection of household goods with the atrium. The presence of *lararia* in the atriums of Pompeii testify to the continued use of that part of the house in family religion.

21. Fiorelli (supra n. 16); and M. Della Corte, in P. Soprano ed., *Case ed abitanti di Pompei* 3d ed. (Naples 1965). Attributions in these works are based on epigraphical evidence of various sorts (and varying authority).

22. On these, see P. Castren, *Ordo Populusque Pompeianus: Polity and Society in Roman Pompeii (ActaInstRomFin* 8, 1975).

23. The latter fact has clearly perplexed P. Veyne in P. Veyne ed., *A History of Private Life: I. From Pagan Rome to Byzantium* (Cambridge, Mass., and London 1987), who writes: "But there are more sumptuous homes [in Pompeii] than there are shops. Were the rich in Pompeii more numerous than the poor? One has to assume, I think, that the richer homes were often rented out to a number of poorer families, each of which occupied several rooms" (p. 134). Veyne's suggestion is only plausible in the event of a complete breakdown of the patronage system. Very likely, the answer to Veyne's question lies in the as yet insufficiently explored areas of Pompeii outside the city walls.

On the other hand, Pompeii's disproportionate number of expensive houses certainly endeared the site to many social historians of the nineteenth century. The interest in Pompeii shown by M. I. Rostovtzeff and his student T. Warsher is presumably due to the extraordinary vitality enjoyed there by the bourgeoisie. In an essay ("M. I. Rostovtzeff") that originally appeared in *Cambridge Journal* 7 (1954) 334–46, A. Momigliano wrote, "Born in a country where the bourgeoisie was hard to find, he came to idealize the Hellenistic and Roman bourgeoisie." See now A. Momigliano, *Contributo alla storia degli studi classici* 1 (Rome 1955) 341–54, esp. 350.

24. The study of the humbler buildings in Pompeii (shops, inns, and the like) begins with Giuseppe Fiorelli, director of the excavations from 1860 to 1875, whose fervent political ideals probably gave him inspiration in this choice. See now J. Packer, "Middle and Lower Class Housing in Pompeii: A Preliminary Survey," in B. Andreae and H. Kyrieleis eds., *Neue Forschungen in Pompeji* (Recklinghausen 1975) 133–46, and "Inns at Pompeii: A Short Survey," *CronPomp* 4 (1978) 5–51. While Packer's study of middle- and lower-class housing in Pompeii tends to de-emphasize the importance of the bourgeoisie, Veyne (supra n. 23) challenges its very existence. In doing so, Veyne virtually ignores (or distorts?) the evidence provided by the remains of Pompeian atrium houses. In Veyne's discussion of private life during the Roman imperial period, the Pompeian evidence, with deliberate intention, receives only passing consideration throughout.

R. Meiggs, *Roman Ostia* 2d ed. (Oxford 1973) 251–62, discusses the changing fate of the *domus* and *insula* at Ostia. Despite the fact that atrium houses were pulled down in the second century A.C. to make way for *insulae*, some single-family houses were also built in the period. In late antiquity the *domus* regained prominence at Ostia, but in the form of peristyle houses that did not conform to a standard plan.

25. According to Tamm (supra n. 1) 54 and n. 9, the introduction of peristyle court-yards altered the architectural and social dynamics of the traditional Roman atrium house. The peristyle increased in importance relative to the atrium, taking over social functions formerly belonging to the atrium. *Triclinium* replaced *tablinum* as the social center of the house, so to speak. These changes are assumed to have taken place in the ideal plan of the atrium house between the time represented by the Pompeian House of the Surgeon (third century B.C.) and (e.g.) the House of the Vettii (first century A.C.). Although there seems to have been a general development to this effect in the later Empire (see Ellis [chap. 6 in this volume] and Wallace-Hadrill [supra n. 1] 88–94), evidence from Pompeii suggests that it had not taken place by 79 A.C. The fact that at least a dozen or so houses were found with stationary money chests (*arcae*) in the atrium is a sign that monetary transactions were made in the vicinity (supra n. 18).

Zanker (supra n. 1) has attempted to show how a number of Pompeian house-gardens (or "theme-parks") seem to imitate and draw inspiration from the great luxury villas that lined the coast from Sorrento to Anzio. In their emphasis on the growing importance of peristyles, *triclinia* and villa-like gardens as centers of family and social life in later Pompeian *domus*, Tamm and Zanker can be seen to challenge the viability of the atrium house as an architectural ideal in the early imperial period.

26. Tamm (supra n. 1) 54, citing earlier literature.

27. The fundamental study of Roman luxury is to be found in L. Friedlander in G. Wissowa ed., *Darstellungen aus der Sittengeschichte Roms in der Zeit von August bis zum Ausgang der Antonine* 9th ed. (Leipzig 1920). A valuable study of luxuriousness in Roman public architecture (with many references to the moralists) is H. Drerup, *Zum Ausstattungsluxus in der römischen Architektur: Ein formsgeschichtlicher Versuch* (Orbis Antiquus 12, Münster 1957). Drerup begins his study of luxurious decoration in Roman architecture by discussing what he deems to be the most important evidence on the subject, literary testimony from the first centuries B.C. and A.C. (pp. 3–13). Citing passages from, among

others, Cato, Livy, Sallust, Varro, Pliny, and Cicero, Drerup concludes that moralistic censure of architectural splendor was largely limited to buildings of a private nature; expensive public monuments to the greater glory of the state and its gods were rarely reproached (p. 8).

28. Pliny *HN* 36.4–8.

29. The example of Metellus is found in Velleius Paterculus's *Roman History* 1.11.5: "Metellus was the first of all to build a temple of marble . . . thereby becoming the pioneer in this form of munificence, or shall we call it luxury?" The translation is by F. W. Shipley, *Velleius Paterculus and Res Gestae Divi Augusti (The Loeb Classical Library*, London and New York 1924) 26–27.

30. Cic. *Off.* 1.138. Translation by W. Miller, *Cicero: De Officiis (The Loeb Classical Library*, London and New York 1913) 140–43.

31. Ibid.

32. On Vitruvius as defender of architecture, see A. Horn-Oncken, *Über das Schickliche: Studien zur Geschichte der Architekturtheorie (Abhandlungen der Akademie der Wissenschaften in Göttingen, phil.-hist. Klasse, dritte Folge* 70, Göttingen 1967) esp. 118–39.

33. *De Arch.* 6.5.1–2. The translation is from M. H. Morgan, *Vitruvius: The Ten Books on Architecture* (New York 1960) 181–82.

34. *Dignitas* was the measure of a man's worth. In Roman society of the late Republic and the Empire it would hardly be an exaggeration to say that it was quantifiable through the number and kind of offices a man held and the number and kind of his adherents. *Auctoritas* was related to *dignitas* as an objectified product or expression of it. (The word sometimes stands for the quality it expresses.) Like money in capitalist society, *auctoritas* serves as currency in hierarchical society, one of its meanings captured in the modern term *influence*. Although the accumulation of wealth in species and in property must have played a significant part in the quest for *dignitas*, it is not, as every student of history knows, an accurate measure of it. The real measure was power (*potestas*)—political power. For a discussion of the meaning of *auctoritas* and *potestas* as they relate to the emperor Augustus, see H. H. Scullard, *From the Gracchi to Nero* 4th ed. (London 1976) 219 nn. 7, 9. For recent remarks on the relationship between the *domus* and the *dignitas* of its owner, see T. P. Wiseman, "*Conspicui postes tectaque digna deo*: The Public Image of Aristocratic Houses in the Late Republic and Early Empire," in *L'Urbs: Espace urbain et histoire (Ier siècle av. J.C.–IIIe siècle ap. J.C.) (Collection de l'École Française de Rome* 98, Rome 1987) 393–413; and R. P. Saller, "*Familia, Domus* and the Roman Family," *Phoenix* 38 (1984) 351–55. On Vitruvius's use of *auctoritas* as a technical term of art criticism, see J. J. Pollitt, *The Ancient View of Greek Art* (New Haven and London 1974) 311–18.

35. Petron. *Sat.* So realistic is the description of the house of the wealthy freedman, Trimalchio, that Amedeo Maiuri wrote an instructive commentary on the text, drawing numerous illustrations from the houses of Pompeii and Herculaneum, in A. Maiuri, *La Cena di Trimalchione de Petronio Arbitro: Saggio, testo e commento* (Naples 1945). See also P. Veyne, "Vie de Trimalchio," *Annales économies-sociétés-civilisations* 16 (1961) 213–47 and "Trimalchio Maecenatianus," in *Hommages à A. Grenier (CollLatomus* 58, Brussels 1962) 1617–24 (both works cited by J. Andreau in his study of a real Trimalchio, *Les affaires de Monsieur Jucundus [Collection de l'École Française de Rome* 19, Rome 1974] 165). See also Zanker (supra n. 1) 521.

36. The sharp words of Vitruvius have had a lasting impact:

Hence, it is the new taste that has caused bad judges of poor art to prevail over true artistic excellence. . . . Their understanding is darkened by decadent critical principles, so that it is not capable of giving its approval authoritatively and on the principle of propriety to that which really can exist. (*De Arch.7.5.4*)

The translation is from Morgan (supra n. 33) 211–12.

37. Vitruvius's famous passage criticizing contemporary painting established the grounds for our chronology of the styles of Pompeian wall painting, and embedded his moral message for good:

Now it is not foreign to our purpose to explain why a false method overcomes the truth. The aims which the ancients sought to realise by their painstaking craftsmanship, the present attains by coloured materials and their enticing appearance. The dignity which buildings used to gain by the subtle skill of the craftsman, is not even missed owing to the lavish expenditure of the client. (*De Arch. 7.5.7*)

The translation is from F. Granger, *Vitruvius: On Architecture* 2 (*The Loeb Classical Library*, London 1934) 108–9.

38. Vitr. *De Arch.* 7.5.3. Translation from Morgan (supra n. 33) 211.

39. "Named from the statue of a dancing satyr found in it, this house [excavated between 1830 and 1840] was among the largest and most elegant in Pompeii. It illustrates for us the type of dwelling that wealthy men of cultivated tastes *living in the third or second century b.c.* built and adorned for themselves" (Mau [supra n. 1] 288, emphasis added). I emphasize Mau's chronology because I believe that many students of Pompeii have accepted it while ignoring the obvious fact that the house remained no less important in 79 a.c. (a point that I discuss later on in this essay). Although the date of Pompeii's destruction is no more than an accidental *terminus ante quem,* archaeological method and experience with urban centers should urge the greatest caution in speculating about remote periods. It is expected that stratigraphic evidence to be presented in the eventual publication of the House of the Faun will greatly clarify this chronology.

40. Mau (supra n. 1) 228–89.

41. On the parts of the house normally open to the public, see Vitr. *De Arch.* 6.5 as quoted in the text of this chapter. The ownership of the House of the Faun must have changed with the fortunes of the city and has not been determined with certainty. As a town house, its only serious competitor is the House of Pansa (VI vi 1). From the point of view of structure, plan, and, presumably, decor, however, it is manifestly superior to all rivals.

42. When accurate plans of the house are finally published, it may be possible to demonstrate some striking proportional relationships that make this house unique in Pompeii. The ratio of the atrium width to length seems to be 5:8 (according to Mau [supra n.1] 291, about thirty-three by fifty-three feet), an arithmetic approximation of the "golden" ratio. Though not found among the proportions recommended by Vitruvius for larger atriums, it falls between his types I and II. See the discussion in the text (infra) of the relevant passage, *De Arch.* 6.3.5. See Knell (supra n. 2) 192–96 for the flexibility of the Vitruvian atrium house model, which allows the architect to combine atrium types, proportions, and sizes to produce "more than 100 variously proportioned or decorated houses" (p. 196). S. F. Weiskittel, "Vitruvius and Domestic Architecture at Pompeii," *Pompeii and the Vesuvian Landscape* (Washington, D.C., 1979) 25–34, surveyed the proportions of twenty-seven atriums in Pompeii. It is interesting to note that none of the houses

that he surveyed approaches the harmony of plan observable in the House of the Faun.

43. Now in the Naples Archaeological Museum, 10020.

44. Although the mixing of the orders is contrary to Vitruvius's principles (see *De Arch.* 1.2.6), he is the first to record the three orders as canonical. An imperial building like the Colosseum, in which all three orders appear in ascending proportion, can be called Vitruvian, but the House of the Faun antedates him considerably and thus becomes an important document in the history of architecture.

45. It is unfortunate that Weiskittel (supra n. 42) omits this house from his statistical survey of Pompeian houses.

46. See Dwyer (supra n. 19) 19–52.

47. The painting is now in the Naples Archaeological Museum, 9819. The inscription is *CIL* 4, 879. See Della Corte (supra n. 21) no. 284.

48. Dwyer (supra n. 19) 21–22.

49. Today, as in so many other cases, nearly all trace of paintings in the house is lost.

50. *De Arch.* 6.3.5. Translation from Granger (supra n. 37) 27–29.

51. On the dimensions of the atrium of the House of the Faun, see supra n. 42.

52. Vitr. *De Arch.* 6.3.8.

53. The garden itself with its population of little demigods is a little Arcadia, one of several identifiable motifs found in the decoration of the peristyles of Pompeii. See Dwyer (supra n. 19) 38–48; and Zanker (supra n. 1) 496–98.

54. Naples Archaeological Museum 5002. Bronze statuettes were a mark of true wealth, and are much less common than marbles in Pompeii. We know from the excavation of houses like the House of the Bronze Bull (V i 7), the House of Fortune (IX vii 20), the House of the Centennary (IX viii 3/6), and others that bronzes were consistently used as centerpieces either in or visible from the atrium in order to achieve maximum decorative effect. See C. Moss, "'Patrician' Taste and the *Casa del Fauno*," *AJA* 89 (1985) 342.

55. See E. Falkener, *The Museum of Classical Antiquities* 2d ed. (London 1860): "The most gorgeous [ceiling], perhaps, was that of the *tablinum*. It consisted of a large circle in a square panel, boldly mounted, and enriched with stucco ornament, with ultramarine, vermillion, and purple colouring, together with a profusion of gilding" (pp. 66–67). Though Falkener did not succeed in obtaining a drawing of the ceiling, his work does not appear to have been in vain. An otherwise unidentified drawing matching his description appears in the fourth plate (no. 8) of the "Casa di Marco Lucrezio" fascicle of F. and F. Niccolini, *Le case ed i monumenti di Pompei, disegnati e descritti* 1 (Naples 1854).

56. Falkener (supra n. 55) 73–78. The view of the garden afforded from the *tablinum* is immediate and imposing—so much so as to make the entire miniature garden appear to be part of the decorative ensemble of the *tablinum*. With its arrangement of small sculpture it struck Falkener, a man of taste, as something resembling a marionette theater.

57. Naples Archaeological Museum 8992; W. Helbig, *Die Wandgemälde der vom Vesuv verschütteten Städte Campaniens* (Leipzig 1868) no. 1140.

The location of the *triclinium* in this house recalls that found in houses of earlier periods (viz., of the "Limestone" and "Tufa" periods [third through early second centuries B.C.]). See L. Richardson, Jr., "A Contribution to the Study of Pompeian Dining-Rooms," *Pompeii, Herculaneum, Stabiae: Bolletino dell'Associazione internazionale amici di Pompei* 1 (1983) 61–71.

On the importance of private dinners under the late Republic and early Empire, see J. H. D'Arms, "Control, Companionship, and *Clientela:* Some Social Functions of the Roman Communal Meal," *Studies in Roman Society* (EchCL 28, n.s. 3, 1984) 327–48. D'Arms asks whether wall and floor decoration—to which we should add sculptural decoration—may have been placed so as to give the person occupying the place of honor (*locus consularis*) a pleasing sight. The decoration of this *triclinium* and the placement of the sculpture in the garden are clearly chosen with something of this in mind. Another case in point is the *triclinium* of the central peristyle of the House of the Citharist (I iv 5/25/28), with the specially placed ensemble of bronze animals in the adjacent peristyle.

58. The final judgement must, of course, await the publication of the excavations of the German Archaeological Institute. One old house that does seem to have undergone changes connected with its reemployment as a hotel is the House of Sallust (to be published by Anne Laidlaw).

59. It might be objected that other "late" houses like the House of the Gilded Cupids (VI xvi 7) or the House of Fortune (IX vii 20) present plans that seem to subordinate the atrium to a peristyle, and are thus representative of some new evolutionary stage of development. This theory rests on the belief that the *triclinium* displaced the *tablinum* as the ritual center of the *domus* in the early Empire; see Tamm (supra n. 1). Consequently, the House of Marcus Lucretius would appear to be anomalous. According to the theory of continuity implicit here, these houses are anomalous.

60. A. Laidlaw, *The First Style in Pompeii: Painting and Architecture* (Archaeologica 57, Rome 1985). This point is often overlooked or even distorted in favor of earlier times. Arguing that the Pompeian evidence is not representative of Roman or Italic houses generally, Tamm (supra n. 1) writes, "The so-called Pompeian standard-house seems to belong to the second century B.C." (citing J. E. Skydsgaard, *Pompeii* [Copenhagen 1970], which I have not seen) (p. 54 n. 7). If Tamm's dating of Pompeian houses were true, her conclusion might be acceptable. Also problematic is her attempt to separate Vitruvius from Pompeii: "I think we must discard this old and unhappily established idea of combining Vitruvius and the old Samnite houses in Pompeii. Vitruvius never wrote about such houses, and if he wrote about Italic houses why should he have Campanian houses of Greek-influenced Pompeii in mind?" (p. 55) In addition to the objections already expressed, there is reason to connect Vitruvius with Campania. Even if we reject P. Thielscher's identification of Vitruvius with the Formian architect L. Vitruvius Mamurra, *praefectus fabrum* under Caesar [RE zweite Reihe 9 (1969) 419–89, s.v. *Vitruvius*], the weight of prosopographical evidence favors a Campanian origin for the author. Nor should "Greek-influenced" Campanian architecture be dismissed as foreign to the Roman tradition even as early as the second or first centuries B.C. The fact remains that the correspondence of the physical evidence with the text should be the final test. In that regard, H. Knell (supra n. 2) 199–200 n. 132 concludes that archaeological evidence proves the "typological accuracy" of Vitruvius's descriptions, which are in "fundamental correspondence" with the plans of preserved Pompeian houses.

61. It would be interesting to note whether the variety of atrium types, etc., mentioned by Vitruvius or the diverse styles of decoration alluded to are in any way responsive to the contemporaneity of older buildings, a feature that must have been evident in the cities of his time. Wallace-Hadrill's analysis of the social function of Roman wall painting (supra n. 1) 68–77 sheds new light on houses that integrate several of the four

Pompeian styles into a unified decor. If the choice of wall decoration is partially motivated by a desire "to refine the hierarchical contrasts between the different social spaces of the house" (p. 77), then "more dimensions than the chronological" (p. 49) are obviously involved.

CHAPTER 2

Painted Perspectives of a Villa Visit: Landscape as Status and Metaphor

Bettina Bergmann

In the mid–first century B.C. a fundamental change occurred in the life-style of wealthy Romans on the Bay of Naples. With the sea freed of piracy, spacious villas appeared along the shore, equipped with private harbors and fisheries. Resorts were built, and pleasure boats dotted the *crater delicatus*, creating a panorama that soon became associated with luxury in a philhellenic mode. As buildings rose, facades on country roads and on the sea were given monumental entrances and lush gardens, and interiors were covered with bright paintings imitating architecture, precious metals, flora and fauna, and even the optical effects of windows, marbles, and framed pictures. In this context appeared, perhaps for the first time, comprehensive views recording the contemporary environment.[1]

Although a general correspondence between painted views, actual land-scapes, and the views described in poetry of the first centuries B.C. and A.C. has been recognized, direct one-to-one comparisons remain elusive. There exists no "portrait" of a place, and despite a few quotations inscribed on paintings, it is unlikely that wall painters had either specific sites or texts in mind while filling the allotted spaces within the larger wall design.[2] There is, however, a felicitous coincidence of a surviving descriptive text, an excavated site, and a body of paintings that reveals a shared repertory of man-made and natural types. In his *Silvae* the poet Statius describes a visit to a rich patron's estate in 90 A.C. This ekphrastic account has been shown to conform in a general way to ruins on the three capes in Sorrento.[3] It has also been compared with selected "villascapes" painted on Campanian walls.[4] What has not been recognized, however, is that the poem, the paintings, and the Sorrentine villas are based

49

on common types, or *topoi*, that have Hellenistic antecedents and become parallel expressions of domestic luxury in the first century A.C.

The *topoi* of landscape emerged in my recent study of approximately three hundred landscapes painted on the walls of houses in Rome and along the Bay of Naples between 60 B.C. and 79 A.C.[5] The main focus of the landscapes is architecture, which appears in two settings, the inland grove and the waterway. These are distinguished by different spatial structures. Inland schemes are primarily vertical, with a structure, usually beside a tree in a wooded setting, marking the axial center. Recurring focal points are the light monuments of the column, the sacred portal, the enclosure, and the larger, more dominant temple, *tholos*, and tower. The waterway tends to be horizontal and is delineated by a juncture of land and sea that is marked by simple shrines and massive substructures. The main subjects of the waterway are the island, mole, or breakwater; the porticus alone; the tower and porticus complex; and the bay and the harbor.

Although the inland grove and the waterway show different spatial formats, they are composed according to the same empirical, additive methods. Patterns of buildings, like the diagonal row of aedicular facades or the oblique porticus, arise from the linear, geometrical scheme of the overall wall and structure the space of the landscapes, revealing Euclidean principles of diminution. Other smaller patterns, like the man and his pack animal crossing a bridge or the figure bending over an altar beside a tree, are secondary, connective units that can be placed in any vacant space in the design. A common background of color and a consistent system of light and shading achieve the semblance of coherent space.

Despite their formulaic nature, the paintings reflect arrangements found in actual architecture and described by contemporary writers who employ topographical *topoi* of Hellenistic epigrams to evoke the views from boats and villas. The recurring schemes in the paintings may thus be regarded as *topoi*, composed of a repertory of generic natural and man-made features, or *topia*. The Roman term *topia* denotes the contrived effects of scenery, whether on open terrain, in a cultivated garden, or depicted in art. Vitruvius mentions an art of landscape painted on walls as *varietates topiorum*, which include harbors, promontories, coasts, rivers, fountains, canals, groves, mountains, flocks, and shepherds. Pliny, attributing this genre to the Augustan artist Studius, groups *topiaria opera* along with villas, porticoes, groves, woods, hills, fishpools, canals, rivers, and coasts. He completes his list of Studius's motifs with people walking, sailing, traveling to villas on donkey or in carriages, fishing, fowling, hunting, or picking grapes. Vitruvius writes that *topia* "reproduce the characteristics of definite spots." In their emphasis on certain recognizable details, the Roman landscape paintings belong to a mode of descriptive realism, achieving an illusion of lifelikeness through variations on a standard scheme.[6]

The shared *topia* of poetry, painting, and villas can best be seen in the poems of Statius, who infuses villa settings with the same landmarks and figures that animate paintings and gardens. Statius is the first to describe villas in long poems, and in his series about art and nature he expresses a primarily visual aesthetic, stressing transitory, illusionistic effects and enlivening his narrative with images of mythological figures and distant places.[7] In *Silvae* 2.2, the first of the series, Statius uses the fiction of a tour to evoke a grander geographical and intellectual sphere and thereby praise his host. The scope or frame of his description is the Bay of Naples, an arena of Greek learning and luxury that mirrors the life and character of his patron Pollius Felix, a citizen of Naples, an Epicurean, and a landholder around the Bay. In the first part of the poem, Statius explains his visit and describes his approach to and arrival at the private harbor and his ascent via a porticus to the upper part of the villa (lines 1–35). The second, longest part describes the *domus*, first from the outside, then from the inside, in a series of catalogues, beginning with art works and proceeding to views and finally to marbles (lines 36–106). In the last part, Statius makes a direct connection between the villa and the patrons Pollius and Polla, employing landscape as a metaphor for their virtues (lines 107–46).

Statius approaches the villa as a geographer, focusing on major landmarks and surveying the region through a sequence of different views. The changing focus of his *periplus* is similar to waterway schemes in which the viewpoint is clearly from the sea. Setting off by boat from Naples, Statius crosses the bay toward the cliffs of Sorrento, a site he introduces with important landmarks and mythical associations. He notes its Minerva Temple, founded by Odysseus, and its proximity to the Straits of the Sirens, and thereby defines the geographical limit of his account, the Punta della Campanella, which divides the gulfs of Naples and Salerno and which through its lighthouse forms an essential link with Capri.

In Statius's day the city of Surrentum, a Greek colony, was a popular resort area for rich Romans; it boasted such extensive villas as that of Agrippa Postumus with its elaborate fisheries and those on the three successive capes of Sorrento, Calcarella, and Massa to the south of the city (fig. 2-1). The promontory villas are notable for their sea and cliffside structures and for the optical connections between their distinct parts and distant landmarks. In each villa the *domus*, a regular blocklike structure, stands on the highest of a series of terraces. A second, maritime section, composed of baths and nymphaea, reaches to the tip of the promontory and down the cliffs to the beach. Between these two main parts are gardens with hemicycles, towers, ramps, and steps, indicating the importance of walks and views.

Were it not for the private beach that Statius describes, one would not readily identify the smallest of the three capes, the Punta della Calcarella, as Pollius's villa. The beach below it, the Marina di Puolo, named after him, was the only safe landing place for visitors arriving by sea. Of the villa, only the substructures of artificial terraces, a few marble steps on the cliffside, and the foundations of a room, possibly an exedra, survive. These remains indicate that the villa of Pollius would have been more modest in its dimensions than the two flanking estates, but would have been planned in the same general way, with an upper *domus* on the hillside and a maritime section on the beach linked together by a ramp or porticus.

Statius first glimpses Pollius's villa from across the bay: "A lofty villa stands and gazes out upon the Dichaearchan deep" against a hillside covered with vineyards (see fig. 2-2).[8] The villa is personified and described as actively looking out on the Bay of Naples, which is here named for Dichaearchus, the legendary founder of Puteoli. A few lines later in the poem, Pollius's villa actually competes with the important city of Puteoli. Characteristically, Statius gives only a general and schematic idea of the villa's appearance. He notes its location between the mountains and the sea, a setting described by earlier literature as ideal for a villa, for it allows access by land and by water and exploits both elements for produce. Most important for maritime villas was the exposure to sweet and salt water for baths and above all to a variety of views.[9]

It is precisely this ideal setting that one sees captured, like an abbreviated version, in a series of landscape paintings of the mid–first century A.C. (see figs. 2-2 and 2-3; also see fig. 2-7).[10] Small in format, the new mode of landscape is characterized by a clarity and a vivid polychromy that evoke a view of or from the coast. Sunlight hits objects directly, creating strong contrasts of light and dark; the sea is blue, trees are bright green, and the yellow, red, and white facades are adorned with glittering decorations. In the numerous variations on this setting in the late Third and Fourth Styles of Pompeian wall painting, the conjunction of land and sea is always marked by an impressive facade, usually a porticus on a large substructure, or *basis villae*. Boats and steps indicate a private landing; regularly spaced trees and lawns, cultivation; and prominent windows in superstructures, a multiplicity of views. It is just these features of Pollius's villa that are singled out as praiseworthy by Statius as he comes closer and his visual field shifts to the private harbor, a small curving inlet beneath the cliffs.

> The crescent waters of a tranquil bay
> break through the curving line of cliff
> on either hand. The spot is of Nature's
> giving; one single beach lies between
> sea and hill, ending towards the land
> in overhanging rocks.
> (lines 13–16)

From its far end he goes to the center, where he sees a bath complex and shrines or statues of deities.

> The first charm of the place is a
> smoking bathhouse with two cupolas
> and a stream of fresh water from the
> land meeting the salt brine.
> Here would the nimble choir of Phorcus
> wish to bathe, and Cymodoce with
> dripping tresses and sea-green Galataea.
> (lines 17–20)

The landing beach, a veritable facade to Pollius's estate, is charged and numinous. Deity is present both in the sea creatures who prefer the man-made baths to natural waters and in the pious offerings made to the protecting gods Neptune and Hercules.

> Before the building the dark-blue ruler
> of the swelling waves keeps watch, and
> guards that innocent home; his shrine
> is it that is wet with friendly spray.
> Alcides [Hercules] protects the happy
> fields; in the two deities does the haven
> rejoice: one guards the land, the other
> resists the angry billows.
> (lines 21–25)

Although nothing remains of these structures, the Marina di Puolo still retains its crescent shape, with its waters stilled by the projecting promontories on either side. From Statius's lines, it is clear that Neptune's statue would have been close to the water and Hercules' closer to the fields inland. However, in another poem set on the Marina di Puolo, Statius describes the building of a temple for Hercules on the site of a small seaside shrine. The temple had not yet been erected at the time of his visit, so he must be referring to the earlier one.[11]

In presenting the main features of Pollius's bay, Statius employs a literary *topos* that is based on geographical description. Virgil had constructed his Libyan harbor in a similar way, shifting from one detail to the next in order of significance. He began by describing the scene horizontally from the sea, moved into the island lying before the harbor and flanking cliffs, surveyed the calm sea surface from above, and finally reached the background of a forest and a nymph cave. This survey influences Lucan's description of Brundisium, as it does Statius's advance towards Pollius's beach from the sea when he focuses first on the shape, then the landmarks, and ends with a mythological image.[12]

The "building blocks" of harbor descriptions employed by Statius and earlier authors can be identified with the patterns of composite bay scenes of the Fourth Style. A common scheme is the U-shaped basin flanked by diagonal lines of cliffs or buildings that lead in from each side of the painting to the level line of the horizon. In two small panels, one a painting from Herculaneum and the other part of a fountain mosaic in Pompeii (figs. 2-4 and 2-5), a tongue of land with a porticus on the left side faces an aedicular structure, a tree, and a portal lining the shore on the right, while a boat enters the harbor in the center. The same shape of the bay and grouping of structures can be seen in the right half of the large peristyle wall in the House of the Little Fountain (fig. 2-6). Here one finds distinct schemes linked together in a bird's-eye view by an ambiguous extent of blue water: on the left is a U- or quadriporticus shown from the closed side, a scheme that appears in small panels and large friezes of the Fourth Style (fig. 2-7); in the center, on a small islet that is reached by a bridge, is another recurring scheme of a tower, a porticus, and a garden, a grouping that occurs elsewhere (fig. 2-8); and on the right the arc of a harbor basin is marked by a porticus and a zigzag wall ending in a ruined tower, a scheme that is both a main subject and a background motif of other landscapes.[13]

Like the groupings on Pollius's beach, the individual structures find parallels in waterway scenes. Of the bathhouse Statius tells us only that is was placed near fresh and salt water on the beach and that it had a double-towered or domed facade. In paintings, a variety of porticoed facades with towers stands near the water. The most ornate of these is two-storied, with a large central apse or exedra and towerlike superstructures with conical roofs; tall trees of a formal garden rise up behind, and quays project from the platform in front of the complex into the sea (fig. 2-9). Such structures resemble seaside villas as well as baths. In the Villa of the Mysteries in Pompeii, a large *basis* supports a porticoed front with a convex exedra and a formal clipped garden, while in the suburban baths at Herculaneum, projecting apsed rooms with large windows rest upon massive arched substructures. Other forms of towered porticoes, like the quadriporticus shown in a bird's-eye view in a small panel from Stabia (fig. 2-10), are similarly ambiguous in function, for the same form appears in carto-graphic vignettes of baths in the Peutinger Table and can be compared with the seaside villa facades such as that of Diomedes in Pompeii.[14] Since the actual and painted complexes could apparently have been baths, villas, or shrines, their primary function must be seen simply as monumental facades that offer shade, vistas, and direct access to the sea.

Just as the natural configuration and architectural features of Pollius's bay appear in earlier literature and in paintings, so do the deities evoked by Statius. Poseidon/Neptune, god of harbors, straits, cliffs, and promontories, is described and addressed at those spots in epigrams placating him and thanking him for a safe landing. Similarly, in several bay scenes, statues of the god stand beside a shrine on the beach or on an isle; twice the renowned Poseidon type by Lysip-pus at the Corinthian Isthmus is shown from the side, elevated on a rocky base, his trident near at hand.[15] More significant for the protection of Pollius's domain is the god Hercules, who actively endorses its construction, is worshiped in a private cult by Pollius, and serves as his model. As with Neptune, veneration of Hercules as protector is depicted in sea scenes. In a small Fourth Style panel from Stabia he sits on a tall pillar, his club beside him, across a stretch of water from a monumental U-porticus—again a structure that could represent a villa, a sanctuary, or a public building.[16]

Even the animation of a coastal site by Galataea in Statius's poem (lines 19–20) finds parallels in Fourth Style paintings, where the nymph floats on waves before elaborate complexes along the shore (possibly the palace of Polyphemus) while the shepherd/Cyclops sits on a crag enticing the nymph onto land. The love story was popular in Hellenistic and Augustan pastoral, serving as a metaphor for the dynamic tension between the two elements.[17] Throughout Statius's poem and in the paintings, land and sea, sea and sky, and art and nature are juxtaposed to evoke a dynamic, numinous site where divine beings delight in man-made structures and the optical illusions created by dis-tance, water, light, and shadow transport one into revery. Galataea's attraction to Pollius's amenities on the shore signifies resolution of the natural conflict of sea and land.

Having landed at the harbor, Statius ascends to the promontory above via a porticus that leads in a zigzag pattern up the cliffs, with each part rising above the last. The porticus, the second monumental facade to Pollius's estate after the bay, is "as vast as a city," triumphal in its regularization of wild terrain, and a sensual delight as one ascends.

Thence a colonnade climbs slantwise up the
cliff, vast as a city, and its long line
of roof gains mastery over the rugged rocks.
Where the sun once shone through clouds of
dust, and the way was wild and unlovely,
now it is a pleasure to go. Even such,
should you scale the lofty height of Bacchic
Ephyre, is the covered way that leads from
the Lechaeum, of Ino's fame.
(lines 30–35)

The porticus was the most prominent facade of most large maritime villas
and was often singled out by authors as a sign of wealth and luxury.[18] Particularly important were the orientation and length of porticoed walks. Statius emphasizes the large size of Pollius's porticus by comparing it with a city, a *topos*
of praise voiced for men's homes and for buildings around the Bay of Naples.[19]
He then compares it with a grander, more famous walk at the Lechaeum, the
harbor of Corinth, the city that controlled communication between northern
Greece and the Peloponnesus and the eastern and western seas. Statius thereby
continues an epigrammatic tradition and gives Pollius's villa universal dimensions.[20]

Not surprisingly, the porticus is also the most frequent structure in landscape paintings from the late Third Style, when it first appears as the main
subject of small panels and large friezes. Common to nearly all porticus schemes
is the large *basis villae* dominating the natural contours of the shore—the formal
garden of regularly spaced, alternating poplars and firs behind and clipped
hedges and lawns in front. Of the various forms and combinations of the porticus, the most common are the U, the L, the T, and the zigzag. In paintings the
zigzag porticus, which is typical in mirror-reversed pendants, usually reaches
from the land into the sea (fig. 2-11). It is clear, however, that porticoes of such
eccentric shape were also cut into cliffs to provide cool access from the shore to
hilltops. The remains of a zigzag ramp can be seen along the rocks of the Capo
di Massa, where it led up from the inlet with its seaside nymphaea to the *domus*
on the promontory above (fig. 2-12). Still today, access from the Marina di Puolo
to the Punta della Calcarella leads via a road of similar shape, clearly the most
efficient means to traverse steep cliffs like those on the Sorrentine coast.[21]

With the porticus Statius ends the first part of the poem dealing with his
arrival and begins the central section about the upper villa. Here he finds many
separate buildings scattered over terraces and oriented in different directions,
with one part facing east, another west, one room opening onto the sea, and

another to the back woods. While the first part of the poem followed the visitor's movements, the structure of the middle section shifts to a series of catalogues that is interrupted by questions and exclamations. Statius employs *topoi* of wonder and admiration and a variety of terms for seeing to explore the contrasts of inside and outside, and of natural and man-made, and thereby conveys the magnificence of Pollius's domain.[22]

> Shall I first admire the genius of the
> place or its master? This part of the
> house looks eastward to Phoebus' morning
> rays; that part detains him as he sets,
> nor allows the exhausted light to disappear,
> when the day is wearied out and the shadow
> of the dark mountain falls on the waters,
> and the proud mansion floats upon the
> glassy flood. Here the sound of the sea
> is in the chambers, here they know not
> the roaring of the waves, but prefer the
> silence of the land. Here are spots that
> Nature has favoured, here she has been
> outdone and given way to the settler and
> learnt gentleness in ways unknown before.
> (lines 44–53)

The villa is transparent, described in terms of the light and sound of its surroundings. Here Statius evokes not only the same subjects and schemes of the paintings, but their optical effects as well. The illusions of reflection, of the indeterminate distance of water, and of the bluish haze on the maritime horizon are noted with delight, as they are by other villa owners. Cicero, for instance, notes that although the sea appears so flat, it can both deny and enhance distance, a phenomenon used effectively by wall painters to unify discrete spatial units.[23] Statius's phrase "and the proud mansion floats upon the glassy flood" recalls particularly those views of porticoed complexes that appear like islands or pleasure boats suspended on an expanse of blue (see fig. 2-9).[24]

The varied ambience of the upper villa was achieved through the building of substructures and terraces. These become triumphal images that manifest Pollius's power in the *agon* between art and nature.

> Here, where you now see level ground,
> was a hill; the halls you enter were wild

country; where now tall groves appear,
there was once not even soil: its owner
has tamed the place, and as he shaped and
conquered the rocks the earth gladly gave
way before him. See how the dwellings
force their entry and the mountain is
bidden withdraw.
(lines 54–59)

Each cape at Sorrento retains the staggered foundations of terraces, platforms for lookouts that created, together with greenery, isolated orbits within the estate (figs. 2-13 and 2-14; also see fig. 2-1). From the outside, such platforms, or *bases villarum,* appeared like hanging gardens with an arcaded quadratic base; inside they offered cool and shady corridors (*cryptoportici*) or contained cool waters in cisterns. Often the massive platforms were included in the planning of views, serving to lead the eye to another focal point. Pliny describes sitting in his garden pavilion, looking through a door over the *cryptoporticus* below, through another window and out to the sea.[25] The remaining houses and villas in Campania still offer glimpses of the wide gaping arches of their bases, as in the Mansion of Fabius Rufus in Pompeii, where terraces and belvederes open onto the lower stories and substructures.

In paintings the *basis villae* fulfills a function similar to that in planned views. Usually reaching out beyond the water's edge, it supports porticoes, towers, and small chapels and is planted with hedges and lawns that are bounded by small fences or balustrades; statues may stand at the edge, and ramps or steps lead down to the water (see figs. 2-2, 2-3, 2-6, 2-7, 2-9, 2-10, and 2-11). The height and breadth of the *basis* make it a prominent feature of the facade that signifies the luxury of being elevated above the tide in shady lookouts with expansive views.

By stressing the beauty of the porticus and the terraces, Statius applauds just the kind of building that had been hotly criticized since the late Republic for its destruction of nature and ostentatiousness, particularly in the domestic realm. In the Flavian era, it became an imperial symbol of technological progress. Architectural inscriptions express admiration for the clear geometry, strength, and durability of such forms, and Pliny the Elder tells how men admired the substructures of the Capitol, the Servian wall strengthened by earthen ramparts, and the city sewers, for which hills were tunnelled through, leaving Rome a hanging city.[26] The waterway, like the other main category of paintings, the inland sacred grove, expresses respect for numinous spots; here, however, that respect is not demonstrated in simple shrines but in concrete wonderworks that restructure, and thereby improve on, natural forms. The paintings suggest what Statius proclaims, namely that such aggressive, man-made forms are pious, inspired, and magical.

Elaborating on this theme, Statius recounts how Pollius has transformed the site, changed mountains into plains and haunts of wild beasts into villas, and made tall woods grow where there was not even land. Pollius is a civilizer, and building is like waging war and taming animals. Just as trees and rocks followed Orpheus, the soil follows Pollius. Once again, Statius uses a poetic allusion with precedents in earlier villa descriptions and domestic decoration. From the second century B.C. villas had served as the settings for performances in which owners would play the protagonist. In the mid-first century B.C. Varro describes how a rich friend entertained his guests by appearing in the guise of Orpheus and surrounded by wild animals that had been trained to follow his tune. Just such a scene is evoked in a Pompeian garden, where visitors and guests encountered a large, frontal image of Orpheus sitting in a landscape among animals, a composition that becomes pervasive in late Roman figural floor mosaics. In Roman domestic decoration, the *topos* of Orpheus among the animals may well suggest an association between mythical hero and *dominus*, an association explicitly made by Statius in describing the poet/patron's magical spell over nature.[27]

Having noted Pollius's massive construction, Statius moves through the villa "from scene to scene," pausing at rooms and lookouts to describe the features and optics of his views. Overwhelmed by the beauties he sees, his eyes tire.

> Why should I recount the numberless
> summits and the changing views? Each
> chamber has its own delight, its own
> particular sea, and across the expanse
> of Nereus each window commands a different
> landscape . . .
> (lines 72–75)

Both the "numberless summits" and the "changing views" can be corroborated by actual remains in Sorrento and by paintings. The importance of viewpoint on the Capo di Sorrento can be seen in the substructures of the maritime part of the villa where a room that is turned diagonally to face Vesuvius and Naples breaks the unity of the plan (see area *B* in fig. 2-14). Separate lookouts on the cape included an exedra, which looked directly past a tower to the city of Sorrento and the flanking cape (see area *A* in fig. 2-14), and a tower on the small island that was reached by a bridge (see area C in fig. 2-14). From the tower on the island one would have had a panorama of the elaborate villas nearby and across the bay as well as of Naples and the busy ports of Baiae and Puteoli. Towers are recurring focal points in paintings, where, as on the Capo di Sorrento, they direct the eye toward further structures and land masses (see figs. 2-4, 2-5, 2-6, and 2-8). The island with a pavilion, a tower, or a shrine, sometimes linked to land by a bridge and often surrounded by boats and fishermen, is another popular scheme in paintings (see fig. 2-6).[28]

The villa on the Capo di Massa, like those on the other two capes, is structured by staggered platforms and open belvederes. From the convex exedra at the end of a long rectangular peristyle on the uppermost terrace, one could have looked over the porticoed garden on the next lowest terrace out to the sea (see fig. 2-12). Such an elevated view of a porticus and a garden before the water is a popular scheme in paintings. Just as one would have encountered Capri from the Capo di Massa, the foreground forms in paintings lead the eye to islands on the horizon that are ringed with porticoes and topped by terraced structures (fig. 2-15). Indeed, the function of the porticus as a directive was appreciated in optical studies. Euclid and Lucretius note the perspectival effects of a colonnade that, when viewed obliquely, result in the gradual contraction of roof and floor to the apex of a cone. This illusion, which is reproduced in the porticoes painted on Roman walls from the mid-first century B.C., became a popular device used to suggest depth and distance in landscapes.[29]

The cape of Pollius would have been planned like those nearby, with the axes and frames of buildings directing one's view horizontally and vertically to the sea and the horizon. Accordingly, Statius's account presents the villa not as a spatial continuum, but as a sequence of objects and areas. The villa is a dynamic image that itself looks out, *spectat, prospectat, prospicit,* and subjugates the land it sees in a succession of framed views.

> Each chamber has its own delight, its own
> particular sea, and across the expanse of Nereus
> (sea) each window commands a different landscape
> (lines 73–75)

Statius uses a *topos* when he describes single views as entire landscapes, with moving nature held in place in selected excerpts like framed paintings. Villa owners likewise recount the quiet hours spent in *diaetae*, where, with all nature centering on them, they could contemplate the sea, the woods, and the rotation of the heavens. Pliny enjoyed the "three seas" captured within a single room of his villa, an impression that one still has looking through the large windows of such seaside complexes as the Villa Arianna in Stabia and from the exedra of the Mansion of Fabius Rufus in Pompeii. The ordered access to nature, which is contained within the geometry of architecture, determined the appearance of actual and painted landscape in the Roman *domus*.[30]

Separate rooms with individual axes, prominent windows, and open galleries like those described by Statius are frequent features in paintings. In one of the small panels from the House of Lucretius Fronto, for instance, buildings of various heights and numerous openings show differing orientations, with some facing the back garden and hills and others the sea (see fig. 2-2). Other coastal complexes are similarly composed of distinct buildings loosely strewn along the shore (see figs. 2-4, 2-5, 2-6, 2-8, and 2-15). It has been pointed out that these could just as likely be small towns as villas; in either case the open, accessible nature of seaside buildings conveys a freedom of movement and an aesthetic enjoyment of landscape that can be contained and brought indoors.[31]

Even the types of places that are seen from the lookouts and windows of Pollius's villa find their painted parallels in the schemes of islands, ports, porticoes, and towers. Statius begins his survey with a catalogue of islands moving from west to east across the bay.

> . . . this one (window) beholds Inarime, from
> that rugged Prochyta is seen; here the
> squire of mighty Hector (Cape Misenum)
> is outspread, there sea-girt Nesis breathes
> tainted air; yonder is Euploea, good omen
> for wandering barks, and Megalia flung out
> to repel the curving billows; and thy own
> Limon grieves that his lord reclines there
> over against him, and gazes at the
> Surrentine mansion from afar.
> (lines 72–82)

The Greek origins of the sites are stressed in their names. The largest island is named Inarime (Ischia)—a name that had already been cited by Virgil— after a passage in the *Iliad* in which Typhoeus was chained "ein arimois." Its one central mountain and its cliffs and beaches would have been studded with numerous villas. Before Ischia lies Procida (named after Aeneas's nurse), which builds a land bridge to the next notable feature, the Cape named for Misenus; Procida's flat plateau, also covered with villas and gardens, dropped abruptly in steep cliffs to the sea. The smallest island, Nesis, with the form of a crater, was the seat of Lucullus's lavish villa. The temple of Aphrodite Euploea, of unknown form, stood on the promontory of Pizzo Falcone, the old city of Naples, signaling luck to mariners. As Statius proceeds, he sets up an *agon* between islands and mainland, distant landmarks and Sorrento. Megalia, the small island near Naples, now the Castel dell'Uovo, protrudes from the mainland to contest the tide. Shifting back and forth across the bay, Statius tells how Limon, Pollius's villa near Puteoli, gazes back at its patron and grieves his absence, thereby actively reflecting the poet's point of view.[32]

As he did with Pollius's villa, Statius personifies the sites he sees across the bay, associates them with distant mythical places, and thereby confuses them with their archetypes. The Aphrodite sanctuary, like that in Naples, is a popular subject in epigrams left by pious builders who describe it as a safe anchorage, in reach of the waves, fully exposed to sunlight and a fair breeze. The setting of the shrine on a promontory near the sea is that of the archetypal Aphrodite sanctuary on Zephyrium overlooking the Canopus. It also corresponds to the colorful shrines in painted scenes (see figs. 2-4, 2-5, and 2-15).[33] The other landmarks noted by Statius, like Puteoli with its massive mole, recur in architectural epigrams and are singled out by Cicero in describing his views across the bay: "O what a glorious view! We can see Puteoli, but we can't see our friend . . . who is very likely taking a stroll in the Colonnade of Neptune. . . ." At another point he tries to sight his own villa in Pompeii, as Statius does Limon.[34]

By amplifying individual, specific views into types, Statius arrives at the same general schemes that the wall painter attempts to individualize with additions of color and detail. Islands like Procida and Ischia appear in paintings on the distant horizon, enveloped in mist with porticoes and fortresses on top and terraces on hillsides (see fig. 2-15). Sunlit chapels and porticoes on the shore signal welcome in the paintings, possibly like the sanctuary of Aphrodite Euploea and Pollius's villa Limon (see figs. 2-4, 2-5, and 2-15). Furthermore, the famous Gragnano harbor painting, as has been often noted, captures the major features of Puteoli's basin, but in a typical scheme; its correspondence to other harbors like that at Alexandria is not due to a failure to document its topography, but to a way of seeing and thinking about the land.[35]

Finally, in a room decorated with precious stones that offers a view of Naples, the Greek world is brought into view. Examining the encrusted walls between windows, Statius describes the regions from which the stones, which he calls "Graia," derive. Both views and marbles embellish Pollius's villa like the *spolia* of captured places.

> Yet one room there is, one higher than
> all the rest, which over a straight track

of sea brings Parthenope to thy sight:
here are marbles chosen from the heart
of Grecian quarries; the stone of Eastern
Syene, splashed with veining, and that
which Phrygian axes hew in mournful
Synnas o'er the fields of wailing Cybele,
whereon the white expanse is bordered by
a rim of purple; here too are green blocks
quarried from the hill of Lycurgus at Amyclae,
where the stone counterfeits the grass;
here gleam the tawny rocks from Numidia,
Thasian marble too and Chian, and Carystian
stone that joys Chalcidian towers (Cumae).
A blessing on thy heart, Grecian land;
nor let the city of Dicarchus that gave
thee birth feel envy! We shall prove better
owners of our poet-ward.
(lines 83–97)

The interpenetration of outside and inside and the shifting focus between art and nature create a blurred, hallucinatory experience in which vista and vision are confused. Marbles are "splashed with veining," green blocks "counterfeit the grass." The desire to deceive the eye with artifice underlies the illusionistic paintings of architecture and gardens that appear in domestic decoration in the late Republic, as it does the fashion for marble incrustation. In fact, it is in paintings imitating inlaid panels created in the second half of the first century B.C. that the first architectural landscapes appear. The yellow monochromes in Oplontis, which clearly imitate relief, show distinct architectural vignettes scattered across their ambiguous surface; like Statius's topographical visions, these vignettes come into focus, then fade as new objects catch the eye (fig. 2-16). Such painted illusions of inlaid stones appear among other signs of wealth such as precious metals, imported works of art, and the pets, fruits, and plants of the private *fundus*. Landscape forms an intrinsic part of the new iconography of materialistic status.

Marbles were in fact as vehemently criticized as porticoes, substructures, and works of art.[36] By juxtaposing views through windows with reflective stones, Statius underlines the proprietary value of the view. In the late Republic and early Empire neighbors went to court over their *prospectus*; and, notably, a view ranked as a *prospectus* only when it was visually subjugated—framed, ordered, and presented in entirety from above; then it was considered beautiful.[37] Horace is critical, claiming:

> Our cares are removed by reason and
> prudence, not by a house commanding
> a wide sea view. We change our sky, not
> our minds by running across the sea.
> We are engaged in a strenuous idleness.[38]

And Seneca condemns the present fashion for views by recalling Scipio Africanus's spartan villa fortress and its small baths with slit windows that were so unlike the large "picture" windows of modern villas.[39]

From the highest point of Pollius's estate, Statius returns to its fertile surroundings, which, like the views and marbles, lend the domain a special status.

> Why should I rehearse the wealth of the
> countryside, the fallows flung out into
> the sea and the cliffs steeped in Bacchus'
> nectar?
> (lines 98–99)

To underline the sublime situation, Statius describes a mythical meeting of land and sea that recalls the earlier attraction of Galataea to Pollius's baths and the patron's magical sway over nature. In autumn, when the grapes begin to ripen, a Nereid "climbs the rocks" and "brushes the seawater from her eyes with a leafy vine-spray, and snatches sweet clusters from the hills." In response, satyrs plunge into the water and Pans from the mountain grasp the sea (lines 100–106). Sea creatures are further charmed and tamed by the harp, as Pollius had tamed the soil with his construction.

In the last part of the poem, Statius focuses directly on the characters of Pollius and Polla. Here the topographical image reflects the spirit of the patron, and the bird's-eye view and the secure harbor become metaphors for his temperance.

> But we, a worthless folk, slaves at the
> beck of transient blessings and wishes
> ever new, are tossed from chance to chance:
> thou from thy mind's high citadel dost look
> down upon our wanderings and laughest at

human joys.
(lines 129–32)

. . . now are the mists dispersed, and thou dost
behold the truth—others in their turn are
tossed upon that sea—and thy unshaken bark
has entered a peaceful haven and quiet resting
place. Continue thus, nor ever loose thy vessel,
her voyage over, to face our storms.
(lines 138–42)

The man-made enclave of a harbor was a popular metaphor for peace, security, and rest. Cicero characterized the quiet retreat enjoyed by Scipio Africanus
in his villa as a return into a harbor, and of his own death he wrote that the
nearer he approached it the more he felt like one who after a long voyage is at
last in sight of land and about to anchor in his home port.[40] The sanctity of entry
points to harbors is recorded in the many epigrams inscribed on them by mariners stopping to sacrifice. These same shrines, breakwaters, moles, and statues
in painted waterway scenes signify a numinous locus and peaceful harbor.[41]

The bird's-eye view, an impossible and purely abstract construct, appears
to be one of the major innovations of the Roman wall painter (see figs. 2-6 and
2-15). This illusion was achieved by manipulating the viewpoint of each component and placing them all below an unnaturally high horizon; lines that should
normally vanish in the horizon lead nowhere, and the eye must begin again, its
dramatic jumps between near and far accommodated by the flat background.
By combining clusters of features, the painter could represent extensive tracts
of sea and land, giving the spectator a sweeping, panoramic view like that of a
landowner or military commander surveying his domain.[42]

The principle of structuring views in parts through windows and columns
and over the forms and edges of buildings was based on prevailing spatial
concepts. The Romans had no inclusive term like the modern *landscape*. Ancient
authors conceived of *landscape* in the plural, as the sum of natural and man-
made objects whose association forms one segment of the visual world. In the
ancient concept of landscape, the parts take precedence over the unified arrangement because each part has its *topos,* or physical envelope, and it is the
relation of one *topos* to another that creates a *choros,* or area. Thus descriptions
refer to place in the plural as *topia,* which is the diminutive form of *topos: topion,*
a term only known from the Roman period.[43]

In each part of his account, Statius singles out the favored aspects of the
maritime villa—its setting between hills, land, and sea; the private, still harbor;

the monumental porticus; the terraced gardens with various lookouts; the *diaetae* with framed views and reflective stones. His viewpoints are those of the paintings: the geographer's scope, the diminishing oblique porticus, the staggered series of buildings, the distant sites across the sea, and the scattered reflected illusions. By bringing the salient features of Pollius's villa visibly before the eyes, Statius fulfills the purpose of his *ekphrasis*. His poem, like the paintings, typifies and exalts a domestic context in which architecture imposes order on the land and nature is shaped into perfect views.

NOTES

1. On this phenomenon in general see J. D'Arms, *Romans on the Bay of Naples: A Social and Cultural Study of the Villas and Their Owners from 150 B.C. to A.D. 400* (Cambridge, Mass. 1970); P. Zanker, "Die Villas als Vorbild des späten pompejanischen Wohngeschmacks," *JdI* 94 (1979) 460–523; H. Mielsch, *Die römische Villa: Architektur und Lebensform* (Munich 1987); E. B. MacDougall ed., *Ancient Roman Villa Gardens* (Washington, D.C., 1987); and R. Neudecker, *Die Skulpturenausstattung der römischen Villen in Italien* (Mainz 1988).

2. On inscribed paintings, see A. F. Gow ed., *The Greek Anthology: Hellenistic Epigrams* 2 (Cambridge 1965) 52; and P. Ciprotti, "Brevi note su alcune scritti pompeiane," in B. Andreae and H. Kyrieleis eds., *Neue Forschungen in Pompeji* (Recklinghausen 1975) 276; K. Lithey, "Dipinti pompeiana accompagnati di epigrammi greci," *Annali dell'Instituto di corrispondenza archeologica* 48 (1876) 294–314. On the difficulty of comparing paintings with texts, see the review of J. M. Croisille's *Poesie et art figure de Neron aux Flaviens. Recherches sur l'iconographie et la correspondance des arts a l'époque imperiale* (CollLatomus 179, Brussels 1982) by A. Wallace-Hadrill, "Ut pictura poesis?" *JRS* 73 (1983) 180–83; a recent attempt to make such a comparison is E. Leach, *The Rhetoric of Space: Literary and Artistic Representations of Landscape in Republican and Augustan Rome* (Princeton 1988).

3. On the correspondences between *Silvae* 2.2 and the Capo di Sorrento, see J. Beloch, *Campanien* (Breslau 1879; 1890) 269–74; F. Vollmer, *P. Papinii Statii Silvarum libros ed. et expl.* (1898) 338; and E. Kirsten, *Süditalienkunde* (1975) 269–73; between the poem and the Punta della Calcarella: P. Mingazzini and F. Pfister, *Surrentum (Forma Italiae* 5, 1946) 54–70; H. Cancik, "Eine epikureische Villa," *Die altsprachliche Unterricht* 11.1 (1968) 62–75; and d'Arms (supra n. 1) 220–22 n. 34. On the poem in general, see R. Argenio, "La villa sorrentina di Pollio Felice," *Rivista di Studi Classici* 18 (1970) 186–97; and N. R. Nisbet, "Felicitas at Surrentum (Statius, *Silvae* 2.2)," *JRS* 68 (1978) 1–11.

4. M. Rostovtzeff, "Pompejanische Landschaften und römische Villen," *JdI* 19 (1904) 115; A. Taisne, "Peintures de villas chez Stace," *Caesarodunum* 13 (1978) 40–53; and Croisille (supra n. 2) vol. 2, pp. 257–66.

5. B. Bergmann, *Coast and Grove: Architectural Landscapes in Roman Painting* (Princeton, forthcoming).

6. Vitr. *De Arch.* 7.5.2; Pliny *HN* 35.116–17. On Studius, see R. Ling, "Studius and the Beginnings of Roman Landscape Painting," *JRS* 67 (1977) 1–16; and C. Daremberg and M. E. Saglio eds., *Dictionnaire des antiquités grecques et romains* (Paris 1877–1919) s.v. *topia* (G. Lafaye).

7. H. J. Van Dam, *P. Papinius Statius*, Silvae, *Book II: A Commentary* (*Mnemosyne*, Supplementum 82, Leiden 1984) 187–280; and H. Cancik, *Untersuchungen zur lyrischen Kunst des P. Papinius Statius* (Spudasmata 13, Hildesheim 1965).

8. Translated passages are taken from J. H. Mozley trans., *Statius Silvae* (*The Loeb Classical Library*, Cambridge, Mass. 1982) 95–107.

9. On the ideal setting of villas, see Cato *Agr.* 1.3.1–7; Columella *Rust.* 1.5; H. Dohr, *Die italischen Gutshöfe nach den Schriften Catos und Varros* (Cologne 1965) 16–23; O. E. Schmidt, *Cicero's Villen* (Darmstadt 1899; 1972); E. Lefevre, "Plinius-Studien: Römische Baugesinnung in der Landschaftsauffassung in den Villenbriefen (2.17.5–6)," *Gymnasium* 84 (1977) 519–41.

10. At present the few relatively secure dates for landscapes are based on inscriptions and phases of building construction. While recent finds have confirmed the developments through the Second Style postulated by A. Mau and refined by H. G. Beyen in *Die pompejanische Wanddekoration vom zweiten bis zum vierten Stil* 1–2, 1 (The Hague 1938–60), from the Third Style the development of painting occurred as a series of shifts in taste, workshop practice, stylistic revivals, and phases of retardation; see the review of F. L. Bastet and M. de Vos's *Proposta per una classificazione del terzo stile pompeiano* (Rijkswijk 1979) by W. Ehrhardt in *Gnomon* 54 (1982) 577–88; see also W. Ehrhardt, *Stilgeschichtlicher Untersuchungen an römischen Wandmalereien von der späten Republik bis zur Zeit Neros* (Mainz 1987). Evidence of such shifts has been found in analyses of walls painted before and after the earthquake that show different combinations of motifs and designs; see M. de Vos, "Primo stile figurato e maturo quarto stile negli scarichi provenienti dalle macerie del terremoto," *Meded* 39 (1977) 35–42; and V. M. Strocka, "Ein missverstandener Terminus des vierten Stils: Die Casa del Sacello Iliaco in Pompeji (I,6,4)," *RM* 91 (1984) 125–40. For a useful review and bibliography of the state of research on Roman painting through 1980, see H. Mielsch, "Funde und Forschungen zur Wandmalerei der Prinzipatszeit von 1945 bis 1975, mit einem Nachtrag 1980," *ANRW* II 12.2, 157–264. Based on the hypothetical development deduced from the external evidence, the landscapes fall into five main phases. The new, late Third Style discussed here appears in Pompeii in the House of Lucretius Fronto in approximately 45 A.C. The greatest number of landscapes was made in the early Fourth Style before the earthquake, roughly between 50 and 62 A.C.

11. "The Temple of Hercules at Surrentum," Stat. *Silv.* 2.1. On the location of the shrines, see Van Dam (supra n. 7) 206–7.

12. Virg. *Aen.* 1.159–69; Luc. 613–25; and H. D. Reeker, *Die Landschaft in der Aeneis* (Spudasmata 27, Hildesheim 1971) 19. For a list of ancient harbor descriptions, see Van Dam (supra n. 7) 201.

13. As, for example, in the landscape in the House of the Argo in Herculaneum (II 2).

14. For reconstructions of the villas of the Mysteries and Diomedes, see Mielsch (supra n. 1) 39, 122; on the scheme of "le Quae" in maps, see A. Levi and M. Levi, *Itineraria Picta: Contributo allo studio della Tabula Peutingeriana* (Rome 1967) 85–90. The same problems of identification exist with the porticoed "Sosandra Baths" in Baiae and the villa at Anguillara Sabazio, which have been seen both as villas and as baths; see Mielsch (supra n. 1) 54; and M. Boriello and A. d'Ambrosio, *Baiae-Misenum* (Forma Italiae 1.14, 1979) 63.

15. Epigrams describing such statues are Antiphilus 11, *Anth. Pal.* 10.17; Alpheus 1, *Anth. Pal.* 9.90; and a dedication to Poseidon at the Corinthian Isthmus: Maccius 8, *Anth. Pal.* 6.233. On the type, see Paus. 10.36.8; and E. Walde, "Die Aufstellung des aufge-

stützten Poseidons," *AM* 93 (1978) 99–107. Figures of Poseidon appear in the white frieze from the Villa Farnesina in the Museo Nazionale, Rome; in a yellow monochrome, Naples Archaeological Museum 9493; in a rectangular panel, Naples Archaeological Museum (no inventory number); and in an unframed vignette, Naples Archaeological Museum 9401.

16. On Hercules' importance for Pollius and his Epicurean associations, see Van Dam (supra n. 7) 208. The landscape from Stabia featuring a statue of Hercules is in Naples Archaeological Museum 9479.

17. A particularly good comparison with Statius's lines is a lost painting from Pompeii (V iv 51)) recorded in a drawing in the German Archaeological Institute in Rome; see C. Dawson, *Romano-Campanian Mythological Landscape Painting* (New Haven 1944) pl. 24, fig. 64. For a list of the ancient representations of Galataea and Polyphemus, see B. Fellmann, *Die antiken Darstellungen des Polyphemabenteuers* (Munich 1972) 133–36. The literary passages include Virg. *Ecl.* 2.19, 7.37, 9.39; and Ov. *Met.* 13.738.

18. Especially Hor. *Carm.* 2.15.16; D'Arms (supra n. 1) 126–33; and Van Dam (supra n. 7) 212. Mielsch (supra n. 1) 58 correctly dismisses the interpretation of the porticus paintings as representations of "Portikusvillen."

19. Strabo describes the Bay of Naples as "one continuous city" in 5.4.8; Pliny *Ep.* 2.17.27 compares parts of the Laurentum with many cities. For similar references see Van Dam (supra n. 7) 212–13.

20. For an interpretation of this complex allusion and earlier poetic descriptions of Corinth, see Van Dam (supra n. 7) 214–16.

21. Mingazzini and Pfister (supra n. 3) 135, fig. 30, map 7. Other examples of the zigzag porticus in paintings are the landscapes in Pompeii (VI ii 14), Naples Archaeological Museum 9749 and 279p.

22. On the *topoi* of wonder and seeing, see Van Dam (supra n. 7) 221–22.

23. *Fragm. Acad.* 2 (Nonius 65). Similar optical effects are described by Cicero in *Acad. Pr.* 2.80 and *Nat. D.* 2.99; for others see Van Dam (supra n. 7) 223–26.

24. Such ambiguous "floating" complexes appear in Naples Archaeological Museum 9409 and 9434.

25. Pliny *Ep.* 2.17.20. On the origins of the *basis villae* in the second century B.C., see Mielsch (supra n. 1) 40.

26. Pliny *HN* 36.24.203–104. On this aesthetic, see H. Drerup, "Architektur als Symbol," *Gymnasium* 73 (1966) 181–96; and Z. Pavlovskis, *Man in an Artificial Landscape: The Marvels of Civilisation in Imperial Roman Literature* (Leiden 1973); on the ancient criticism of excessive *luxus* in domestic architecture, see Dwyer, chapter 1, and Ellis, chapter 6 in this volume.

27. Varro *Rust.* 3.13.2. Orpheus charming trees and beasts with his music is a *topos* since Eur. *Bacch.* 560. The painting of Orpheus is in the House of Orpheus (VI 14 20). For a list of representations of Orpheus among the animals in Roman art, see F. Schoeller, *Darstellungen des Orpheus in der Antike* (Freiburg 1969) 23–40. On the literary and theatrical aspect of the villa, see Mielsch (supra n. 1) 37–38 and Kondoleon, chapter 5 in this volume.

28. Other examples are Naples Archaeological Museum 9391 and 9463.

29. Euc. Prop. 4; Lucr. 4.424–29. A. Borbein, "Zur Deutung von Scherwand und Durchblick auf den Wandgemälden des zweiten pompejanischen Stils," in B. Andreae

and H. Kyrieleis eds., *Neue Forschungen in Pompeji* (Recklinghausen 1975) 61–70, discusses the possible influence of Lucretius on perspective vistas in Roman wall paintings, particularly the architectural views and garden paintings of the Second Style.

30. Pliny *Ep.* 2.17.5. For other passages on rooms with separate views, see Van Dam (supra n. 7) 239–40; on *diaeta*, 246. Seneca denounces this kind of architecture in *Ep.* 89.21. On the aesthetic and creation of ideal views, see H. Drerup, "Bildraum und Realraum in der römischen Architektur," *RM* 66 (1959) 151; L. Bek, *Towards Paradise on Earth: Modern Space Conception in Architecture. A Creation of Renaissance Humanism* (*Analecta Romana Instituti Danici* 9, Copenhagen 1979) 164–203; and F. Jung, "Gebaute Bilder," *AntK* 27 (1984) 71–122.

31. Mielsch (supra n. 1) 58.

32. On the etymology of the place names used by Statius in this catalogue, see Van Dam (supra n. 7) 241–46; and Beloch (supra n. 3) 83 (Euploea), 87 (Nesis), and 210–11 (Procida). The same catalogue is used by Statius in *Silv.* 3.1.147–53.

33. Particularly to the seaside shrines depicted in Naples Archaeological Museum 9391, 8583, and 9408. On Aphrodite sanctuaries in epigrams, see Apollonides 25, *Anth. Pal.* 9.791; Antipater 93, *Anth. Pal.* 9.143; Anyte 15, *Anth. Pal.* 9.144; Mnasalces 15, *Anth. Pal.* 9.333; Str. 17.800; and H. von Hesberg, "Bemerkungen zu Architekturepigrammen des 3. Jahrhundert v. Chr.," *JdI* 96 (1981) 71.

34. Puteoli: Philip 57, *Anth. Pal.* 9.708; Antiphilus 3, *Anth. Pal.* 7.379. Puteoli is evoked by Statius again in *Silv.* 3.5.75. While on Hortensius's estate in Bauli, Cicero claimed that he could see the Cumanum of Catullus but not his Pompeianum; although nothing lay between them, his eyesight was just too weak (*Acad.* 2.80).

35. Naples Archaeological Museum 9514; J. Kolendo, "Le port d'Alexandrie sur une peinture de Gragnano?" *Latomus* 61 (1982) 305–11; M. L. Bernhard, "Topographie d'Alexandrie: Le Tombeaux d'Alexandre et le Mausolee d'Auguste," *RA* 47 (1956) 129–56; and C. Picard, "Pouzzuoles et le paysage portuaire," *Latomus* 18 (1959) 23–51.

36. Pliny mentions that the fashion of cutting marble into thin slabs, of which the earliest instance was in the palace of Mausolus at Halicarnassus, was introduced in Rome by Mamurra when he covered the walls of his house on the Caelian (*HN* 36.48–50). For a list of ancient criticisms, see Van Dam (supra n. 7) 246–47.

37. Cicero relates that Clodius wanted a house on the Palatine with a *prospectus* (*Dom.* 44.116); see also A. Rodger, *Owners and Neighbors in Roman Law* (Oxford 1972) 124–40; and H. J. Horn, "Respiciens per fenestras prospiciens per cancellos: Zur Typologie des Fensters in der Antike," *JAC* 10 (1967) 30–60.

38. Hor. *Ep.* 1.11.26.

39. Sen. *Ep.* 11–13.86.1.

40. Cic. *Off.* 3.2; *Sen.* 19.71. Petronius has Trimalchio order "ships under full sail" to be carved on his tomb (*Sat.* 70.11–71.12). On the symbolism of the harbor in general, see C. Bonner, "Desired Haven," *Harvard Theological Review* 34 (1944) 49–67.

41. Antipater of Thessalonica 113, *Anth. Pal.* 9.408; Crinagoras 34, *Anth. Pal.* 10.24; D. Wachsmuth, *Untersuchung zu den antiken Sakralhandlungen bei Seereisen* (Diss. Freie Universität, Berlin 1967).

42. G. Wataghin Cantino, "Veduta dall'alto e scena a volo d'uccello," *RivIstArch* n.s. 16 (1969) 30–107; P. H. von Blanckenhagen and C. Alexander, *The Paintings from Boscotrecase* (Heidelberg 1962) 56; and id., "Narration in Hellenistic and Roman Art," *AJA* 61

(1957) 81. On the significance of the bird's-eye view see D. Fehling, "Ethnologische Überlegungen auf dem Gebiet der Altertumskunde," *Zetemata* 61 (1974) 39–58; and P. de Lacy, "Distant Views: The Imagery of Lucretius 2," *CJ* 60 (1964) 50.

43. Ptol. *Geog.* 1.19. On the spatial concept of *topos* and *choros*, see H. R. King, "Aristotle's Theory of Topos," *CQ* 44 (1950) 76–96; and F. Lukermann, "The Concept of Location in Classical Geography," *Annals of the American Association of Geographers* 51 (1961) 194–210.

CHAPTER 3

Sculptural Collecting and Display in the Private Realm

Elizabeth Bartman

"Have you not observed on coming in," said he, "a very fine statue set up in the hall, the work of Demetrios, the maker of portrait-statues?"

"Do you mean the discus-thrower," said I. . . .

"Not that one," said he, "for that is one of Myron's works, the discus-thrower. . . . Neither do I mean the one beside it, the one binding his head with a fillet, a handsome lad, for that is Polycleitos' work. Never mind those to the right as you come in, among which stand the tyrant-slayers modelled by Critius and Nesiotes; but if you noticed one beside the fountain, pot-bellied, bald on the forehead . . . the image of a real man. . . . he is thought to be Pellichus, a Corinthian general."[1]

In a well-known description of a visit to a Roman *domus*, one of the characters in Lucian's *The Teller of Lies* vividly evokes a statue-filled interior. Although the reliability of the author might be questioned—after all, the narrator is a "teller of lies"—nonetheless the validity of his description is confirmed by numerous sculptural finds from Roman houses and villas. Because it highlights several features typical of collections of sculpture during the imperial period, Lucian's passage forms a convenient starting point for discussion of Roman sculptural patronage in the private sphere.[2]

Like the display seen by Lucian's narrator, many collections were remarkably diverse in their subject, style, and date. Frequently they included copies of well-known masterpieces of Greek pedigree whose prestigious past bestowed the status of erudition upon the owners and whose expense marked the owners

71

as persons of wealth. This essay will explore the criteria by which these statues were selected and the meanings attached to them in their Roman surroundings. Because so many images were already familiar to the audience, sculptural display seems to have acquired importance as a device for imparting individual meaning to an ensemble. Whether formal, historical, or thematic, this meaning bears witness to the presence of an often complex program lying behind what is sometimes mistaken for a strictly decorative sculptural scheme.

The statues seen by Lucian's narrator made a visual impact whose effect is difficult to reconstruct today. Although large numbers of statues survive from antiquity, they often cannot be associated with a particular context. Being movable—if not easily portable—freestanding statuary tends to migrate from its original setting. Statues could be reused by a new owner in a new setting or be grouped together simply en route to their disposal.[3] As a result, few sculptural collections are found both intact and in situ. Not even an ostensibly "closed" context such as a house sealed by Vesuvius's unexpected eruption can provide certain evidence for an original statuary arrangement. Many of the sculptures from the Villa at Oplontis were in storage pending a renovation;[4] and, at least at Pompeii, the tendency to reuse statuary in new contexts makes it unlikely that any freestanding sculpture stands in the setting for which it was originally commissioned.[5]

Even those sculptural groups found undisturbed, and presumably intact, pose difficulties. A cache of statues that has been carefully hidden may not represent the entirety of a collection. Usually consisting exclusively of bronzes, such finds may instead be hoards of the most valuable and portable pieces of the collection.[6] Moreover, most sculptural groups that have come to light date from the late imperial period, thus almost certainly representing the final rather than the formative phase of an assemblage. While this later phase is by no means artistically inferior to its predecessors, the visual impression that it makes is relevant only for that late phase. Since we remain woefully lacking in archaeological evidence for earlier displays, our knowledge of the taste of the first republican patricians who adorned their houses and villas with sculpture is based largely on later literary sources.[7]

The interior of the *domus* described by Lucian is filled with statues linked in no obvious manner by theme, style, or any other feature. If the statues correspond to statuary types now recognized by scholars, two can be understood to represent athletes executed in a classical mode[8] while another, the "tyrant-slayers" Harmodios and Aristogeiton, renders two historical personages of late sixth-century Athens in the so-called Severe Style.[9] The remaining two statues seem to be portraits, and at least one of them, of Pellichus, is executed in a highly realistic style presumably Hellenistic in date. To what extent the narrator conflates scattered images cannot be known, but it does seem likely that the various works he mentions stand fairly close to one another and were meant to be seen as an ensemble.

The iconographic and stylistic diversity so marked in the assemblage described by Lucian would have been familiar to the Roman audience, for eclecticism defined many collections.[10] The owner of the House of Fortuna Annonaria at Ostia typifies the eclectic taste of the Roman patron during the imperial era. Datable by its latest works to the mid–third century A.C., the collection comprised two portrait busts and images of Aphrodite, Artemis, Athena, Hera, and Fortuna.[11] Diverse in style and size as well as subject, the images loosely reproduce prototypes that range in date from the fifth to the third centuries B.C. Similarly, the sculptural cache found in a Roman house at Antioch comprised members of the Dionysiac retinue who cavorted among more staid images of Meleager, Ares, Aphrodite, a grouse, and several imperial portraits.[12] Here no single theme or even genre prevailed in the mix of historical realism, mythology, and decoration found in the group.

More extensive collections formulated (presumably) by wealthier patrons differed from the smaller collections not in the character of their sculptural components but rather in the considerably more luxurious settings provided for them. Two examples from diverse parts of the Empire illustrate this point: the so-called Palazzo delle Colonne at Ptolemais in Cyrenaica and the villa at Chiragon in Gaul. At the sumptuously furnished Palazzo, a complex of Hellenistic and Roman marble statues of divinities such as Aphrodite and Dionysos were found with Egyptian portraits in basalt and granite.[13] In the extensive collection of the Gallo-Roman villa at Chiragon, believed to date from the third century A.C., portraits of members of the imperial circle dating from Augustus to Philip the Arab supplemented traditional decorative works such as images of the gods and heroes and members of the Dionysiac retinue.[14]

While the diversity seen in these sculptural groups, all rather late in date, may reflect a lengthy process of building a family collection, nonetheless, an eclectic character may have been sought intentionally. To the Roman, eclecticism was a virtue, rife with connotations of wealth, power, and tradition. The very first collections on public view in Rome had been eclectic: the *Atrium Libertatis* built and decorated by Asinius Pollio, for example, exhibited statues of centaurs, nymphs, and muses, gods such as Jupiter, and Dirce tied to a bull.[15] Disparate in their subjects, these statues seem to have had little in common other than their Hellenistic past. The holdings of Julius Caesar's Temple of Venus Genetrix were mixed in media as well as style, with coins and gems joining paintings and statuary in the display.[16] Enshrining some of the most magnificent treasures of the Greek world, these late republican collections embodied the new wealth pouring into the capital and the power possessed by those who obtained it. In the tradition of these fantastic collections based on plunder, the displays formed by private citizens for the *domus* or villa typically combined statues diverse in theme, style, date, and even scale.

Given the wide range of possibility, it seems likely that the selective judgment of the individual Roman patron was actively engaged in determining the final appearance of the sculptural ensemble. It is not easy, however, to determine the criteria by which the Roman collector chose statuary to decorate his urban town house or country villa. Both the surviving statuary and the literary sources provide some evidence that must be used with caution. The statuary can be interpreted in various ways—was a statuary type popular because of its subject or the artistic manner in which that subject was interpreted?—and the literary sources are rarely explicit. Certainly no single set of motives can be assumed to have directed every patron.

In recent scholarship, theme has been widely regarded as the decisive factor for the patron's choice of art works because it embodies the concept of *decor* known to have played so extensive a role in Roman artistic thought. In the context of sculptural decoration, *decor*, or appropriateness, dictated the placement of images of athletes in the gymnasium and portraits of playwrights in the library.[17] Cicero documents this aim of decoration in his letters to Atticus, of course, when exhorting him to purchase statues and herms appropriate for the palestra and gymnasium.[18] Statuary finds in public spaces such as theaters and baths[19] and private spaces such as the gardens of the Pompeian *domus* richly attest to the prevalence of the tradition.[20]

The emphasis placed on iconography as the primary factor that determined the selection and display of works of art unnecessarily restricts the Roman definition of *decor*, which referred as much to aesthetic factors, such as the majesty of a statue, as to theme.[21] Moreover, misinterpretation of the concept of *decor* contributes to an oversimplified view of the motivations that underlay the decoration of Roman private spaces. For example, in elaborate villas where scores of sculptures were displayed, a strictly thematic interpretation can become unwieldy. Adorned with more than eighty statues, the Villa dei Papiri in Herculaneum offers a prime illustration.[22] In an effort to identify a prevailing theme in this extensive collection, historians have devised elaborate and overly inventive interpretations. Some interpret the villa's decor as symbolic of the Epicurean ideal of a cultural education and an active political life, while others perceive an allusion to a paradisiacal afterlife.[23] The very fact that completely different interpretations can be proposed raises doubts about the primacy of theme as a criterion of selection. Even a small collection such as that housed in the Villa at Oplontis poses similar difficulties. Its excavator has convincingly interpreted a series of marble centaurs as symbolic of the conflicting natural forces of civilization and barbarism,[24] but it remains unclear how a group of Julio-Claudian portraits found nearby can be integrated into this otherwise neat tableau.

Further skepticism about interpreting the significance of a sculptural display in exclusively iconographic terms emerges when one considers why certain renderings of a subject achieved wider popularity than others. Of the many images of satyrs available to the copyist and patron, for example, why was the late fourth-century B.C. type known as the Resting Satyr (fig. 3-1) so overwhelmingly favored? Certainly other statues could have fulfilled its thematic role equally well. Yet with more than one hundred extant replicas, the Resting Satyr outstrips any other satyr as a statuary type favored for copying.[25] Similarly, the Heracles Farnese was preferred to all other renderings of the brawny hero.[26]

To some extent, of course, a replica's popularity fed on itself.[27] Once established as part of the artistic canon, a statuary type's future longevity was assured. Plaster casts taken from either the original or one of its copies could transmit the image to the far corners of the Empire. Likewise, copybooks could disseminate the imagery, albeit in a less precise manner. Such technical aids made a sculptural type accessible to an ever-widening circle of patrons.

Although important, theme was but one criterion by which works of art were selected by the private patron. Literary sources, occasionally corroborated by archaeological finds, attest that age, genealogy, associative value, and formal qualities all seem to have been considered as well. As regards sculpture, several other factors must also be taken into account. Copies were judged by the same criteria as originals.[28]

Numerous sources record the attraction that age held for collectors of sculpture.[29] Julius Caesar, for one, was an avid collector of old statues.[30] Moreover, the presence of "antique" sculptures in several collections offers clear archaeological evidence of the prestige attached to the age of a work of art. In the Palazzo delle Colonne at Ptolemais, for example, Egyptian statuettes from the Saite period stood on display with an assemblage of Greco-Roman gods, erotes, and satyrs. The large number of these statues, believed to predate the first-century A.C. installation by many years, suggests that they were acquired and displayed deliberately as artifacts from an earlier time and culture.[31] Similarly, a late-imperial Gallo-Roman villa in Aquitaine housed a collection that included some sculptural curiosities. Here two Celtic images in limestone were exhibited with fifty-six marble sculptures of gods and heroes representing familiar images from the Greco-Roman repertory.[32] Even in the case of copies of classical prototypes, age might emerge as a virtue. As will be argued later in this essay, some collectors owned older and newer replicas of the same work and consciously set up a contrast between them.

While age in itself was regarded with favor, age combined with a distinguished genealogy was even more highly touted. Latin authors frequently record the boastings of art collectors who claimed prestigious historical associations for their possessions. Thus Martial's client Novius Vindex claimed to own a bronze statuette that had previously belonged to Hannibal and Alexander the Great,[33] and Caracalla was said to own drinking vessels and weapons that had once been Alexander's.[34] Preposterous in their claims, these exaggerated pedigrees ("smoke-begrimed genealogies," Martial calls them)[35] must have been fairly commonplace, as they are repeatedly satirized in the literature.

A variety of other associations could enhance a statue's popularity in more general ways. Sculptures belonging to private collections may well have quoted from public monuments whose statuary displays were famous. For example, two statuettes depicting the slaughter of the Niobids (figs. 3-2 and 3-3) found in a house at Inatos on Crete might allude to the impressive ensemble associated with the Horti Lamiani in Rome.[36] The designer of the Cretan group has extracted two figures, Niobe shielding her daughter and an attacking Artemis, to adapt a monumentally conceived work to a domestic context. By reducing the large-scale originals to a statuette format, he scaled them appropriately for their new setting. Similarly, the consul C. Piso Frugi Pontifex is said to have copied the Danaids of Augustus's Temple of Apollo on the Palatine for his house, the so-called Villa of the Papyri at Herculaneum.[37] And the owner of the house described by Lucian may have intended a reference to the tyrant-slayers on the Capitoline with his own version of the group.[38] Allusions by private patrons to public works of this kind are credible when one considers the evidence for the practice of quotation at the imperial level. The Polyphemus group installed by Domitian at his Castelgandolfo villa almost certainly recalled earlier sculptural tableaux from imperial property at Baiae and Sperlonga.[39] If the associative value of sculpture were self-aggrandizing to an emperor, surely it spurred ordinary collectors as well to capitalize on the allusive powers of the sculptures they owned. The use—or, more properly, reuse—of these sculptural types would have established their owner as both visually learned and culturally au courant.[40]

The portraits of imperial personages so often found in private collections bore their own particular historical connotations, marking their owners as persons of power and social connections.[41] Such images were typically combined with traditional mythological representations, as the previously mentioned house at Antioch and the House of Fortuna Annonaria at Ostia attest. This practice had a precedent in the Hellenistic world; for example, a collection assembled in the last decade B.C. for a villa at Knossos includes a portrait head of Ptolemy and various statuettes of gods and draped figures.[42] While suggesting the piety felt by the imperial subject toward his leader, these portraits also fulfilled a more self-serving function for their owners—they commemorated the owner's relationship with the imperial house. When the gallery of imperial personages extended over several generations or dynasties, as it did in many villas,[43] it graphically portrayed the distinguished lineage of a patron long connected with the imperial circle.

Of all the criteria by which a private patron chose or commissioned sculptural decoration, the formal aspects of the work have been most often undervalued or even disregarded by modern scholars. Yet statues were certainly appreciated for their purely aesthetic qualities. The Roman collector in need of a marble satyr to grace the sylvan setting of his garden may have chosen the Resting Satyr mentioned earlier from the large number of images of the same subject because of the same formal, technical, and expressive qualities that are recognized today—a sophisticated composition, rich play of textured surfaces, and hint of emotional depth in a Dionysiac creature of the woods.[44]

The viewer's aesthetic appreciation was often enhanced by his admiration of technical prowess. Rendering the sculptural virtues of the Resting Satyr posed a challenge to the copyist, and his successful fulfillment of that challenge announced his superior ability as an artist. Just as the Greeks had celebrated artistic skill or *technē*, so too the Romans esteemed technical virtuosity. Pliny alludes to this fact in his frequent mention of statues, apparently complex in their composition, as being "carved from the same block of marble."[45] In addition, sculptors often proudly displayed their technical expertise by piecing marble in order to create bold sculptural compositions.[46] Such tours de force, challenging the intrinsic structural limits of the material, established the sculptor as a master of his medium.

Lucian's dialogue implies that attribution to a famous name was another important factor in the selection of works of art. However, the name of a statue's sculptor seems not to have been a primary consideration of most Roman patrons. Admittedly, there is some evidence for the falsification of signatures,[47] but, in general, a famous name did not guarantee the popularity of a statuary type. Some of the most esteemed statues by sculptors of great fame were virtually ignored by the copying industry and the collectors who supported it.[48] The Apoxyomenos of Lysippos provides a telling example of this disparity between reputation and popularity as a "collectible."[49]

Given Lucian's satirical bent and the title of the dialogue under discussion, it is unlikely that the attributions cited were meant to be taken literally. Rather, the name-dropping in which the host of Lucian's narrator engages may be meant to reveal either his lack of education or his boorishness. If the attributions themselves are wrong, the host appears to the audience as ignorant, but if the works are taken to be originals made by the master himself, when in fact they are copies, he is guilty of gross naïveté. Whatever the status of the works that are cited, Lucian's passage reveals that the names of Greek masters were quite familiar in certain circles. If the writings of the critics and encyclopedists are any measure, the fine points of artistic connoisseurship were not unfamiliar terrain to Rome's cultural elite in the second century A.C.

On a more prosaic level, the host of Lucian's narrator may merely be referring to copies of famous works by the names of their originals (a practice that persists today). In any case, the passage reinforces our knowledge that the sculptural copy played an important role in the Roman statuary collection. Finds throughout the Empire confirm its prominence, although it is clear that only imperial citizens of considerable wealth could afford to commission large-scale copies of famous works.[50] The prominence of the copy results from two conditions: first, the absence of any objective aesthetic preference for the "original," and, second, the practical exigencies that shaped collecting at the time. Of the various criteria by which works of art were judged, originality ranked rather low. Certainly the many signatures of copyists indicate that there was little stigma attached to the making of a copy.[51] Nor should there have been, for the quality of a replica could easily rival that of the original.[52] In any case, as the sources attest, many viewers—perhaps including the collector in Lucian's dialogue—were unable to tell the difference between an original and a copy.[53] By the late first century B.C., moreover, the acquisition of original works of Classical or Hellenistic date by private individuals was virtually impossible. Many of the Greek cities and sanctuaries had already been plundered for their treasures, while under Augustus there was a strong movement, by persuasion if not coercion, to nationalize private collections of importance that already existed.[54]

In their choice of works to copy, the Romans displayed a catholic taste. As apt to commission works of the Hellenistic style as of the Classical, they copied a wide gamut of artistic works, from freestanding statuary to enormous urns decorated with relief carvings.[55] Despite the range of their tastes, however, they confined their selection to a limited number of sculptural models. Of the thousands of Greek statues that would have been available for copying, fewer than one hundred were copied.[56] These same types, recurring throughout the Empire, clearly reflect a standardization of sculptural imagery. The case of the Resting Satyr noted earlier illustrates this phenomenon well.

To the modern observer, the repetition of these types verges on monotony. To a Roman, however, such repetition had certain positive connotations. A replica of a familiar statuary type ensured social acceptance for its owner and provided the patron with a sense of cultural belonging, of *romanitas*.[57] With its allusion to a prestigious masterpiece of the Greek past, moreover, the copy established its owner as a person of refinement who belonged to the cultural elite.

While originality in itself was not a criterion for the selection of a sculptural work, nonetheless there is considerable evidence that discerning patrons installed their "conventional" images in novel ways in order to endow their collections with a personal, and in that sense "original," meaning. In some instances the display involved only the sculptures, but the most ambitious examples of this aspect of collecting relate the sculpture to other elements of interior decor such as painting and mosaics, whose formal and thematic coordination has been the focus of much recent study. Although only a few examples are well documented, this interaction hints that statuary joined walls, ceilings, and floors as the fourth ingredient of a decor unified thematically and aesthetically.[58]

Many of the sculptures displayed in the House of Loreius Tibertinus at Pompeii (II ii 2), for example, presented Egyptian themes that complemented the Egyptianizing painting and architecture of a pavilion room overlooking the garden, the so-called *diaeta* of Isis.[59] While none of the Egyptian sculptures that have been found seems to have actually stood in the room, the repetition of Egyptian motifs served to coordinate the decor of several spaces.[60] The number of statues and paintings conveying these same themes that survive from other settings suggests that an Egyptian decorative formula was one of the clichés of Roman interior design.[61]

The villa at Piazza Armerina provides evidence for the use of this mode of coordinating interior design in the later period.[62] Among the few sculptural finds from the villa was a large-scale statue of Apollo Lyceios that stood in an apsidal room whose floor was paved with a mosaic depicting Orpheus singing to his audience of animals.[63] As the divine patron of music and the arts, Apollo appropriately stood physically above the mortal musician depicted on the floor.[64]

A second mode of design favored by the patron as a means of integrating decor and personalizing its sculptural component was the sculptural pendant. By exploiting the potential of context to alter the visual and formal impact of a statue, the pendant infused familiar images with new meaning by the simple act of juxtaposition.[65] Because as few as two statues were involved, the pendant also proved to be a design tool of extraordinary versatility. When used in a space cluttered with statues, the pendant provided a visual focus; when used alone, it conveyed a "finished" or planned look.

Martial's fourteenth book of epigrams is sometimes interpreted as literary evidence for the presence of pendants in Roman sculptural display. Each devoted to a single work of art, the poems were believed by Karl Lehmann to describe an actual collection, that of the Temple of the Divine Augustus in

Rome.[66] On the basis of Martial's text, Lehmann drew a plan of the temple's cella in which he juxtaposed works of related theme—two paintings of the loves of Zeus, Danae and Europa; two statuettes representing Heracles; and a painting and relief depicting sensuous young beauties, Hyacinthos and a hermaphrodite. Thus Lehmann imagined an artistic arrangement composed of multiple pendants executed in diverse media. Unfortunately, it is by no means clear that the hypothetical works described by Martial actually existed or that they were placed as Lehmann imagined.

Numerous archaeological discoveries nevertheless confirm the role of the pendant in Roman private and public decorative schemes. Statuary pendants fall into two major categories, those that stress the thematic bond between the two images and those that emphasize a more formal relationship. Pendants of the first type are usually straightforward in meaning, often depicting thematic contrasts that were commonplace in other media such as mural painting. Statuettes of Artemis and Aphrodite (figs. 3-4 and 3-5) found in a Roman villa in Aquitaine,[67] for example, might have counterposed the two antithetical forces of female sexuality in the same manner as countless pairs painted on the walls of Campanian houses.[68] Late antique in date, the images from provincial Gaul testify to the longevity of this visual motif in Roman art. Their similar scale and identically profiled bases argue strongly that they were commissioned to be displayed as a pair. A more subtle play existed between two portraits of Greek poets found together at the Villa of the Bruttii in Rieti. Representing Anacreon and a writer whose identity remains unknown (the figure is the so-called Borghese poet), the two probably juxtaposed different poetic styles.[69]

Other pendants discovered in Roman private contexts emphasized the formal aspect of the images from which they had been constituted. A favorite form of the pendant involved two identical copies of the same work oriented in opposite directions with respect to the viewer. Hellenistic works such as the Three Graces[70] (figs. 3-6 and 3-7) or the *symplegma* in which a hermaphrodite wrestled a lecherous satyr (figs. 3-8 and 3-9) proved popular for this type of arrangement.[71] While the statuary types themselves embodied a complex intermingling of figures, the pendants emphasized their bifaciality.[72] In doing so they underscored the viewer's expectations of frontality when viewing sculpture.

The statue's composition itself was the basis of a pendant from Aphrodisias composed of two groups, one of Menelaos and Patroclus and the other of Achilles and Penthesilea (figs. 3-10 and 3-11).[73] Although diverse in subject, the two groups echoed one another in their compositions. Both contrasted an erect, living figure and a limp corpse. Indeed, the one is typically regarded as typologically derivative from the other.[74]

Two images of discus throwers found in building *M* at Side (figs. 3-12 and 3-13) contrasted stylistically diverse interpretations of the same subject. A copy of a mid-fifth-century Discobolus (of the type attributed to Myron; see fig. 3-12) was exhibited with a copy of a work of identical subject believed to have been executed several decades earlier (the Pythagorean type; see fig. 3-13).[75] One of the points of the comparison must have been to contrast the freer, more natural-istic rendering of the Myronian figure with the stiffer, more archaic style of the Pythagorean. While its findspot is a public building of as yet undetermined function, nonetheless, there is nothing to preclude the appearance of this type of pendant in a private house.

A final type of pendant joined two versions of the same statuary type. As I have argued elsewhere,[76] the pendant formulated in this manner usually juxta-posed two contrasting stylistic interpretations of the same sculptural type. One of the best documented examples of this type of pendant consists of two replicas of the Pothos of Scopas (figs. 3-14 and 3-15) found in a Hadrianic town house under the Via Cavour in Rome. The pendant works stood prominently in the spacious rooms of the *domus*, along with two other statues of different types (fig. 3-16). While akin in their typology, the replicas differ in their formal details—one exhibits a hardened treatment of both drapery and musculature (see fig. 3-14) in contrast to the blurred surfaces of the other (see fig. 3-15). There is little doubt that the absence of stylistic conformity is intentional, meant to focus the viewer's attention on the subtle nuances that individualized each image. The Via Cavour pendant offers a rare but not unparalleled illustration of the exis-tence of a purely formal level of meaning for a work of art.

When the viewer of the Via Cavour pendant recognized the stylistic diver-sity that characterized the two works, presumably he recognized as well the different histories that lay behind them. Clearly their styles indicate carving at different times. Today we judge one of the statues to be Hadrianic, or contem-porary with the house, while we date the other decades earlier, to the Claudian era.[77] How closely ancient viewers would have dated the same works remains questionable. We can imagine, however, that they might have understood one of the sculptures to be substantially earlier than the other. In the private setting of the *domus,* such a work might have appeared to be an heirloom. Benefiting from the regard traditionally accorded to ancient works, the "heirloom," genu-ine or not, implied long-standing wealth and familial rank.

Conceived for a specific setting, the pendant group from the Via Cavour town house testifies to the use of this decorative motif in the 120s A.C. As a decorative form in the second century A.C. the pendant owes its popularity to the aediculated facades of public buildings such as the aforementioned structure at Side (fig. 3-17).[78] With their many niches, these facades of theaters, baths, and other monumental buildings required statuary for their decoration. While any statuary could suffice as such sculptural "filler," pendants suited the role admirably because the visual or thematic echo they embodied bolstered the underlying symmetry of the architectural program.

Although the number of pendants found in public contexts testifies to their position as a staple of monumental art, in some respects the private realm of the *domus* provided a superior environment for the pendant's viewing and appreciation. In its gracious rooms and verdant courtyards the viewer was likely to find the quiet and leisure necessary for the contemplation of nuances of form and meaning.[79] To be sure, all works of art benefited from such contemplation, but many pendants required especially close examination in order to be understood. For all its bestowal of status upon its proud possessor, the sculptural decor of the private dwelling could also serve to engage visitors in the formal refinements of the visual arts.

By tailoring statuary to its setting on both a functional and an aesthetic level, Roman patrons and their designers invested familiar sculptural forms with new significance. With their combination of both the familiar and the novel, however, the figural arrangements they created spoke a visual language that could be understood by any audience.

NOTES

1. Lucian, *Philopseudes* 18 (trans. A. Harmon, *Loeb Classical Library* [Cambridge and London 1969]).

2. R. Neudecker, *Die Skulpturenausstattung römischer Villen in Italien* (Mainz 1988), deals with this subject on a larger scale. Because I obtained a copy of the book after completing this essay, I cite only specific references from its catalogue of villa finds.

3. Sculpture from a second-century A.C. villa near Fianello Sabino offers a vivid testimony of the latter fate. The fourteen statues found at the villa represent but a fraction of the original decoration, the rest clearly having provided the raw material for several blocks of lime lying nearby. The find is discussed by D. Facenna, *NSc* ser. 8, vol. 5 (1951) 55–74; and B. Andreae, *AA* 1957, 265–67, figs. 64–66. Of high-quality workmanship and material, the remaining sculptures depict members of the Dionysiac retinue, nude athletes, and gods such as Heracles and Artemis. Most stand slightly less than one meter in height. At present the statues are in the Museo Nazionale delle Terme in Rome, but await publication. For the female dancer, see B. Andreae, "Statuette einer Tänzerin aus Fianello Sabino," *Festschrift F. Matz* (Mainz 1962) 73–79.

4. S. de Caro, "The Sculptures of the Villa of Poppaea at Oplontis: A Preliminary Report," in E. MacDougall ed., *Ancient Roman Villa Gardens* (Washington, D.C. 1987) 87; and Neudecker (supra n. 2) 241–42, no. 71. For further examples, see E. Dwyer, "Sculpture and Its Display in Private Houses of Pompeii," *Pompeii and the Vesuvian Landscape* (Washington, D.C. 1979) 63 and n. 70.

5. H. Döhl and P. Zanker, "La scultura," in F. Zevi ed., *Pompei 79* (Naples 1984) 202.

6. As an example, see the group of bronze statuettes found carefully buried in a trench in the modern Athenian suburb of Ambelokipi. Dating to the second century A.C., the cache reproduces well-known types such as the Lateran Poseidon (G. Daux, *BCH* 92 [1968] 741–48).

7. As in so many artistic matters, the Romans were presumably influenced by Hellenistic practices. On these traditions and their pervasive impact on the decoration of Roman houses and villas, see V. Harward, *Greek Domestic Sculpture and the Origins of Private Art Patronage* (Diss. Harvard 1982); and two articles by P. Zanker, "Die Villa als Vorbild des späten pompejanischen Wohngeschmacks," *JdI* 94 (1979) 460–523, and "Zur Funktion und Bedeutung griechischer Skulptur in der Romerzeit," in *Le classicisme à Rome aux 1er siècles avant et après J. C. (Fondation Hardt, Entretiens sur l'antiquité classique* 25, Geneva 1978) 283–314. Zanker argues that a standardized program of sculptural decoration was already firmly established in the villas of the hellenized Roman aristocracy of the first century B.C. Moreover, in the latter article, Zanker detects few changes in the sculptural decor of wealthy residences over time: "Norms formulated early on remained influential in the imperial period. . . . Even the incredibly rich statuary decoration of Hadrian's Villa seems to have been a *mixtum compositum* of the various *topoi* of decoration in the late republican villa" (p. 300).

8. For the Discobolus of Myron, see B. Ridgway, *The Severe Style in Greek Sculpture* (Princeton 1970) 85; and for the Polycleitan Diadumenos, see P. Zanker, *Klassizistische Statuen: Studien zur Veränderung des Kunstgeschmacks in der römischen Kaiserzeit* (Mainz 1974) 11–13.

9. Ridgway (supra n. 8) 79–83.

10. Zanker, "Funktion und Bedeutung" (supra n. 7) 300.

11. R. Meiggs, *Roman Ostia* 2d ed. (Oxford 1973) 433–34. On the sculptures, see R. Calza and M. Squarciapino, *Museo ostiense (Itinerari dei musei, gallerie e monumenti d'Italia* 79, Rome 1962) 34, no. 16 (Athena); 36, no. 5 (Artemis); 40, no. 8 (archaistic head of a kore); 41–42, no. 13 (Crouching Aphrodite); 70, no. 9 (togate bust of a man); 78, no. 2 (bust of a youth).

12. D. Brinkerhoff, *A Collection of Sculpture in Classical and Early Christian Antioch* (New York 1970).

13. The date of this collection is difficult to establish, as the house was occupied for many centuries. It may be contemporary with the substantial renovations undertaken in the first century A.C. (O. Brogan, *PECS*, s.v. *Ptolemais*). The standard publication on the house and its finds is G. Pesce, *Il "Palazzo delle Colonne" in Tolemaide di Cirenaica (Monografie di archeologia libica* 2, Rome 1950). See Ellis, chapter 6 in this volume, for further reference to the same sculptures.

14. E. Espérandieu, *Recueil général des bas-reliefs, statues et bustes de la Gaule romaine* 2 (Paris 1908) 33–95, nos. 893–1011. Precise information concerning the original placement of the statues is lacking, unfortunately, and it cannot be determined whether these works, so diverse in genre and style, actually stood together in the same rooms.

15. Pliny, *HN* 36.33–34; D. Strong, "Roman Museums," in D. Strong ed., *Archaeological Theory and Practice* (London and New York 1973) 249; and G. Becatti, "Lettere pliniane: le opere d'arte nei *monumenta Asini Pollionis* e negli Horti Serviliani," in *Studi in onore di Aristide Calderini e Roberto Paribeni* 3 (Milan 1956) 199–210.

16. Pliny *HN* 35.26, 35.156, and 37.11; and Cass. Dio. 51.223.

17. Zanker, "Funktion und Bedeutung" (supra n. 7) 284. For ancient testimony on this mode of thought, see Vitr. *De Arch.* 1.2.5–7, 7.5.4, and 7.6.5; and the discussion of *ratio decoris* in J. J. Pollitt, *The Art of Rome, c. 753 b.c.–337 a.d: Sources and Documents* (Englewood Cliffs, N.J. 1966) xiv-xv.

18. Cic. *Att.* 1.6.2, 1.9.2, and 1.10.3. For a new discussion of the letters of Cicero and the importance of "appropriateness" in the collection and display of sculptures by Roman patrons, see M. Marvin, "Copying in Roman Sculpture: The Replica Series," in *Retaining the Original: Multiple Originals, Copies and Reproductions (Studies in the History of Art* 20, Washington, D.C. 1989) 29–45.

19. For the statuary programs of theaters see G. Bejor, "La decorazione scultorea dei teatri romani nelle province africane," *Prospettiva* 17 (1979) 37–46; and M. Fuchs, *Untersuchungen zur Ausstattung römischer Theater in Italien und den Westprovinzen des Imperium Romanum* (Mainz 1987). For baths, see H. Manderscheid, *Die Skulpturenausstattung der kaiserzeitlichen Termenanlagen (Monumenta Artis Romanae* 15, Berlin 1981); and M. Marvin, "Freestanding Sculptures from the Baths of Caracalla," *AJA* 87 (1983) 378 n. 190.

20. On this topic, see Döhl and Zanker (supra n. 5) and E. Dwyer, *Pompeian Domestic Sculpture: A Study of Five Pompeian Houses and Their Contents (Archaeologica* 28, Rome 1982).

21. J. J. Pollitt, *The Ancient View of Greek Art* (New Haven and London 1974) 343–47.

22. The sculptural finds from this villa have received substantial attention. Among the most recent treatments are Neudecker (supra n. 2) 105–14 and 147–57, no. 14; M. Wojcik, *La Villa dei Papiri ad Ercolano: Contributo alla ricostruzione dell'ideologia della nobilitas tardorepubblicana* (Rome 1986); and G. Sauron, *"Templa serena:* À propos de la 'Villa des Papyri' d'Herculaneum: contribution a l'étude des comportements aristocratiques romains à la fin de la république," *MEFRA* 92 (1980) 277–301. D. Pandermalis, "Zum Programm der Statuenausstattung in der Villa dei Papiri," *AM* 86 (1971), remains fundamental.

23. For a recent view against a single, prevailing interpretation, see H. Mielsch, *Die römische Villa: Architektur und Lebensform* (Munich 1987) 101. Zanker, "Funktion und Bedeutung" (supra n. 7), calls the Villa of the Papyri "the clearest example of the use of decoration with statuary to evoke a multiplicity of associations, to confer upon individual sections and the villa as a whole an aura which exalted the intellect and sensibilities of the owner, and, in brief, to make the sphere of life characterized by *otium* a place of Greek culture" (p. 286).

24. De Caro (supra n. 4) 127.

25. The typology of the Resting Satyr has been recently discussed by B. Vierneisel-Schlörb, *Glyptothek München: Katalog der Skulpturen* 2, *Klassische Skulpturen des 5. und 4. Jahrhunderts v. Chr.* (Munich 1979) 353–69, no. 32. Other well-known types that failed to achieve the popularity of the Resting Satyr include its derivative, the flute-playing satyr (C. Picard, *Manuel d'archéologie grecque: La sculpture* [Paris 1948] 3^2 531, fig. 218); and the Drunken Faun in Munich (D. Ohly, *Glyptothek München: Griechische und römische Skulpturen* [Munich 1977] 20–21, pl. 9).

26. On this type see D. Krull, *Der Herakles vom Typ Farnese: Kopienkritische Untersuchung einer Schöpfung des Lysipp* (Frankfurt 1985).

27. See Marvin (supra n. 18).

28. The literary references that follow refer primarily to works of art in general rather than to copies in particular. As they illustrate the basic cultural attitudes of the time,

however, they can, with some obvious exceptions, be applied to the realm of copying as well.

29. Many of these antique treasures were bronze: *veteres ceraeque aerisque figuras* (Stat. *Silv.* 1.3.4) and *artes veterum manus* (Stat. *Silv.* 2.2.6). Old easel paintings (Pliny *HN* 35.4; Plut. *Aratos* 13) and silverplate (Pliny *HN* 33.157) were also coveted by some collectors.

30. Suet. *Iul.* 47.

31. C. Kraeling, *Ptolemais: City of the Libyan Pentapolis (The University of Chicago Oriental Institute Publications* 90, Chicago 1962) 9; and D. Nasgowitz, *Ptolemais Cyrenaica* (Chicago and London 1980) 28.

32. See L. Valensi, "Deux sculptures romaines de la villa de St-Georges-de-Montagne," *RLouvre* 23 (1973) 7.

33. Mart. *Epigrams* 9.43.

34. Cass. Dio. 72.7.1.

35. Mart. *Epigrams* 8.6.

36. Herakleion Archaeological Museum 265 and 266. The statuettes lack full publication, but have been briefly noted by S. Marinatos, *AE* 1934–35, 4–17, pls. 1–2; and I. Sanders, *Roman Crete* (Warminster 1982) 151. On the Niobids from which they seem to derive, see G. Mansuelli, *Galleria degli Uffizi: Le sculture* 1 (Rome 1958) 101–21, nos. 70–82. The Uffizi Niobids are believed to have decorated a nymphaeum on imperial property, the Horti Lamiani (C. Vermeule, *Greek Sculpture and Roman Taste* [Ann Arbor 1977] 48; and M. Cima and E. La Rocca, *Le tranquille dimore degli dei: La residenza imperiale degli horti Lamiani* [Venice 1986] 30).

37. P. Zanker, "Der Apollontempel auf dem Palatin: Ausstattung und politische Sinnbezüge nach der Schlacht von Actium," in *Città e architettura nella Roma imperiale* (*AnalRom* suppl. 10, 1983) 27–31, figs. 3–4; and E. Simon, *Augustus: Kunst und Leben in Rom um die Zeitenwende* (Munich 1986) 21–24, figs. 9–14.

38. Part of a statue of Aristogeiton was found on the Capitoline (Palazzo dei Conservatori, 2404 [Helbig[4] 1646]). On its location on the Capitoline, see F. Coarelli, *Guida archeologica di Roma* (Rome 1974) 46.

39. The Castelgandolfo Polyphemus is discussed in the context of the Polyphemus group from Sperlonga by B. Andreae and B. Conticello, *Die Skulpturen von Sperlonga* (*AntP* 14, 1974) 74, no. 1 and figs. 16–20, foll. p. 108. See also Neudecker (supra n. 2) 139–44, no. 9. For the Baiae group see B. Andreae, "Le sculture," in F. Zevi ed., *Baia: Il ninfeo imperiale sommerso di Punta Epitaffio* (Naples 1983) 46–66, figs. 77–109.

40. In addition to reproducing specific statues, private owners may have installed their works in a manner that recalled their famous precedents; see Mielsch (supra n. 23) 112.

41. Even the empress Livia was not above making such references, for her villa at Prima Porta included the now-famous statue of Augustus in military garb. See Neudecker (supra n. 2) 203–4, no. 46.

42. W. Catling and G. Waywell, "A Find of Roman Marble Statuettes at Knossos," *BSA* 72 (1977) 85–106.

43. For an example see the villa at Chiragon, where the gallery of imperial portraits ranged in date from the last decades B.C. to the mid–third century A.C., in subject from Augustus to Philip the Arab. See Espérandieu (supra n. 14) 41.

44. Although the Satyr is often attributed to Praxiteles, the statue's association with a "name" sculptor would not in itself ensure the work's popularity, as will be discussed.

The effeminate, curvaceous figures that Praxiteles created, however, appealed enormously to Roman tastes.

45. Sculptures of Laocoon and his sons and of Dirce tied to the bull are described as *ex eodem lapide* (Pliny *HN* 36.34).

46. A. Claridge of the British School at Rome has been exploring the practice of piecing. The publication of "Techniques of Obtaining Joins in Marble Sculpture," a paper given in the symposium at the J. Paul Getty Museum in April 1988, is forthcoming.

47. Phaedrus *Fabulae* 5.4–6. Other instances are documented in *EAA*, s.v. *Falsificazione*.

48. B. Ridgway, *Roman Copies of Greek Sculpture: The Problem of the Originals* (Ann Arbor 1984) 2.

49. Pliny *HN* 34.62 mentions this Lysippan work, which is known only in two copies, the well-known statue in the Vatican (Helbig[4] 254) and a reversed copy in the Museo Nazionale Romano (A. Giuliano ed., *Museo Nazionale Romano: Le sculture* 1,1 [Rome 1979] 335–37, no. 199).

50. Large-scale copies of the *opera nobilia* so familiar from public findspots have only infrequently come to light in Roman houses. When they do appear, their context suggests a patron of wealth. For example, large replicas of well-known fourth-century B.C. types were found in a marble-revetted *domus* under the Via Cavour in Rome, to be discussed later in this essay, and the equally rich Palazzo delle Colonne in Ptolemais housed large-scale versions of much-copied figures of Artemis and Aphrodite; cf. Pesce (supra n. 13) 80–81, pl. 51 (Artemis Rospigliosi), and 81, nos. 53–54 (two variants of the Aphrodite Frejus). To date no large-scale copies of earlier works have been found in the more modest settings of Pompeian houses. According to Zanker, "Villa als Vorbild" (supra n. 7) esp. 476–77 and 492–98, the deliberate miniaturization of popular statuary types was a characteristic of the prevailing *Wohngeschmack* of early imperial Pompeii. In Zanker's view, a desire to emulate the otiose, hellenized lifestyle of the Roman villa led city dwellers to affect a villa-like decor in their town houses; sculpture was de rigueur for the proper "look." Since the urban *domus* of Pompeii was, by definition, less spacious than the idealized villa, certain standardized sculptural ensembles were, of necessity, often reduced in scale.

51. Two well-known examples are the Weary Heracles, a work attributed to Lysippos but signed by the Athenian copyist Glycon (Naples, Archaeological Museum 6001), and a copy of Pheidias's Athena Parthenos signed by Antiochos (Rome, *Museo Nazionale Romano* 8622 [Helbig[4] 2828]). Two versions of the Hera Borghese found at Baiae were signed by two different copyists (P. Zancani Montuoro, *BullComm* 61 [1933] 41–43, no. 8, pl. 4 and fig. 14 [signed by Aphrodisias], and 43–45, no. 9, figs. 15–16 [signed by Caros]).

52. Pliny mentions Zenodoros's duplication of bronze beakers made by Calamis (*HN* 34.47); Plutarch refers to eleven copies of a sacred bronze shield that ensured the survival of early Rome (*Numa* 15.2–4); and Lucian praises a Roman copy of Zeuxis's painting of centaurs (*Zeuxis sive Antiochus* 3). Although these copies were made in media other than sculpture, the anecdotes indicate that the copy's technical superiority to the original was not an unfamiliar notion to an ancient audience.

53. Dionysios of Halicarnassus suggests that the average person was unable to distinguish between a copy and an original (*Dem.* 50 and *Dinarchus* 7). Dionysios, however, does not specify the medium. Discerning viewers must have recognized that most copies, at least of sculptures, involved a shift of medium from bronze to marble.

54. J. J. Pollitt, "The Impact of Greek Art on Rome," *TAPA* 108 (1978) 165.

55. Although erroneous in many details, the approach of G. Lippold, *Kopien und Umbildungen griechischer Statuen* (Munich 1923), is still fundamental. For a more recent treatment of the subject, see Ridgway (supra n. 8).

56. This is a rough estimate, based on a perusal of standard discussions of Greek sculpture such as Picard (supra n. 25) and M. Collignon, *Histoire de la sculpture grecque* 2 vols. (Paris 1892–97). When one considers that some types such as the Heracles Farnese are known in more than a hundred copies, the degree of repetition becomes all the more apparent; see Krull (supra n. 26).

57. This seems to be so despite the obvious Greek provenance of most images. For examples of sculptural copies found in the Roman provinces, see M. Abramic, "Antiken Kopien griechischer Skulpturen in Dalmatien," in *Festschrift für Rudolf Egger: Beiträge zur älteren europäischen Kulturgeschichte* 1 (Klagenfurt 1952) 303–26; and M. Bieber, "Copies of Greek Statues in the Roman Provinces," in *Hommages à Albert Grenier (CollLatomus 58, Brussels 1962) 288–93.

58. For recent research on domestic decor (exclusive of sculpture), see A. Barbet, *La peinture murale romaine: Les styles décoratifs pompéiens* (Paris 1985); and H. Joyce, *The Decoration of Walls, Ceilings, and Floors in Italy in the Second and Third Centuries A.D.* (Rome 1981).

59. For example, statues of Isis, Bes, and a sphinx, some executed in glazed terracotta in imitation of true faience. V. Spinazzola, *Pompei, alla luce degli scavi nuovi di Via dell'Abbondanza (anni 1910–23)* (Rome 1953) 382–87, 395, figs. 432–37, 450–51, and 454; and L. Richardson, Jr., *Pompeii: An Architectural History* (Baltimore and London 1988) 340–41.

60. In keeping with prevailing fashion, the statuary stood in as conspicuous a place as possible, either on the axis with the entrance to the house or in the garden; see Döhl and Zanker (supra n. 5) 202. For a statue in a comparable location, see the bronze dancing satyr from the House of the Faun in Pompeii. Restored by C. Moss, "'Patrician' Taste and the *Casa del Fauno*," *AJA* 88 (1985) 342, as having stood on a marble pedestal at the backmost edge of the *impluvium* in the atrium, the statuette stood on axis with the entrance but at a higher level than its present location in the fountain permits.

61. M. de Vos, *L'Egittomania in pitture e mosaici romano-campani della prima età imperiali* (Leiden 1980).

62. In the public sphere, see the use of the Weary Hercules motif in the decoration of the *tepidarium* of the Baths of Caracalla, both in two freestanding statues (see Marvin [supra n. 19] 355–57, pl. 47) and in a figured architectural capital now in a storeroom on the north side of the building (E. von Mercklin, *Antike Figuralkapitelle* [Berlin 1962] 158–59, no. 385a, figs. 751–53).

63. R. Wilson, *Piazza Armerina* (London 1983) 24; and Neudecker (supra n. 2) 176–77, no. 30. For a plan of the villa at Piazza Armerina in this volume, see Ellis (chap. 6 in this volume) fig. 6–3. The room under discussion lies on the south side of the central peristyle.

64. The room has been interpreted as a music hall, but this attribution is based on its decoration rather than specific architectural attributes; see Wilson (supra n. 63) 24. For further discussion of the decor at Piazza Armerina, see Ellis (chap. 6 in this volume).

65. Admittedly, some pendants were probably not conceptions original to the setting in which they appeared, but instead, repetitions of preexisting pairs. Like pendant paintings, some sculptural pendants probably became hackneyed through overuse.

66. K. Lehmann, "A Roman Poet Visits a Museum," *Hesperia* 14 (1945) 259–69.

67. Now in the Musée d'Aquitaine in Bordeaux (Artemis) and the Louvre, Paris (Aphrodite). See Espérandieu (supra n. 14) 220–21, nos. 1243 and 1244. For more recent treatment see Valensi (supra n. 32) and E. K. Gazda, "A Marble Group of Ganymede and the Eagle from the Age of Augustine," in J. H. Humphrey ed., *Excavations at Carthage, 1977, Conducted by the University of Michigan* 6 (Ann Arbor 1981) 150–54.

68. M. Thompson, "The Monumental and Literary Evidence for Programmatic Painting in Antiquity," *Marsyas* 9 (1960–61) 38.

69. A tripod may have been placed between them, as a physical reference to their literary "competition." For a recent discussion of the statues, see Neudecker (supra n. 2) 182, nos. 35.12 and 35.13, pl. 20; and M. Moltesen, "From the Princely Collections of the Borghese Family to the Glyptothek of Carl Jacobsen," *AnalRom* 16 (1987) 200. Moltesen argues that the statues are contemporary copies from the same workshop, although based on originals of different periods (pp. 192–93).

70. Two copies found at the baths in Cyrene are believed to have stood oriented in this manner. For a reconstruction, see E. Ghislanzoni, "Gli scavi delle terme romane à Cirene," *Notiziario archeologico* 2.1 (1916) 150, fig. 23 (reproduced as pl. 17.1 in Manderscheid [supra n. 19]). Their "reversed" orientations are confirmed by the different treatments of the bases on which the figures stood. See E. Paribeni, *Catalogo delle sculture di Cirene* (Rome 1959) 108, no. 301, pl. 144, and 109, no. 303, pl. 145.

71. For a discussion of such finds, see D. Levi, *Antioch Mosaic Pavements* (Princeton 1947) 185, and B. Ashmole, *A Catalogue of the Ancient Marbles at Ince Blundell Hall* (Oxford 1929) 16–18, no. 30. Of the replicas listed by Ashmole, *a* and *b* in Dresden (P. Herrmann, *Verzeichnis der antiken Originalbildwerke der staatlichen Skulpturensammlung zu Dresden* [Dresden 1925] 45, nos. 155 and 156) and *e* and *f* in Rome (Palazzo dei Conservatori, Helbig[4] 1715) were certainly found together.

72. That this meaning was intended can be seen from a second- or third-century A.C. floor mosaic found in the House of the Boat of Psyche at Antioch; see Levi (supra n. 71) 167, 183–84.

73. For initial publication of the statues, see K. Erim, "Aphrodisias: Results of the 1967 Campaign," *TürkArkDerg* 16.1 (1967) 67–68.

74. E. Künzl, *Frühhellenistiche Gruppen* (Diss. Univ. of Cologne 1968) 152–55.

75. J. Inan, *Roman Sculpture in Side* (Ankara 1975) 13–18, no. 1, pls. 6 and 7 (Pythagorean), and 19, no. 2, pls. 8 and 9. The suggestion that the two stood together as pendants was made by A. Linfert in a review of Inan, *BJb* 79 (1979) 781.

76. E. Bartman, "*Decor et Duplicatio*: Pendants in Roman Sculptural Display," *AJA* 92 (1988) 211–25.

77. Bartman (supra n. 76) 216–18.

78. Because of its superior resources and more frequent patronage, the public sphere is likely to be the trendsetter in this regard, but there is little definitive chronology with which to document the path of influence.

79. Pliny *HN* 36.27.

CHAPTER 4

The Decor of the House of Jupiter and Ganymede at Ostia Antica: Private Residence Turned Gay Hotel?

John R. Clarke

Perhaps no art is more private than erotic art, especially when created for a domestic context. The genre was frequently evoked in the decoration and furnishings of Roman houses. In the Roman *domus*, erotic decor encompassed a broad spectrum of functions and meanings, ranging from symbolic and reverent references to the powers of fertility and prosperity, through superstitious faith in *erotica* as an apotropaic force, to banal enthusiasm for pornography. Numerous wall paintings of erotic scenes are known. The finest of these come from *cubicula D* and *E* of the Villa under the Farnesina,[1] believed by several scholars to have belonged to Augustus's daughter and his son-in-law Agrippa.[2] Meant to be seen by the couples who slept there, the paintings both form part of an elegant late–Second Style decoration and underscore the relation of this subject to the room's function. Whatever the source for this practice of illustrating acts of lovemaking in little bedroom paintings, it is a tradition with a long life. The *cubiculum* in the southwest part of the House of the Centenary at Pompeii has two explicit scenes of sexual intercourse,[3] and as late as 250 A.C. similar pictures adorned bedroom 5 of the House of the Painted Vaults at Ostia Antica.[4]

The genre was also well suited, of course, to the decoration of public brothels. The explicit paintings of Pompeii's *lupanar* represent a variation on these *Kama-Sutra*-like pictures of couples—presumably married ones—enjoying the pleasures of sex in their elegant private bedrooms. More like advertisements of what was available to clients than marital aids, these paintings are executed in a frank and artless way, with a reduced palette and a minimum of ambience.[5] Interestingly, however, similar artless images can also be found in private houses. For example, room x^1 of the House of the Vettii received three equally explicit paintings that were executed in exactly the same style as that of the *lupanar*, perhaps by the same artist.[6] The issue of social class may be relevant here. Pompeii's *lupanar* appears to have served the lower classes of the city. In the House of the Vettii, both the location of the erotic paintings—in a small cul-de-sac next to the kitchen—and their crude quality suggest that the paintings were meant for the eyes of a favorite servant (perhaps the cook) rather than for the masters of the house.

Erotic subject matter also decorated a wide variety of luxury and utilitarian objects found in the Roman *domus*. For example, sophisticated representations of lovemaking also adorn fine silver vessels from the Augustan period. Two cups found among the treasures in the silver hoard of the House of the Menander may represent Mars and Venus.[7] Although of unknown provenance, the silver vessel discussed later on in this essay (see fig. 4-3) is, like the Menander cups, Augustan in style and meant for a cultured, wealthy patron. In the same period numerous Arretine-ware vessels with erotic representations were manufactured for persons of more slender means.[8] To an even less refined level belong the ubiquitous lamps with artless scenes of coupling that may have been used for illuminating bedchambers.[9] All of these portable objects demonstrate that Roman appreciation for erotic art in the decor of the home crossed class boundaries, a conclusion already suggested by the variable quality of erotic wall painting, which ranged from the naive scrawlings of the *lupanar* artist to the elegant boudoir paintings of the Farnesina master.

A unique painting in the House of Jupiter and Ganymede in Ostia offers an opportunity to examine an instance of Roman erotic interior decoration that apparently belonged to a specialized and intriguing social context. The painting gives its name to the *insula* apartment in which it is found and was first published along with the architecture of the *insula* in 1920 by the excavator, Guido Calza. In 1986 I restudied this painting and discovered hitherto unknown details of its iconography that must now be integrated into a new interpretation of the meaning of the painting to its Roman audience. To do so, it will first be necessary to consider the nature of the building for which it was intended.

In the middle of his 1920 excavation report on Regio I, Insula iv, 2, at Ostia Antica, Guido Calza's tone changes ominously. He has been discussing the substantial modifications of the ground-floor apartment that took place fifty years after it was built. After noting the care and refinement of these changes, he says:

> But if the house was degraded neither in its appearance nor in its value [by these modifications], it seems by contrast to have been destined for a most degrading use. For, as we shall see, the graffiti

read on some of its walls boast of the numerous obscenities commit-
ted within these walls.[10]

After examining the evidence, Calza concludes that this apartment, the
finest and largest of the entire complex, was enlarged and redecorated to serve
as a hotel for male homosexuals. In keeping with the spirit of his times, Calza
refrains from using the term "homosexual"; he spares the gentle reader by using
instead the Latinized Greek word *cinaedus*. Calza builds his gay-hotel hypothesis
on three different sorts of evidence: the changed layout of the house; the meaning of the graffiti; and the painted images of the house's largest room, whose
centerpiece is the representation of Jupiter and Ganymede.

As the plan (fig. 4-1) shows, the House of Jupiter and Ganymede (labeled
Casa III) was the largest of three units occupying the western portion of a whole
city block. Brickstamp evidence and building technique indicate that the whole
complex was built around 130. On the southwest corner of the building, at the
intersection of the Via di Diana and the Via della Casa dei Dipinti, is a shop
space. The house's secondary entrance is next to this corner shop, farther to the
east on the Via della Casa di Diana. On the plan one can see the gap between
our structure and the row of shops along the eastern part of the block.

It is reasonable to assume that the two identical apartments to the north
(called Casa I and Casa II on Calza's plan) were planned as rental units, leaving
Casa III, the larger, more luxuriously appointed quarters occupying the southwest corner of the block, for the owner. We know that in Roman times the
owner or landlord preferred the ground-floor apartment, and the best of these
imitate the spaciousness and formality of the traditional single-family dwelling
or *domus*. The House of Jupiter and Ganymede originally had two separate
entrances. The principal entry (1) leads to a large courtyard (3) surrounded by
a covered walkway or *ambulacrum* (2), in this way providing a circulation pattern
similar to that of the *domus*. A secondary entry leads to the *ambulacrum* from the
Via della Casa di Diana. Furthermore, room 4, accessible both from the courtyard and the *ambulacrum*, is enormous and opulently decorated. It is about 6
meters tall, extending vertically through the second story, and is 6.75 by 8.75
meters in area. This room's great size is an indication of the wealth of the
patron, particularly if we compare it with the most luxurious houses at Pompeii.
It is almost a third larger than both the *tablinum* in the Villa of the Mysteries (5.75
by 7.25 m.) and the great *oecus* of the House of the Vettii in Pompeii (5 by 8 m.),
and only three-tenths smaller than the largest dining room in Pompeii, that of
the House of the Menander, which measures 11 by 7.5 meters.

The plan also illustrates, by means of parallel hatching, the modifications
to this large luxury apartment in the period between 184 and 192. The graffito

"VII K L COMMODAS," or "on the seventh day before the Calends of Commodos," scratched on the wall of the *ambulacrum* dates this wall-painting campaign, since the emperor Commodus's proclamation of 184 renaming the month of September after himself was repealed after his murder in 192.[11] The decoration of this wall, and in fact that of all the painted wall surfaces that have survived in this house, covers the modifications to the original plan. These were six in all:

1. A wooden staircase was placed in room 11 to connect the ground-floor apartment with one of the upstairs apartments.
2. Room 10 and the remainder of 11 became shops facing the street.
3. A room, unnumbered on the plan but usually called the "Gastzimmer" or "guest room," was added at the eastern end of the *ambulacrum*. It had no doors, only a curtain hanging between the two partition walls framing its entrance.
4. Room 13, a corner shop, was detached, and the second entrance to the ground-floor apartment was blocked.
5. Probably to improve the support for the upper stories, the great door to the courtyard in front of the entrance to room 9 was closed, and the door to the *tablinum* was made into a window.
6. Room 7's door to the *ambulacrum* was closed, and rooms 8 and 6 got new doorways to vestibule 1.

The purpose of these modifications was to enlarge the house by adding the rooms of the upstairs apartment and to gain greater control of street access by closing off the secondary entrance and by opening doorways to either side of the vestibule. This new configuration of the spaces suggested to Calza a private hotel, for now the apartment was too large for a single family. Why else do away with the suite of street-side rooms except to increase the privacy of the ground-floor rooms? And why else do away with the secondary entrance and add facing doorways at the principal entrance except to be able to monitor comings and goings? This kind of entryway, according to a recent interpretation, belongs in a gay brothel. In a vase painting (fig. 4-2) a woman sits in a kind of booth or box office at the entryway to the right, flanked by the male owner of the establishment. Both watch a young customer mounting his purchased playmate with the help of a staff.[12]

A fine silver cup of the Augustan period carries this situation forward in time to the Roman period (fig. 4-3).[13] The clear representation of a room's interior and the presence of an onlooker looking through one of the battens of a door[14] suggest that the lovemaking is taking place in a hotel or brothel. Other details make this even more convincing than the vase painting as a scene in a specially designed gay hotel or house of prostitution rather than a private home. The young couple occupy a bed in a room outfitted for lovemaking, complete with a convenient strap that one of the men uses (much like the staff in the vase painting) to help him assume a pleasurable position. The refined relief technique and use of a precious metal indicate that this object was intended for a patron of means; the upper-class status of the lovemakers is signified by their clearly Augustan hairstyles and facial types and the allusion to Augustus's favorite male deity, Apollo, in the lyre at the left and the bearded male's laurel wreath.

These representations suggest, but do not prove, the existence of gay brothels for the upper class. Literary sources are equally inconclusive. Amy Richlin has collected and analyzed the literary evidence for the circumstance of male homosexuality in Roman society of the late Republic and early Empire. Whereas sources suggest that relations between adult males and youths, usually slaves, were expected and normal, sex between adults of the same age receives no mention.[15]

Graffiti, usually much closer to life than to literature, have much to say about sexual mores.[16] For Calza, in fact, the meaning and location of the graffiti were more important factors than the new arrangement of spaces in convincing him that this was a well-appointed hotel for gays. On the right wall of the "guest room" were scratched pictures of several ships, a male figure, and a pair of duelling gladiators, one called TAURUS. Near these is *Ti Ermadion cinaedus*, or, "You're a faggot, Ermadion." Superimposed in two different lettering styles nearby were two different verses (fig. 4-4). The first reads:

> *hic ad Callinicum futui*
> *orem anum amicom mare . . .*
> *nolite in aede . . .* [or] *nolite cinaede . . .* [17]

The second graffito is equally graphic:

> *Livius me cunus*
> *lincet Tertulle cunus . . .*
> *Efesius Terisium amat*[18]

In the stairhall things seemed to be just as busy as in the "guest room." There we read that Agathopus, Primus, and Epaphroditus had a threesome and that Cepholus and Musice came together (literally).[19] The explicit meaning of the word used here, *convenire*, is established both in a famous heterosexual graffito at Pompeii (*Secundus cum Primigenia conveniunt*) and in Apuleius (*Met. 4.27*).

Two aspects of these graffiti puzzled Calza. First, most of the graffiti from the houses at Pompeii mention sexual acts between males and females, and frequently the females mentioned are prostitutes, *ancellae* or *togatae*. One graffito naming a household slave a *cinaedus*, in atriolo *v* of the House of the Vettii, was subsequently scratched out, presumably by the person so named.[20] None of the graffiti in the House of Jupiter and Ganymede name females, and none of the males called faggots registered their objections by attempting to erase anything. Second, the rooms where the graffiti were found form part of the circulation system of the house; no one could be having sex in either room without the rest of the household knowing about it, for the "guest room" had only a curtain, no permanent door, and the stairwell room formed the only route from the ground floor to the upstairs rooms. The owner would have had to know what these rooms were used for. If the graffiti were written by servants, why are there no female names, and why were they written in these rather public spaces?

At this point Calza abandons the physical evidence of the building and the graffiti and turns to the interpretation of the wall painting, but it is worth asking further questions. Could the graffiti have belonged to a later period of economic decline, when even fine houses like this were abandoned? The answer is no, because the graffiti themselves have an upper temporal limit. They were covered when the house was replastered forty years later, in about 235–45.[21] This means that the remodeling, the wall decoration, and the graffiti belong to the last period of Ostia's great economic prosperity, not to the period of its decline in the later third century. In this period of prosperity there could have been a need for a hotel catering to a special sort of clientele.

How does the layout of the House of Jupiter and Ganymede fit into what we know of hotel plans in the Roman period? Tönnes Kleberg's study of hotels in Roman antiquity ignores the House of Jupiter and Ganymede in favor of smaller buildings with much simpler plans and with easy access to busy streets.[22] These *cauponae*, or little restaurant-bars with rooms (and often prostitutes) for rent, were decidedly for the lower classes; middle- or upper-class gentlemen would never be seen there.[23]

Comparison of the plan of the House of Jupiter and Ganymede with that of the common whorehouses reveals little in common. The previously mentioned *lupanar* at Pompeii, for instance, has about one-tenth of the space of the House of Jupiter and Ganymede. The plan (fig. 4-5) suggests that it was built for quick turnover, and it has nothing in common with plans of either the single-family *domus* or the multifamily apartment building. Instead of rooms, there is a central passageway surrounded by ten cramped cubicles with flimsy partitions. The explicit paintings of heterosexual intercourse are oriented toward the central reception/circulation area, in keeping with their purpose as advertisement.[24]

On the other hand, if we look at the location of the House of Jupiter and Ganymede and ask, "Is this a likely place for a hotel?" the answer is most certainly yes. All the examples of hotels noted by Kleberg at Pompeii, Herculaneum, and Ostia are near the amphitheater, forum, city gates, theater, or baths.[25] The House of Jupiter and Ganymede is one block to the west of Ostia's central Forum. Across the street from the House of Jupiter and Ganymede is a *caupona* serving wine and food, and the Forum Baths are nearby.

Ostia in the second and early third century A.C. was a cosmopolitan city filled with men of commerce whose concern was supplying Rome, a city of over a million inhabitants, with the goods it consumed. Some of these *negotiatores*, probably those of the lower classes, lived there permanently, but shipping magnates and prosperous entrepreneurs may have preferred to reside in Rome or their native port of supply. The "shop-sign" mosaics of the Piazzale of the Corporations at Ostia vividly record the far-flung geographical origins of businessmen active in Ostia. It seems likely that certain well-heeled Roman commercial travelers, like some of their modern counterparts, may have preferred a well-appointed hotel that looked with approval on their homosexual activities.

Calza's theory of the purpose of the House of Jupiter and Ganymede seems the most logical explanation for the unusual architectural and occupational history that he has reconstructed for the building from archaeological and epigraphical evidence. The plausibility of Calza's case is further enhanced by the iconography of the great hall whose central element is the painting of Jupiter and Ganymede. Here architectural context and interior decoration appear to be in complete harmony, both with each other and with identification as a gay hotel for wealthy patrons.

The wall paintings of the *tablinum*-like reception room (room 4 in fig. 4-1) in the House of Jupiter and Ganymede constitute the largest extant painted surface at Ostia Antica (figs. 4-6 and 4-7). Its ambitious decorative program consists of four horizontal registers with *aediculae* in the center of each wall. There were originally pictures in the centers of each *aedicula*. Calza described the fragments of the central picture on the left-hand wall, no longer visible. One-third of the panel was preserved, showing a young, nude Dionysus standing, with his left arm folded behind the nape of his neck, a bell-shaped object (perhaps cymbals) in his right. He was revealing himself to a clothed female, probably a maenad.[26] In the upper zone, directly above this picture, was a representation of Flora, the Italic goddess of flowers. Calza tells us that she wore a green mantle and held a garland woven of fruit and flowers. Opposite her, in the same position on the room's right wall, is a young, nude Dionysus with long, curly hair. He holds a fillet in his left hand and a bunch of grapes in his right. A red chlamys is draped over his shoulders.

The rear wall is the best preserved. Above the picture of Jupiter and Ganymede appears Venus Anadyomene (see fig. 4-7). This representation of

Venus rising from the sea, based on a famous painting by Apelles of Kos,[27] occurs elsewhere at Ostia in a mid-third-century painting in the Terme del Faro and in the mid-fourth-century mosaic of the House of the Dioscuri. Calza notes that all of these divinities belong to the younger Olympus, standing for eternal youth and joy.[28]

The remaining single figures represent generic types rather than specific gods and goddesses. They fit into three categories: the bearded males represent "philosophers"; the beardless males, "poets"; and the draped, flying females, "maenads" or "nymphs." Because of their lack of a specific pictorial context and their obviously decorative function in the ensemble, it is risky at best to assign them precise meanings.

If there is a key to the room's iconography, it must lie in the central picture of the rear wall (see figs. 4-7 and 4-8). By analogy to many fully preserved decorations with similar aedicular schemes, the central picture of a room's rear wall, opposite the entry and commanding the room's axis, is the most important.[29] The closest parallel is *oecus p* of the House of the Vettii at Pompeii, often called the Ixion Room because of the subject matter of the aedicular picture in the center of its rear wall.[30] Many aspects of the Ixion Room's late Fourth Style decoration survive a hundred years later in the Ostian room of Jupiter and Ganymede: the socle consisting of faux-marble revetment, slots with shallow architectural perspectives, flying or floating figures in front of monochrome panels, and, the most important element, a cycle of aedicular pictures in the median zones with statuelike groups above them in the upper zone.

What of this key picture? It must be noted at the outset that the painting has suffered greater losses than are evident even from slides and photographs. Ostian wall painting has been much maligned for its poor quality vis-à-vis Pompeii, but only very rarely do we see more than the fresco underpainting at Ostia. All the finished surfaces, added over the dried fresco, have been lost. Bearing this in mind, one must remember that one is often looking at guidelines never meant to be seen when studying the paintings of Roman Ostia.

Faced with the difficulty of studying this important ruined central picture from slides or photographs, I made a tracing over the painting using transparent acetate and a marking pen (fig. 4-8). Making a tracing forces one to see the guidelines in the fresco underpainting very clearly and allows one to separate out the "static" caused by partially adhering upper layers, damages, calcification, and inept modern restoration.

All that remains of Jupiter's thunderbolt, for instance, is the fresco underpainting in porphyry red. Jupiter is seated on a throne with a footstool. The porphyry-red underpainting of his cloak and the outlines of his feet are just visible. The underpainting shows that Zeus's right hand reaches toward

Ganymede's neck and chin. He is not caressing him on his cheek, as Calza would have it. This gesture would never be lost on a Roman or Greek audience, for from at least the sixth century B.C. on it always signifies amorous intent. Leo Steinberg, who traces its survival into Renaissance religious painting, calls it the "chin-chuck."[31] Greek black-figured vase painting presents numerous examples of courting scenes between the bearded adult male *erastes* or lover and the beardless, often barely pubescent boy, the *eromenos* or beloved. In every case the *erastes* touches the boy's chin in the precise way Jupiter touches Ganymede's—with the hand open, thumb near the chin and fingers at the neck (fig. 4-9). What is lacking here is the accompanying attempt to fondle the youth's genitals, which J. D. Beazley called the "up and down" pose.[32] This is difficult here because Jupiter is seated.[33] Ganymede is reciprocating in some way. A common gesture among the courtship scenes (also illustrated in fig. 4-9) shows the beloved responding to the chin chuck by grasping his lover's wrist. This gesture seemed to work best in the reconstruction drawing (fig. 4-10), with the seated Jupiter's torso in a three-quarter view, his head in profile. Rather than restoring Ganymede's missing right arm to hold a cup of ambrosia, the wrist-grasp seems preferable because the figures are so close to each other and Ganymede leans back and tilts his head up to look at Jupiter.

Sculptural representations of Ganymede with the Eagle, such as that in the British Museum, share several features in common with our painted version. The Phrygian cap, the chlamys or cape draped over the shoulders, the upturned gaze, and the *contrapposto* stance appear in both sculpture and painting. Our painter reversed the position of the feet while retaining Ganymede's stance, and of course in the painting his right arm reaches for Jupiter. Although these parallels seem to reveal the painter's awareness of sculptural prototypes, given the enormous paint losses in this area, accurate reconstruction seems out of the question. For example, Jupiter's left hand, restored here as resting on his modestly draped lap, is entirely conjectural.

Whereas Ganymede's Phrygian cap, *contrapposto* stance, and red chlamys secure his identification, the female figure occupying the left-hand fourth of the painting is much more problematic. Calza thought she could be Aphrodite, asserting—like the Aphrodite Anadyomene above—the right of every kind of love. But he noted that her clothing and features suggested Hera, in an almost undignified attitude, in no way participating. Or perhaps she was Hebe, the former cupbearer of the gods who had lost favor to the new boy. None of these interpretations is possible. While tracing this female figure, I discovered the outlines of feathers and a swan's neck and head in her lap. She must be Leda.

There is a white form in Leda's lap. Close inspection of that white form reveals black outlines of feathers on the white plaster of the ground. The swan's head and neck are at the right, and its curved wings begin at Leda's waist. Paint losses prevent us from knowing just how large the swan was, but comparison with sculptural types makes it probable that it was lap-size. A Leda in the Archaeological Museum in Venice represents a type sometimes attributed to Praxiteles; it is dated to the last quarter of the fourth century B.C.[34] It emphasizes Jupiter's divinity in a strange way. Since in the Greek mind gods are like mortals in form, but are just larger, this type enlarges the swan to emphasize that this is a divine visitation. Leda is nude and knows exactly what is happening to her. Her nudity and the enormous size of the swan rule this type out as a source for our painted Leda.

On the other hand, an early fourth-century B.C. type, often attributed without foundation to Timotheos, has many points in common with our painting (fig. 4-11). In this Antonine copy of the type, Leda wears a chiton that is fastened at the shoulders; one clasp has gotten undone so that half of her body is exposed to the swan. Leda's left arm holds up a huge cloak to protect that small swan, which she pulls toward her with her right hand. This representation dramatizes the version of the myth in which Zeus, smitten with passion for Leda, persuades Aphrodite to help him get her. Aphrodite turns herself into an eagle and pretends to threaten Zeus, who has turned himself into a swan. Leda, alarmed and compassionate, tries to shelter the swan; we see her at the moment when she raises her cloak to protect it. Of course this allows Zeus to have his way with Leda.

A painted version of this early fourth-century sculptural type decorates the south wall of room *e* in the House of the Vettii at Pompeii (fig. 4-12). There Leda occupies the center of the upper zone, facing Danae on the opposite wall, while Jupiter regards both of his mortal conquests from the west wall. Leda is clearly seated, a chair leg appearing at her left knee, her feet on a rocky footstool. Her chiton has fallen into her lap and she has drawn the protecting cloak over her head with her right arm. The swan has alighted on her left knee, his head poised as if to gaze at her or kiss her. Since the figure of Jupiter is the only remaining copy of Apelles' painting for the temple of Diana at Ephesos,[35] it is reasonable to assume that the artist was also attempting to reproduce with some degree of fidelity a painted composition based on a canonical sculptural type for Leda.[36]

Whether drawing from a painted or a sculpted source, it is easy to see how our painter might have used this type. The half-unfastened chiton becomes a fully fastened one with two shoulder clasps. Leda's dramatic *contrapposto* stance also translates, albeit in a somewhat deadpan fashion, into an ambiguous, approximately seated position. Her right hand, which overlaps the picture frame, does not seem to be holding the swan. Instead the swan presses himself into her lap so that his back is toward the viewer. Leda's left arm gestures upward as in the sculpture but does not hold drapery. Instead her slightly upraised and outstretched left hand seems to be a gesture of presentation, particularly in combination with her frontal pose. She looks out at the viewer.

In fact, Leda's position, crowded into the left-hand quarter of the picture, her awkward, disengaged pose, and her detachment from the courting scene as a kind of "third wheel" all suggest that the artist wished to express Jupiter's preference for a male mortal lover over a female one—at least for the moment.

The reconstruction drawing wavers between a lap-size and a man-size swan. It is likely that our painter intended the smaller bird. He seems to have based his representation of the swan itself on a ready-made type he was quite familiar with: that of the ubiquitous images of swans that appear as decorative elements in wall painting. In fact, our artist reinforced the Jupiter/Leda connection in the symbolism of the birds that frame this picture: to the right and left are Jupiter's eagles, but beneath it is a representation of a swan. Enlarged, and pressed against Leda's lap and legs, it solved for the painter the iconographical problem of justifying Jupiter's bisexuality in his choice of mortal lovers.

Although there are no representations of Jupiter, Ganymede, and Leda in the same pictorial composition, these two mortal loves of Jupiter were often arranged as pendants in sculpture. In these sculptural groups, in contrast to our painting, each figure has equal importance. A drawing of a silver cup, discovered in 1861 at Cullera near Valencia, presents four of Jupiter's mortal loves (fig. 4-13). Leda is on the far left with her swan and Ganymede on the far right with his eagle. Between the two are Zeus with Semele and Zeus with Callisto.[37] Four sixteenth-century drawings document a sarcophagus, now lost, in which Leda and Ganymede are more properly pendants. Sichtermann has recently shown that the version in the Codex Corburgensis is closest to the original (fig. 4-14).[38] Here the pendant composition is elaborated by the portrait of the deceased in the center with theatrical masks below and two mourning putti, torches downturned, at the outer edges. If the arrangement of the drawing is accurate, the recumbent figures of Ganymede and Leda were arranged symmetrically, Ganymede on the viewer's left and Leda on his or her right. This sarcophagus, and another in Budapest,[39] probably dating to the second century after Christ, could have been contemporary with our painting.

A more dramatic pendant display of Leda and Ganymede comes from a monument called Las Incantadas in Thessalonika, Macedonia; it was dismantled and removed to the Louvre in the last century.[40] The original setting is illustrated in a drawing by Stuart and Revett.[41] Pilasters with relief figures on both sides decorated the upper storey of a colonnade. The monument has been dated to the second or third century A.C. One of the double-sided pilasters has Leda on one side and Ganymede on the other. The Leda (fig. 4-15) is clearly based on the type attributed to Timotheos. She is draped and holds the swan in her lap. Although her pose, like that of the other figures in Las Incantadas, has been rearranged to fit the frame, this Leda also parallels our painted version.

It seems that the idea of arranging sculptural images of Leda and Ganymede as pendants also extended into domestic decoration. Elaine Gazda has suggested that the Ganymede from the House of the Greek Charioteers at Carthage may have been arranged with Leda as a companion piece.[42] Gazda noted two possible locations for pendant display. Traces of two foundations at the centers of the long walls of the *triclinium* may have held Ganymede on one side with Leda opposite, or there may have been niches for them at the two small fountains that flank the intercolumniations to the left and right of the entrance to the *triclinium*.

When the wall paintings of the room of Jupiter and Ganymede are compared to the decorative programs of upper-class Roman houses, one significant difference emerges. The original aspect lies in the homoerotic iconography of Jupiter, Ganymede, and Leda, which has no known parallel in Roman domestic wall painting. On the other hand, the mythological mode into which the theme of homosexual love is cast is a hallmark of interior decoration in the residences of the elite. Representations of heterosexual lovers drawn from Greek mythology are a staple element in the decor of *tablina* and *oeci*. Erotic subject matter, when allusively encoded in mythological imagery, was apparently considered acceptable decoration for public areas of the private house. Except for its homosexual theme, the decor of the hotel foyer in the House of Jupiter and Ganymede would have been equally appropriate to the room's presumed original function as a reception room for a wealthy private apartment.

Among the most popular heterosexual parallels for the painting of Jupiter and Ganymede are scenes of the archetypal Olympian lovers, Mars and Venus, in their bedroom. Whereas Mars and Venus are usually depicted in an intimate moment, nearly nude, with only cupids present,[43] in *tablinum h* of the House of Lucretius Fronto their boudoir is crowded with five onlookers in addition to Cupid, whose quiver hangs from the bed while he unstrings his bow. Maiuri has called this tableau a charming *scène galante* in the spirit of a fashionable eighteenth-century Parisian boudoir.[44] Curtius proposed that the scene takes place in the house of Hephaestus, and that the figure with wings on his forehead is Hermes.[45] Maiuri interpreted a second, almost identical version of this composition as an allusion to the wedding of Mars and Venus; he named the god with winged forehead Hymen.[46]

More recently, Michel has deemed the onlookers in the boudoir of Mars and Venus merely one example of a conventional motif invented and popularized by Roman copyists who wished to make their Greek mythological models more immediately engaging to a Roman audience. In Michel's view, the observers inserted into mythological paintings were generic types who needed no identity consistent with the content of the scene. Their purpose was to direct the attention of the Roman viewer and, occasionally, to add a frisson of voyeuristic titillation to his or her enjoyment of erotic themes.[47]

Michel's provocative ideas can be applied with illuminating result to the decorative program of the House of Jupiter and Ganymede. The figure of Leda, who turns to confront the viewer and gestures toward the group of Jupiter and Ganymede, fits neatly into Michel's category of the "camouflaged observer." Leda is a mythological character who can be thematically integrated into the scene she observes. Nevertheless, her primary compositional function is to guide the viewer's gaze and to intensify the viewer's response to the central picture of the wall—a homosexual encounter between the ruler of Olympus and a mortal youth. Perhaps with intentional irony, Leda, one of Jupiter's heterosexual conquests, actually heightens the homoerotic content of the composition as a whole. Does she also invite the viewer, a prosperous guest who may hire a compliant male companion during his stay, to identify with Jupiter, the god about to dally with a beautiful young man of inferior status?

In subject matter, setting, and style, the painting of Jupiter and Ganymede reveals nothing to contradict Calza's hypothesis that it adorned a gay hotel for wealthy patrons. The homoerotic theme is certainly suited to such an establishment. The painting's location in a reception room is equally appropriate, at least to judge from the brothel at Pompeii, where cruder *comparanda* were on display in the central passageway. In contrast to the unpretentious little placards in the working-class *lupanar*, however, the painting of Jupiter and Ganymede was pitched to a more cultured clientele. Neither its discreet treatment of mythological erotica nor its megalographic composition would be out of context in an upper-class private house.

It seems likely, however, that the artist who put Ganymede and Leda in the same frame was deliberately underscoring the fact that Jupiter loved and made love to both male and female mortals, although here he prefers Ganymede. Rather than registering disapproval, as Calza thought, Leda's frontal pose and openhanded gesture invite the viewer to consider the coexistence of two kinds of love—homosexual and heterosexual—in the person of the supreme Olympian deity. The artist who achieved this conflation as the central decoration of the most important room of a hotel for homosexual men knew that the message (including its ironic overtones) would not be lost on the establishment's clientele.[48]

NOTES

1. I. Bragantini and M. de Vos, *Le decorazioni della villa romana della Farnesina* (*Museo Nazionale Romano, Le Pitture* 2, 1, Rome 1982), D: 189, pls. 85–86; E: 285–86, pl. 174.

2. P. H. von Blanckenhagen, *The Paintings from Boscotrecase* (*RM*, Ergänzungsheft 17, 1963) 59–60, follows H. G. Beyen, "Les *domini* de la Villa de la Farnesine," *Studia varia Carolo Guilielmo Vollgraff a discipulis oblata* (Amsterdam 1948) 3–21.

3. One is illustrated in M. Grant, *Eros in Pompeii* (New York 1975) 36; see also M. and A. de Vos, *Pompei Ercolano Stabia* (Bari 1982) 213, plan, 215.

4. B. M. Felletti Maj, *Le pitture della Casa delle Volte Dipinte e della Casa delle Pareti Gialle* (*Monumenti della pittura antica scoperti in Italia* 3, 1–2, Rome 1961) 38, dates these paintings to 240–50 A.C., illustrated in fig. 9; pl. 5, 1; pl. 6, 3.

5. Grant (supra n. 3) 32–33.

6. Illustrated in Grant (supra n. 3) 52.

7. A. Maiuri, *La Casa del Menandro e il suo tesoro di argenteria* (Rome 1932) vol. 1, 321–330, figs. 125–128; vol. 2, pls. 31–35.

8. *CVA* Metropolitan Museum 1, pl. 34.1 a-b, bears a representation of a homosexual scene of a youth with a boy on a couch framed by ithyphallic herms.

9. Seven examples pictured in Grant (supra n. 3) 106–7.

10. G. Calza, "Gli scavi recenti nell'abitato di Ostia," *MonAnt* 26 (1920) 362.

11. A. W. Van Buren, *CR* 37 (1923) 163–64.

12. E. Keuls, *The Reign of the Phallus* (New York 1985) 293. Keuls's interpretation is not entirely convincing: see P. H. von Blanckenhagen, "Puerilia," in L. Bonfante and H. von Heintze eds., *In Memoriam Otto Brendel* (Mainz 1976) 37–41.

13. The cup is in a private collection, on anonymous loan to the Basel Museum. C. Vermeule, "Augustan and Julio-Claudian Court Silver," *AntK* (1963) 39, pl. 14, 2 and 4, for views of both scenes. Vermeule maintains that the couple illustrated here (his pl. 14,2) have the features of Tiberius and Drusus the Younger. A modern copy of the cup in the Ashmolean Museum is illustrated in C. Johns, *Sex or Symbol?* (Austin 1982) pl. 25 and fig. 84. Recently, several scholars have questioned the authenticity of this cup because of its similarity to forged Arretine pottery. See Michael Vickers, "Arretine Forgeries Revealed," *The Ashmolean* 18 (1990) 5.

14. For the representation of onlookers in Pompeian wall painting, see D. Michel, "Bemerkungen über Zuschauerfiguren in pompejanischen sogenannten Tafelbildern," *La regione sotterrata dal Vesuvio: Studi e prospettive* (Naples 1982) 537–98.

15. A. Richlin, *The Garden of Priapus: Sexuality and Aggression in Roman Humor* (New Haven 1983) 220–26; see also J. Boswell, *Christianity, Social Tolerance, and Homosexuality* (Chicago 1980) 61–87.

16. Richlin (supra n. 15) 81–86.

17. "Here I screwed the mouth and anus of my sea-going friend. Don't do [something] in the temple . . . [or] Don't do [something] with or to a faggot." The phrase *ad Callinicum* is added for emphasis, literally, "to victory!" It is unfortunate that there are gaps in the text, for it would be interesting to know what the reader is not supposed to do in the temple or with the homosexual. Note also that one of the orifices named in the graffito is illustrated in the *U* of *futui*.

18. "Livius that faggot [literally *cunt* used as a synonym for faggot] licks me. Tertullus,

you're a cunt too." J. N. Adams, *The Latin Sexual Vocabulary* (London 1982) 116–17, notes that *cunnus*, when used of a male homosexual, equals *culus*, and by extension a *cinaedus*. Here *lincet* (= *lingit*) indicates anilingus or fellatio. The last line provides another bit of sexual gossip by proclaiming that "Efesius [a male, presumably from Ephesus] loves Terisius [another male]."

19. Van Buren (supra n. 11) 164 suggests alternate readings: for Calza's *Agathopus et Primu et Epaphroditus tre convenientes* he suggests *Agathopus et Prima et Mod(e)stus tres convenientes*, putting a female into the threesome; for *Cepholus et Musice duo convenientes* he reads *Nicephorus et Musice due convenientes*, adding that *Musice* is a female name.

20. de Vos (supra n. 3) 170.

21. Calza (supra n. 10) 368.

22. T. Kleberg, *Hôtels, restaurants et cabarets dans l'antiquité romaine* (Uppsala 1957) passim.

23. Kleberg (supra n. 22) 93–94.

24. Reg. VII, Ins. xii, 18–20; de Vos (supra n. 3) 202–4.

25. Kleberg (supra n. 22) 49–53.

26. Calza (supra n. 10) 397.

27. J. J. Pollitt, *The Art of Greece, 1400–31 B.C.: Sources and Documents* (Englewood Cliffs, N.J., 1965) 165–67.

28. Calza (supra n. 10) 396.

29. R. Brilliant, *Visual Narratives: Storytelling in Etruscan and Roman Art* (Ithaca and London 1984) 78.

30. Illustrated in H. Kähler, *The Art of Rome and Her Empire* (New York 1965) 66.

31. L. Steinberg, *The Sexuality of Christ in Renaissance Art and in Modern Oblivion* (New York 1983) 3.

32. J. D. Beazley, "Some Attic Vases in the Cyprus Museum," *ProcBritAc* 33 (1947) 199.

33. G. Neumann, *Gesten und Gebärden in der griechischen Kunst* (Berlin 1965) 67–69; K. J. Dover, *Greek Homosexuality* (Cambridge, Mass. 1978) 93–96; Keuls (supra n. 12) 277–83.

34. G. Lippold, "Leda und Ganymedes," *SBMünch* 3 (1954) pl. 2,3.

35. P. Mingazzini, "Una copia dell'Alexandros Keraunophoros di Apelle," *JBerlMus* 3 (1961) 7–17, argues that this image of a beardless Zeus is a close replica of the painting of Alexander holding a thunderbolt described by Pliny (*HN* 35, 36, 92).

36. Another painted variant of this type is in the Casa dei Capitelli Colorati (VII iv 51), room *f*, in K. Schefold, *Vergessenes Pompeji* (Bern 1962) fig. 166. Leda, standing, holds her right hand up while her veil swirls around her head and the swan looks up at her. There is a chair behind to Leda's left.

37. S. Reinach, *Répertoire de reliefs grecs et romains* 2 (Paris 1912) 242, figs. 1–3.

38. H. Sichtermann, "Leda und Ganymed," *MarbWPr* (1984) 43–57. Sichtermann illustrates the four drawings: fig. 1, Codex Coburgensis; fig. 2, Dal Pozzo's sketchbook; fig. 3, Pierre Jacques's sketchbook; fig. 4, Giovanni Bellini's sketchbook.

39. S. Burger, *ArchErt* 100 (1973) 42ff., figs. 1–10.

40. Lippold (supra n. 34) 3; L. Guerrini, "*Las Incantadas* di Salonicco," *ArchCl* 13 (1961) 53–55.

41. C. Gurlitt ed., *The Antiquities of Athens, Measured and Drawn by James Stuart and N. Revett (1762–1764)* (reprint London 1922) pl. 98.

42. E. K. Gazda, "A Marble Group of Ganymede and the Eagle from the Age of

Augustine," in J. H. Humphrey ed., *Excavations at Carthage, 1977, Conducted by the University of Michigan* 6 (Ann Arbor 1981) 177.

43. For instance, in the painting from the House of Mars and Venus, Naples Archaeological Museum, illustrated in L. Curtius, *Die Wandmalerei Pompejis* (Hildesheim 1960) pl. 1.

44. A. Maiuri, *Roman Painting* (Geneva 1953) 78.

45. Curtius (supra n. 43) 250–51; and Hom. *Od.* 8.333–42. In this interpretation, the luxurious bed will trap the lovers, and Hermes is one of the Olympians who comes to see the entrapped couple. Difficulties remain, since Hermes should have wings on his feet, not his head, and the couple is not yet caught in Hephaestus's nets.

46. On the Third Style *tablinum* of Pompeii I vii 19, see A. Maiuri, *NSc* (1929) 362–64, pl. 19. Maiuri also suggests that the figure with winged head is Hypnos; M. Della Corte, *RM* 57 (1942), 34, concurs. Against this interpretation see K. Schefold, *Die Wände Pompejis: Topographisches Verzeichnis der Bildmotive* (Berlin 1957) 36: Mars and Venus surprised by the gods. Pompeii VII ii 23 (House of the Punished Cupid) had a painting in *tablinum* f, now in Naples, in which Mars and Venus appear in the same pose, but without the additional figures; K. Schefold, *Pompejanische Malerei* (Berlin 1972) pl. 21.

47. Michel (supra n. 14) 537–98.

48. For an account of the revival of the imagery of Ganymede for wealthy, educated patrons in the Renaissance, see J. M. Saslow, *Ganymede in the Renaissance: Homosexuality in Art and Society* (New Haven 1986).

CHAPTER 5

Signs of Privilege and Pleasure: Roman Domestic Mosaics

Christine Kondoleon

The most abundant evidence available to the scholar of Roman art in the private sphere consists of hundreds of floor mosaics found throughout the Empire. Although mosaics were largely dependent on the pictorial conventions of painting and the stock repertory of a given workshop, there are exceptional compositions that illustrate a high degree of innovation. The originality—an unusual subject or arrangement—of such compositions may have been determined by the patron, and often they were inspired by the practices of everyday life. In other words, the decoration of Roman domestic interiors can reveal certain aspects of Roman social realities. The decoration of privileged spaces, that is, the luxuriously appointed town houses and villas throughout the Mediterranean, reflects, in some of their more uncommon compositions, public and private events sponsored by and directly connected to the interests and activities of the patrons.

Often the selection of figural themes and their placement—primarily in the *triclinia*, peristyles, and gardens—were determined by long-established decorative traditions; however, the introduction and institutionalization of these compositions was a projection of interests and tastes inextricably tied to the process of Romanization. For example, mosaic compositions of events staged at amphitheaters throughout the Empire were especially popular. The activities of the amphitheater were an integral part of Roman civic experience and a public means by which the elite expressed political power and privilege. The games and their accompanying spectacles and processions carried a definite social connotation of *romanitas* and of prosperity.

The fact that a rich variety of these spectacles is illustrated in many domestic mosaics suggests an association between public benefactions and private patronage. Similar relationships can be recognized in other spheres of Roman social life and customs—dining or private entertainments. These themes, their arrangements, and their placement within the Roman house underline the interaction between contemporary social institutions and artistic representation. It is possible to reconstruct, with the aid of literary sources, the cultural context of certain mosaics. The following discussion seeks to outline broadly the possibilities of this approach.

One model of the dialogue between reality and representation is an account by the early Roman author Varro. He describes a banquet held within a game preserve on an aristocrat's estate (Quintus Hortensius) during which the guests are presented with a dramatic performance of Orpheus charming the wild beasts with music.[1] The various animals described correspond to those typically found in the imperial hunts staged in the Roman amphitheater. The popularity of Orpheus as a subject for mosaic decorations of dining areas may, in fact, have been inspired by theatrical episodes performed for private banquets. Mosaics showing Orpheus soothing the exotic beasts, normally seen in the amphitheater, are typically found in reception halls of Roman villas. A wall painting of Orpheus from a Pompeian garden might have been a townsman's attempt to evoke the luxury of such a banquet and setting. This observation is supported by a series of megalographic paintings of wild beasts that cover the garden walls of several Pompeian houses. Sometimes these beasts roam freely in their natural habitats without the intervention of man, as they do on the garden wall of the House of Ceius Secundus.[4] Two fountains, which are painted on either side of the animal scenes, seem to empty into the actual gutter of the real garden. These paintings provide an imaginary extension of gardens, and the animals allude to the wild game parks found on grand estates. Such representations fulfill a bourgeois fantasy by associating the owner with the tastes and luxuries of the elite class.

The peristyle often functioned as an interior garden, and its decoration reflected activities, both imaginary and real, set in the garden.[5] The incorporation of fountains and pools within the peristyle underlines the conceptual and formal connections between the garden, peristyle, and atrium within the Roman house. The entertainment pavilion of a third-century house in Volubilis in Morocco illustrates this relationship.[6] In the *triclinium*, a mosaic composition displays Orpheus at the center of a forest of radially set trees and beasts that, if we recall Varro's account, seems appropriately placed as a floor decoration for banquets (fig. 5-1). Immediately adjacent is a colonnaded court with a pool preceded by a black-and-white fish mosaic. While the presence of a marine mosaic near a pool might seem obvious, the overall program is more subtle. This domestic unit in western North Africa, intended for receptions, recreates not only the game preserve with its famed entertainer, but also a real pool adjacent to a fictive fishpond or *piscina,* one of the more opulent appointments of Italian patrician villas. The economic fact that the addition of a fishpond could increase property value was not lost on the owners.[7] Although the use of such schemes was conditioned by tradition, their inspiration should be traced to actual features that connoted status and privilege.

If we now move to the Greek-speaking East, this point becomes clearer. The atrium-peristyle (area *A* in fig. 5-2)—a porticoed courtyard with an *impluvium* at the center[8]—in the House of Dionysos at Paphos on the southwestern coast of Cyprus is the interior counterpart to the colonnaded gardens at Pompeii.[9] The discovery of this luxurious urban residence of over forty rooms, including fifteen mosaic floors and a real fishpond, in an Eastern capital of little historical significance, provides tangible evidence of the assimilation of Roman culture by the upper levels of provincial society. Similar discoveries in the Greek East made in the last two decades indicate that private taste, like civic identity, was surprisingly romanized in the imperial period.[10]

The hunt scenes that cover three porticoes of the atrium-peristyle at Paphos make this point visually. The animals and hunters are arranged in a frieze against a plain background, with only schematic allusions to landscape and setting (fig. 5-3). This composition, as well as several other mosaics in the house, is unusual for the late-second-century date assigned to it on the basis of archaeological evidence.[11] The inspiration for these innovative compositions may be tied to the patron. An analysis of the hunters, beasts, and props revealed that they represent a particular type of hunt performed by professional *venatores* within the confines of the amphitheater, rather than hunts practiced out in nature for sport or for the procuring of wild beasts for the arena.[12]

An especially gruesome episode graphically locates these hunts in an arena setting. In a corner of the north portico (see area *A1* in fig. 5-2) we witness the bloody finale of a combat between a leopard and a wild ass (fig. 5-4). The headless ass with blood dripping from his neck stumbles behind a leopard, who carries the ass's head in his maw. The leopard walks toward an arched structure that corresponds to the gates that gave the beasts access to the arena from their cages. This and other visual evidence, such as details of costume and equipment, prove that the Paphian hunts reflect the realm of the amphitheater.

Moreover, the presence of trees and hills in these hunts, though at first evoking a natural outdoor setting, indicate rather a type of arena spectacle known as a *silva.* This category of spectacle, to which the Paphian hunts belong, was rarely described in written sources or in art.[13] Sufficient evidence exists, however, to confirm not only that the arena was artificially transformed into a natural hunt terrain, but that such scenic reconstructions were copied by artists. An account of the games given by the emperor Probus in 281 A.C. preserves the most elaborate description of the creation of a pseudonatural setting within the arena.[14] Probus ordered his soldiers to pull up real trees by their roots and plant them in the Circus Maximus so that it would look like a verdant forest. Herds of grass-eating animals were let loose in this shady wood and the spectators were invited to participate in the hunt. Once the crowds entered the arena, the *venatio* assumed a power that broke the barriers between reality and illusion, and the forest was no longer an artifice, but a palpable environment. Although the text for this event is generally deemed hyperbolic in regard to the number of animals and trees employed, it must have been based on an actual *silva*. The Paphian mosaics represent professional hunts and the landscape elements should be read as theatrical props.

The very fact that the Paphian hunts are rare recreations of the *silvae* invites further speculation about whether they represent a specific event. Several mosaics, especially those from North Africa, do record real moments from the games and were intended as honorific commemorations of the munificence of the benefactor.[15] Throughout the provinces gladiatorial shows, chariot races, staged hunts, and theatrical performances were given by local magistrates as part of their official obligation.[16] Those who were ambitious to bolster their community standing and power actively competed to sponsor the most splendid shows. One such event is recorded with explicit documentation in a mosaic found in a seaside villa at Zliten along the northern coast of Libya.[17] In a large room of unspecified function, four long mosaic panels frame a central area that is filled with mosaic and *opus sectile* (fig. 5-5). The panels contain a detailed account of the arena activities, including gladiatorial combats, wild-beast baiting, and musicians (fig. 5-6). Like the hunts at Paphos, these scenes unfold in a frieze of colorful figures placed against a solid ground. The two-dimensionality and paratactic composition are striking in contrast to the realistically depicted costumes and technical paraphernalia. Although the dating of the Zliten mosaic is controversial, the style of the composition is closer to late antique works than to any of the earlier Roman periods to which it has been assigned. The Zliten amphitheater scenes and the Paphian staged hunts—already noted as unusual for the archaeologically founded date of the late second century—must be seen as original creations within their respective provinces.[18] A logical explanation for these unprecedented types may be sought in the role of the patron who, in each case, might have commissioned a pictorial account of a specific event.

That the episodes depicted at Zliten closely correspond to those experienced firsthand in the amphitheater is underlined by a Pompeian relief (fig. 5-7).[19] The triple frieze from Pompeii illustrates the whole performance of the games, which typically occurred over a series of days: in the upper register, the procession, which was accompanied by musicians and presented the sponsor and all the fighters in resplendent attire; in the middle, scenes of gladiatorial combat; and below, incidents from the wild-beast hunts. Such sculptured friezes are directly connected to the benefactors of the games who put them up as memorial plaques in theaters or as tomb reliefs.

The visual analogies between the mosaics and reliefs suggest a similar intention for the mosaics. The narrative realism employed in these mosaics and reliefs could be applied to the explicit documentation of a specific event. The Zliten amphitheater mosaic was conceived with the energy of a fresh creation full of new information and is unparalleled in its account of full-scale games.

The dominant presence of the hunting panels within the Paphian house bespeaks their importance and the owner's intention to associate himself with the elite who donated the games to ensure their community standing and political power. The arena became a public extension of the private game parks, and the representation of spectacles, whether as historical record or imaginary projection, a sign of privilege linked directly to the Roman social order.

A late second- or early third-century mosaic from an unidentified building on the island of Kos in Greece emphasizes the correspondence between representation and real-life performance.[20] The border of the Kos mosaic includes an unusual display of acrobatics that, along with the Greek names for the hunters and beasts, suggests the actuality of the subject treated (fig. 5-8).[21] One of the three mythological panels in the center of the Kos mosaic depicts the Judgment of Paris (fig. 5-9); the other two are largely destroyed. The figures, identified by Greek inscriptions, include Paris, Hermes, Aphrodite, Hera, and Athena. This scene is immediately bordered by the nine Muses and Apollo set into separate panels, and the whole is framed by the frieze of acrobats, stunt riders, and hunters. The juxtaposition of these diverse elements has not been explained. A conventional interpretation might strain at metaphorical meaning when, in fact, the association of these elements in the amphitheater may well have been the sole inspiration for this unusual combination.

The Kos scenes find their literary counterparts in *The Golden Ass*, by Apuleius.[22] In his description of a three-day *munus*, or games, given in Roman Corinth, we are told that the gladiatorial combats and hunts were preceded by dance and dramatic mythological performances. One such episode was the reenactment of the Judgment of Paris. It took place on an artificial wooden mountain planted with trees, meant to represent Mount Ida, upon which sat an actor dressed as the Phrygian shepherd Paris watching over his flock of goats. Not only were all the dramatis personae present—that is, Mercury, Juno, Minerva, and Venus—but they were accompanied by attendant figures such as the Dioscuroi and Cupids. In the final scene, the Graces and Seasons danced onto the stage strewing flowers everywhere. In the Kos mosaic the Muses and

Apollo underline the theatrical nature of the scene and serve a function in the mosaic similar to the one played by the Seasons and Graces in the description of Apuleius, that is, of an attendant tableau. If amphitheater compositions such as the one at Smirat in North Africa are accepted as records of specific events, then why not, given the assurance of a literary parallel in this instance, assume the same for the entire mosaic at Kos?

This explanation for the Kos mosaic admits the possibility of many types of popular spectacles as sources for visual representation. To a large degree Roman audiences knew the figures of myth, tragedy, and legend through the medium of mime and other such theatrical stagings. Roman pantomimes were the most popular type of dramatic spectacle and were often performed during the amphitheater games.[23] This is shown by a first-century A.C. relief from Bulgaria in which actors dressed as monkeys dance and perform a kind of burlesque alongside the fierce beasts and hunters.[24] Martial, in his *Liber de Spectaculis*, recounts several pantomimic performances as part of his description of the Imperial Games in Rome. In a Roman version of "seeing is believing," Martial writes of one of these scenarios—"That Pasiphae was mated to the Dictaean bull believe: we have seen it, the old time myth has won its warrant."[25] What Romans were probably seeing was a condemned female criminal in the role of Pasiphae, forced to simulate intercourse or actually to couple with something in the form of a bull before her public execution. The grotesque realism of such events is shown on several lamps found in the Athenian Agora.[26] Apuleius provides further evidence that real animals were used for these bizarre executions in his description of the Ass's narrow escape from the amphitheater at Corinth where he was about to be mated with a murderess. Martial describes several mythological dramas involving animals, such as those of Orpheus or Prometheus, which served as dramatic vehicles for the execution of criminals. These graphic spectacles were a debased form of mime adapted to suit the gruesome ends of Roman discipline and punishment.

Martial undoubtedly reflects the attitudes of his contemporaries when he declares that "whatever fame sings of, that the arena makes real for thee."[27] Such contemporary accounts provide compelling testimony that these enacted episodes make the imaginary real; they condition the way the public "sees" these myths. The act of attending a performance involves "picture seeing" and can be related to the pictorial arts. Thus, through the study of spectacles, a sense of the "period eye" emerges—that is, the visual experience and habit of society.[28]

In the Roman world, pictorial traditions for mythological subjects were established, but it is also possible that the inspirations for the staging of popular dramas were famous paintings, and that these theatrical reinterpretations, in turn, inspired artists and patrons alike.[29] Certainly the great number of unexplained mosaic figural groups found within one composition or within one architectural complex might be better understood in this light. For example, the odd juxtaposition of Ganymede in a central medallion with eight other medallions filled with amphitheater beasts in an early third-century mosaic from Sousse in Tunisia (fig. 5-10) makes sense if seen as derived from a full figural composition and taking place in the arena: an actor, more likely a criminal, is posed as the handsome youth about to be attacked by some beast in the midst of a hunting display in the amphitheater.[30]

In the arena, myth, like the simulated hunts, became reality for a moment. It is not hard to conceive of an era when the perception of real events and imaginary ones overlapped in the realm of popular culture; the act of viewing all types of spectacles conditioned the public eye and the way artists and patrons directed the depictions of a wide range of subjects. The owners of grand villas, like the one recently published at Piazza Armerina, clearly wished to record themes connected with their public status and their private pleasures, as well as those exhibiting learning, literary pretensions, or allegory.[31]

The elaborate Dionysiac mosaic found in the *triclinium* of the House of Dionysos at Paphos, immediately adjacent to the peristyle (see area *B* in fig. 5-2), suggests an even broader application of the exchange between daily life and artistic representation. The Triumph of Dionysos (fig. 5-11) unfolds in a procession at the entrance to the dining room, flanked at both ends by the Dioscuroi (fig. 5-12); once the guests take their seats they are greeted with a katoptic view of a lush vineyard replete with erotes and male vintagers.[32] The great size of this room (11.5 by 8.5 m.) and the originality of the composition, along with the Dionysiac subjects found in several other rooms, must have been determined by more than decorative considerations. If we take the hunting panels, which by virtue of their location link the major sections of the house, as a pendant to the Dionysiac scenes, a specific program emerges. There are several periods in the year that involved Dionysiac festivities and amphitheater games. Half the month of September was given over to the *Ludi Romani*, during which time all manner of games and performances were conducted.[33] They included elaborate processions of people dressed as Dionysiac characters, Olympian deities, the Muses, Graces, Dioscuroi, and others. It is likely that vintage celebrations dedicated to Dionysos coincided with these autumnal festivities. The same patrons who donated the games undoubtedly funded such festivals and commissioned domestic mosaics.

The location of a mosaic with the busts of the Seasons and a central bust of the Genius of the Year at the entrance to the Paphian house and on axis with the west portico and *triclinium* entrance is an important pendant to the proposed program (fig. 5-13).[34] The popularity of the Seasons as a subject for domestic decoration might also be attributed to the phenomenon of public festivals and private patronage. In actual processions Dionysiac figures were often accompanied by persons representing the Seasons and the Genius of the Year. A famous model for such a pageant is the *Pompē* of Ptolemy Philadelphus as described by Kallixeinos and retold by Athenaeus in the *Deipnosphistae*, where various individuals who personified time—Penteteris, Eniautos, the Horai—marched alongside the Dionysiac cortege.[35] Although it took place in third-century B.C. Alexandria, the memory of this grandiose procession doubtless inspired centuries of abbreviated versions throughout the Mediterranean.[36] Once again, domestic mosaics clearly indicate the active role of such events in the formulation of imagery. At Hippo Regius in Algeria, a personification of time, Aion, is surrounded by female entertainers clad in bikinilike costumes: one holds a musical instrument; the other dances.[37] The inclusion of theatrical masks in addition to the dancing girls suggests that this mosaic was inspired by a contemporary performance, perhaps one associated with a festival.

Representations of popular culture should not surprise us; the benefaction of these events was a public display of privilege and, above all, a duty of citizenship and political power. The effective transference of this message into domestic decoration depended on the realistic portrayal of such events. Certainly, the compositions became codified in time, and artists relied on intermediary sources such as model books for their execution, but their selection and creation could well have been determined by the visual experience of Roman cultural institutions such as the spectacles.

NOTES

1. Varro *Rust.* 3.13. See also P. Grimal, *Les jardins romains* 3d ed. (Paris 1984) 293; and W. Jashemski, *The Gardens of Pompeii* (New York 1979) fig. 116. See also Bergmann's discussion of the same passage in chapter 2 of this volume. Bergmann points out that the *dominus* himself played the role of Orpheus in a performance that must have involved a lot of preparation (the wild animals were trained to follow his tune), directly linking the host/patron with public performances he may have sponsored and attempted to recall at his private al fresco dinner party.

2. See H. Stern, "La mosaïques d'Orpheé de Blanzy-les Fismes," *Gallia* 13 (1955) 41–77, for examples of Orpheus mosaics in reception halls. For the Roman West, see room 35 at Piazza Armerina, discussed in A. Carandini, A. Ricci, and M. de Vos, *Filosofiana: The Villa of Piazza Armerina* (Palermo 1982) 40 and 88–89, where Varro's description is also invoked for a similar interpretation. For the Roman East, see the reception hall of a third-century Roman house at Lesbos in S. Charitonides, L. Kahil, and R. Ginouves, *Les*

mosaïques de la Maison du Menandre à Mytilene (*AntK* suppl. 6, 1970) 18–25, pls. 1, 10 and color pl. I.

3. This T-shaped painting is found on the garden wall of the House of Vesonius Primus at Pompeii. See Jashemski (supra n. 1) 72–73, fig. 116. See Ellis's discussion of Orpheus in regard to the theme of the heroic host in chapter 6 of this volume.

4. Jashemski (supra n. 1) 69–70, figs. 111–12.

5. Grimal (supra n. 1) 260–73. For the most recent discussion on the peristyle, see Y. Thébert, "Private Life and Domestic Architecture in Roman Africa," chap. 3 in P. Veyne ed., *History of Private Life: I. From Pagan Rome to Byzantium* (Cambridge, Mass., and London 1987) 357–64.

6. R. Thouvenot, "Les Maison d'Orpheé à Volubilis," *Publications du Service des Antiquités du Maroc* 6 (1941) 42–46, fig 1; and K. Dunbabin, *The Mosaics of Roman North Africa* (Oxford 1978) 135 and n. 26.

7. J. H. D'Arms, *Commerce and Social Standing in Ancient Rome* (Cambridge, Mass., 1981) 82 n. 43. For a discussion of the social significance of seafood and marine motifs in reception halls of North Africa, see Thébert (supra n. 5) 365–67. It should also be noted that the black-and-white style of the marine mosaic had definite associations with Italic taste, since it was almost exclusively an Italian mosaic style that was occasionally exported.

8. See A. G. McKay, *Houses, Villas, and Palaces in the Roman World* (Ithaca 1975) 45–46, on the evolution of the peristyle form of the atrium.

9. K. Nicolaou, "The Mosaics at Kato Paphos, the House of Dionysos," *RDAC* 1963, 56–72; and id., "Excavations at Nea Paphos, the House of Dionysos: Outline of the Campaigns, 1964–1965," *RDAC* 1967, 100–125, are the two preliminary publications by the excavator. For a study of the mosaics, see C. Kondoleon, *Realities and Representations: The Mosaics of the House of Dionysos at Paphos* (Ithaca, forthcoming).

10. One of the more prominent of these discoveries is the black-and-white marine mosaic found in the Baths at Isthmia; see P. M. Packard, "A Monochrome Mosaic at Isthmia," *Hesperia* 49 (1980) 326–46.

11. The dating is largely based on the pottery analysis; see J. W. Hayes, "Early Roman Wares from the House of Dionysos, Paphos," *Rei Cretariae Romanae Fautorum Acta* 17/18 (1977) 96–102.

12. See Kondoleon (supra n. 9) chap. 6, p. 2.

13. For the most complete discussion of *silvae* in literature and art, see J. Aymard, *Essai sur les chasses romaines* (Paris 1951) 189–96.

14. Ibid., 190; and *S.H.A. Vita Probus* 19.2–4.

15. The most explicit illustration of this can be found in a mid-third-century mosaic from Smirat, Tunisia, showing the patron, Magerius, receiving the acclamations for his donation of the *venationes* that are enacted around him. For the most recent discussion of this example, see P. Veyne, "The Roman Empire," chap. 1 in P. Veyne ed., *A History of Private Life: I. From Pagan Rome to Byzantium* (Cambridge, Mass., and London 1987) 111–13 and 397–98. For the late antique development of *domini* who commemorate public benefactions in private interior decoration, see Ellis (chap. 6 in this volume).

16. For a discussion of the role of spectacles in political life, see K. Hopkins, *Death and Renewal* (Cambridge 1983) esp. 4–7; and Veyne (supra n. 15) 200–2.

17. S. Aurigemma, *I Mosaici de Zliten* (Rome 1926) 131–201, figs. 75–126, 152–54, and,

from room *D* on plan, fig. 11; and Dunbabin (supra n. 6) 278, pls. 1, 46–49, cat. Zliten 1,e.

18. For the extensive bibliography on the dating of the Zliten villa mosaics, see D. Parrish, "The Date of the Mosaics from Zliten," *Antiquités africaines* 21 (1985) 137 n. 1. Parrish argues convincingly for a Severan date for these mosaics.

19. The relief was found outside the Stabian Gate and was probably from a large tomb; it is now in the Museo Nazionale in Naples. See Th. Kraus and L. von Matt, *Pompeii and Herculaneum: The Living Cities of the Dead* (New York 1973) 52, fig. 53.

20. L. Morricone, "Scavi e ricerche a Coo (1935–1943), relazione preliminare: Cronaca d'Arte II," *BdA* 35 (1950) 227, figs. 37–40; and P. Asimakopoulou-Atzaka, "Katalogos Romaikon Psiphidoto Dapedon me Anthropines Morphes ston Helleniko Choro," *Hellenica* 26 (1973) 231–32, no. 23. The late second-century date is assigned by the excavator, Morricone, on the basis of technique and the fact that these mosaics were lifted in the third century, probably for the construction of the Western Baths.

21. See L. Robert, *Les gladiateurs dans l'orient grec* (Paris 1940) 37 n. 1, who judges the Kos mosaic an actual record because of the Greek legends; see also a relief from Apri (Thrace) with similar acrobatic stunts, ibid. 90–92, pl. 24, no. 27.

22. Apul. *Met.* 5.29–32.

23. On the popularity of mimes and other theatrical spectacles associated with the amphitheater, see L. Friedländer, *Darstellungen aus der Sittengeschichte Roms* (Leipzig 1920) 125–47; and M. Bonaria, *Romani mimi* (Rome 1965) passim.

24. See D. Levi, *Antioch Mosaic Pavements* 1 (Princeton 1947) 275–77, esp. 276 n. 75, fig. 108.

25. Mart. *Spect.* 5. Translation taken from W. C. A. Ker, *Martial: Epigrams* 1 (*The Loeb Classical Library*, London and New York 1925) 6–7.

26. A. Hönle and A. Henze, *Römische Amphitheater und Stadien* (Freiburg 1981) 58, fig. 31.

27. Mart. *Spect.* 5: *Quidquid fama canit, praestat harena tibi. . . .* See supra n. 25.

28. The concept of the period eye was introduced by M. Baxandall, *Painting and Experience in Fifteenth Century Italy* (Oxford 1972) esp. 40.

29. For example, when Gordian I was aedile in Rome he sponsored *silvae,* among the twelve exhibitions given for each month, that were directly inspired by a painting in his ancestral residence; see *S.H.A. Vita Gordiana* 3.5–8.

30. From the *triclinium* of the Maison de l'Arsenal, see L. Foucher, *Inventaire des mosaïques, feuille no. 57 de l'atlas archéologique: Sousse* (Tunis 1960) 42–44, pl. 20,a, inv. no. 57.092; and Dunbabin (supra n. 6) 269, cat. Sousse 12,a.

31. See Carandini et al. (supra n. 2) esp. 69–86; and for criticism of their approach, see R. J. A. Wilson, "Luxury Retreat, Fourth-Century Style: A Millionaire Aristocrat in Late Roman Sicily," *Opus: rivista internazionale per la storia economica e sociale dell'antichità* 2 (Rome 1983) 535–52, esp. 544–48.

32. See K. Nicoloau, *Ancient Monuments of Cyprus* (Nicosia 1968) 29, pl. 39; and more recently published in *LIMC* vol. 3 pt. 1, p. 527, nos. 129–30, and 3.2, pl. 418; and by J. Balty, "La mosaïque antique au Proche-Orient," *ANRW* II 12.2, 419–20, pl. 42; in these publications the mosaics are misdated to the late third century. For a discussion of the date, iconography, and style of the *triclinium* mosaics, see Kondoleon (supra n. 9) chaps. 3 and 4.

33. See H. H. Scullard, *Festivals and Ceremonies of the Roman Republic* (Ithaca, 1981) 91–92, for a description of this festival.

34. For a discussion of the Seasons mosaic, see Kondoleon (supra n. 9) chap. 5. The mosaic is located in room C on the plan, fig. 5–2, which most likely functioned as a vestibule because it includes a salutatory inscription.

35. For a thorough analysis and recent translation, see E. E. Rice, *The Grand Procession of Ptolemy Philadelphus* (Oxford 1983) esp. 48–51. For an application of this important text to mosaic representations, see D. Parrish, "Annus-Aion in Roman Mosaics," in Y. Duval ed., *Mosaïque romaine tardive* (Paris 1982) 11–25.

36. For support of this opinion, see Parrish (supra n. 35) 16.

37. For the most recent publication of this mosaic, see D. Parrish, *The Season Mosaics of Roman North Africa* (Rome 1984) 48, no. 46, pls. 61b–62. The mosaic is from room 6 in the combined houses, Maison de la Chasse and the Maison de la Pêche, dated to the first quarter of the fourth century. The function of the room is unknown.

CHAPTER 6

Power, Architecture, and Decor: How the Late Roman Aristocrat Appeared to His Guests

Simon P. Ellis

The earlier essays in this volume have made it clear how the houses of Roman aristocrats were designed to display the power of their owners to visitors, clients, and friends. Dwyer has explained how, in first-century A.C. Pompeii, the character of the spaces and the decor in a house were expected to reflect the dignity and rank of the owner.[1] Early Roman authors often complained about the discrepancy between the social origin of a *parvenu* and his luxurious mode of living. The authors of such complaints, writing at an early date, would have been at a loss for words at seeing the extravagantly rich houses of late Roman times.

Between the first and fourth centuries A.C. many profound social changes had taken place, among them the rise of provincial aristocrats. In the first century Roman society was still led from Italy; by the second the majority of rich Romans, whether Italians or provincial in origin, had large houses abroad.[2] In the archaeological record, the enormous number of provincial Roman houses overwhelms the number known from Italy. The literary sources also reflect this change. After a general lack of records from the third century, we are faced with an increasing quantity of criticism, particularly from Christians writing in the fourth. As pagan authors of the earlier period condemned extravagance as unseemly, so Christian authors looked at too much luxury as immoral. A word of caution should be inserted here, however. Bishops tended to exaggerate such vices beyond the real situation in order to hammer home the morals of their sermons,[3] and thus many of their texts must be read with a degree of skepticism.

The provinces will be the focus of our discussion, but we shall begin in

Italy, where aristocratic families continued to thrive. Ammianus Marcellinus gives a vivid description of aristocrats and their dwellings at Rome in the fourth century A.C.

> Their houses are the resort of idle gossips, who greet every word uttered by the great man with various expressions of hypocritical applause, like the parasite in the comedy who inflates the pride of the boastful soldier by attributing to him heroic exploits in sieges and in battles against overwhelming odds. In the same way our parasites admire the beauty of columns in a high facade or the brilliant sight presented by walls of colored marble, and extol their noble owners as more than mortal.[4]

Ammianus was a pagan bureaucrat or soldier and is generally regarded as a trustworthy historian. Because he was incensed by the foppery of the urban Roman aristocracy, however, some exaggeration must be allowed for. The passage from which the extract is drawn nonetheless shows not only that the *salutatio*, or morning greeting of an aristocrat by clients and friends, went on much as it had in the late Republic, but also that the power of the owner, as expressed in architecture, was still appreciated by his guests. In the late Roman Empire, moreover, the guests or clients ascribed to the owner certain heroic qualities on the basis of his architectural achievements. The ideology of the period is made clear by Ammianus's characterization of the owner as hero and the client as parasite. We can elucidate this ideology by examining certain innovations in domestic architecture and some of the visual imagery that complemented them.

The spread of Roman culture to provinces around the Mediterranean included the use of Roman forms of housing, particularly in the western provinces. The interpretation of this wide range of Roman provincial housing has posed many problems, not least as regards the function of rooms. Provincial housing did not adopt the Italian, or Pompeian, tradition of a reception suite composed of atrium and *tablinum*.[5] This major difference between Italy and the provinces is enough to make one raise the question of the relevance of Italian Roman authors (particularly Vitruvius) when we are considering provincial housing. Literary references to provincial housing are usually too oblique to allow direct identification with the archaeological evidence. Certainly, there are occasions when we can try to identify room functions on the basis of literary descriptions, but in very few instances can the function of a room be proven with any certainty. To try to avoid the problems of literary evidence many scholars have attempted to identify room function directly from provincial houses themselves.

The richest Roman provincial houses had a peristyle court in the center of the house. The court was entered by a passage from the street (or the yard in the case of a villa). Opposite the entrance, on the far side of the peristyle, was the largest, most richly decorated room in the house. The rich decor and large size lead us to assume that the room was where the owner received guests whom he would want to impress. Conventionally scholars have called this room the *triclinium* or *oecus*, following the literary texts. The *triclinium* was named after the three rectangular couches used for dining, which were located around the sides of the room. Indeed, the mosaic floors of some of the large rooms in the provincial houses have plain white panels on which the dining couches would have been set. From this it is clear that the large, rich room opposite the house entrance was often used as a dining room.

The most important architectural development of late Roman times was the widespread use of the apsidal dining room, associated with the semicircular couch or *stibadium*.[6] The couch was known in the first century A.C., when an apsidal *triclinium* (the *cenatio Jovis*) was constructed in the *Domus Augustana* of Domitian. To J. B. Ward-Perkins, the apsidal state banquet hall, audience hall (*aula regia*), and basilica in the Palace of Domitian represent the "apse mak[ing] its first formal appearance in Roman architecture as the setting for the semi-divine majesty of the Roman emperor."[7] In private houses, however, the *stibadium* only became popular in the late third century A.C., when the dining room was provided with an apse and one semicircular couch replaced the traditional three rectangular couches. Each rectangular couch held from one to three people, whereas one semicircular couch could hold up to seven. Nevertheless, many aristocrats chose to retain the traditional number of dining couches. The substitution of three semicircular couches for three rectangular couches gave the room the shape of a triconch. Triconch *triclinia* are very common in several provinces from the fourth century A.C. onward.[8]

Dinners had always been central to Roman life. Entertaining guests was not simply a matter of meeting friends, but was important in creating political alliances and in demonstrating status. Guests would often be the "clients" of their host who were bound to return his hospitality with political support.[9] Attempts have been made in consequence to see the development of the triconch *triclinium* as a product of a society in which the aristocrat was wielding more patronal power and was copying the architecture of the imperial palace or the church.[10] Apsidal dining halls in aristocratic private houses and imperial palaces have a related form and function, but the former need not derive directly from the latter. By the fourth century A.C., the apse, as an architectural form

designed to frame and exalt the figure or object enclosed, had become commonplace in a wide variety of public and private building types. The specific origin
of the trefoil-shaped *triclinium* most probably lies in the sphere of domestic
architecture.[11] Once the idea of dining on *stibadia* in an apsidal dining hall
gained popularity among aristocrats, the triconch design, in my view, probably
evolved naturally out of the traditional usage of three couches per *triclinium*. A
change in the nature of patronal power, which we will examine later, may also
have contributed to the popularity of apsidal dining halls.

We can identify two other types of reception rooms in late Roman provincial houses.[12] They are found only in a small number of houses, which are all
the largest and richest in each town or district. Because of their extraordinary
size these houses have often been called palaces, but there is no direct evidence
to suggest who owned any of them. All one can say for certain is that the
owners were high-ranking provincial aristocrats.

One type of room seems to be a private audience chamber. It can be
identified in three houses—the "palace" above the theater at Ephesus, the "palace" of the governor or bishop at Aphrodisias, and the "Palace of the Dux" at
Apollonia (fig. 6-1).[13] The room is typically a large chamber fitted with a single
apse. It is preceded by a vestibule and located near the main entrance to the
house. In the house at Apollonia the vestibule lies right next to the street; in the
house at Ephesus it is entered by a long passage from the street. The chamber
in each of the houses can also be entered close to the apse. None of the chambers has a mosaic floor. The room in the Apollonian house has four small
rectangular niches, or "cupboards," cut into its south wall. The location of the
room next to the street suggests that it was a public room, placed close to the
street to stop visitors from penetrating far into the house and disturbing its
privacy. In other words, this type of room was used to meet with people who
were not intimates of the family. Dining rooms are not entered close to the apse,
and so some kind of audience chamber seems to be the most likely function.
Single-apsed rooms were used as audience chambers in contemporary palatial
architecture. The best example is the Constantinian Basilica at Trier.[14]

The second type of reception room, which I shall term the grand dining
hall, will be the focus of the rest of this paper. This room is found next to the
triclinium of the house. It can clearly be identified in three houses (fig. 6-2)—a
villa at Mediana near Niš, the "Palace of Theodoric" at Ravenna, and the House
of Bacchus at Djemila.[15] At Ravenna the room is a triconch adjoining the large
single-apsed *triclinium*, and both rooms open onto the same side of the peristyle.
The triconch grand dining hall is separated from the peristyle portico by a
vestibule. At Mediana a hexagonal central area has two rectangular niches and
one semicircular niche opening from it. The other two sides of the hexagon may

also have held niches, but modern wall foundations hinder investigation here. A fountain in the center of the room seems to be a characteristic of local domestic architecture.[16] The Mediana room also opens onto the same peristyle portico as an adjacent large, single-apsed *triclinium*. A vestibule and an antechamber separate the grand dining hall from the peristyle. The grand dining hall at Djemila is by far the most magnificent of the group. It has seven apses, each of which would have held a *stibadium* dining couch. Each apse is framed by columns, and the hall is preceded by a vestibule with two columns on each short side. The room is adjacent to the *triclinium* of the house, but does not share its peristyle. Although one could enter the peristyle courtyard through a side door in the vestibule of the grand dining hall, the main entrance to the seven-apsed hall is a separate passage from the street.

The function of these rooms as dining halls has been well established by comparison with true palatial architecture in Rome and Constantinople.[17] These latter rooms are described as dining rooms by early medieval texts. In Constantinople a fifth- to sixth-century A.C. parallel is provided by the Palace of Lausus, which has been excavated near the hippodrome. It consists of a hall with seven apses, seventy meters in length, that is entered from a circular vestibule. In front of the vestibule is a semicircular portico that faces the street.

Precise dating of these late antique houses provided with audience chambers or grand dining halls has proven difficult. The Mediana house appears to be the earliest in the group and is said to be of the late third century A.C., after the style of its mosaics. Both the "Palace of Theodoric" at Ravenna and the House of Bacchus at Djemila underwent a long development throughout much of the Roman period. The dining hall at Ravenna has been dated to the early sixth century A.C., but many doubts about the chronology remain.[18] On the basis of a new analysis of the stratigraphy, mosaics, and historical context of the House of Bacchus at Djemila, M. Blanchard-Lemée has recently concluded that the seven-apsed grand dining hall was constructed during the mid–fifth century A.C. as a final architectural embellishment to the largest private residence in the city.[19]

The great Sicilian villa at Piazza Armerina (fig. 6-3) can be added to the series of late antique mansions equipped with a multiplicity of impressive reception and entertainment suites. Although Piazza Armerina was long thought to have been a palace with imperial associations, it is now known that there are several similar private villas in Sicily.[20] Despite the controversy over the ownership of Piazza Armerina, the authorities now seem to agree that its date falls in the early fourth century A.C. Formal comparison with contemporary houses elsewhere in the Empire allows a more precise identification of several of the villa's most imposing rooms. The single-apsed hall (room *T* in fig. 6-3) that dominates the transverse corridor paved with the Great Hunt mosaic (room C in fig. 6-3) is often called an audience chamber on the order of those cited here in the "palaces" of Ephesus, Aphrodisias, and Apollonia.[21] The apsidal hall at Piazza Armerina, however, does not share the characteristic street-side position of audience chambers in the "palaces" of Asia Minor. Rather, it is axially aligned with the central peristyle of the villa, in a location where we would expect to find the *triclinium*.[22] For that reason, I would identify the apsidal hall in the central reception suite at Piazza Armerina as a *triclinium* and the triconch, with its own independent peristyle (room G in fig. 6-3), as a grand dining hall. The separate peristyle for the triconch ensures privacy for the main house in the same way as the separate entrance to the grand dining hall in the House of Bacchus at Djemila. The grander style of architecture at Piazza Armerina has allowed this separate entrance to be expanded into a separate peristyle.

We can thus trace a progressive line of development in the reception and dining rooms of aristocratic houses in the Roman provinces. Most provincial houses of the early and middle imperial period had only one reception/dining room, the *triclinium*, located on the peristyle opposite the entrance to the house. From the third century A.C. onward, however, three types of more specialized reception rooms began to appear, in various combinations, in the houses and villas of the provincial elite: the *triclinium*, the audience chamber, and the grand dining hall. The *triclinium* and audience chamber were probably used to receive and entertain clients or less important guests, while the grand dining hall was most likely reserved for the most important and influential friends. The grand dining hall at Djemila could seat up to thirty-five people, which would have been quite an impressive gathering of aristocrats.

The role of the *triclinium* in domestic architecture of the Roman provinces therefore changed considerably over time. In earlier times all receptions probably took place in the *triclinium*, the only large room in the provincial house. Thus the *triclinium* first had a widening role, from dining room to general reception room, before the introduction of other reception rooms reduced its role again in late antiquity. It is likely, in view of the large size of the single-apsed *triclinia* at Mediana, Ravenna, and Piazza Armerina, that in late antiquity the room still maintained a function that included more than simple dinners, but the nature of this wider role remains unknown.

The immediate reasons for the introduction of the audience chamber and the grand dining hall were a desire for privacy and a need to differentiate among the different social classes of guests. The poor client was to be overawed in the audience chamber, the *amicus* may have been invited to the *triclinium*, and the dignitary was to be conducted to the grand dining hall.[23] For Vitruvius the peristyle was a public space, but for the late Roman aristocrat it became increasingly private, and his reception facilities were designed to control access by visitors.[24] To promote privacy, late antique audience chambers and grand dining halls could be provided with separate entrances from the street (as in the "palaces" of Ephesus, Aphrodisias, and Apollonia and in the House of Bacchus at Djemila) and independent peristyles (as at Piazza Armerina). In early Roman houses the public areas of the house were not clearly separated from the private areas. The late Roman aristocrat carefully defined the architectural context in which his public encounters took place. He separated public and private and used the architecture to manipulate social encounters in a way that had never been done in earlier periods.

In early Roman houses the public areas of the house were not clearly separated from the private areas. Wallace-Hadrill points out that early Roman houses had various grades of privacy.[25] The most intimate receptions took place in the bedroom (*in cubiculo*). The rooms of the Pompeian house were distributed around one major peristyle to which most guests had access. In the house of the late Roman aristocrat guests of different ranks were routed through the house on different paths. Many of them never saw the peristyle, let alone the main *triclinium*. There was thus a strong hierarchy of access. The depth to which a guest penetrated the building and the route he took emphasized his degree of intimacy with the owner. The use of different routes and an organized hierarchy of access has been held by architectural analysts to represent a strong control of social relations.[26]

I have argued elsewhere that these architectural developments were a reflection of an increasing concentration of wealth and the more autocratic nature of late Roman systems of patronage.[27] Riches became restricted to an elite group with contacts in the imperial administration. During the later fourth and fifth centuries A.C., this elite became the main power in cities with declining local government. The inefficiency of local government led the poor to seek help from high-ranking patrons, and patronal power was largely effected through assemblies of clients in rich houses. It is not possible to repeat here the part played by the architectural decline of cities and the growing abandonment of many middle-class Roman houses, both of which movements began in the fourth century A.C. However, the topic can be approached from another direction by asking how the aristocrat managed to impose his power on his clients in his own house. I have suggested that he may have consciously manipulated the architecture to express his power, and I now want to propose that he also manipulated the decor of the grand dining hall to the same end.

The vast majority of Roman provincial houses are only preserved at foundation level. Only in rare cases do we know anything about the upper parts of their walls, and we have nothing in the way of wall paintings that compares with the range of murals from Pompeii.[28] In some instances marble dining tables have been found.[29] Sometimes the *stibadium* couch had a masonry foundation,[30] and sometimes its position is marked by a semicircular panel in the mosaic of the floor.[31] Since the upper part of the room is usually missing, the mosaic floor tends to be the only preserved indication of the decor of a room.

In the center of the seven-apsed grand dining hall of the House of Bacchus at Djemila is a mid-fifth-century A.C. mosaic panel depicting a hunt (fig. 6-4). At the top of the mosaic a villa owner rides triumphantly in front of his property. His cloak, his position at the top of the scene, and the fact that he is the only horseman identify him as the person in charge. Below him three other men confront various animals. We may presume that the owner of the villa depicted in the mosaic is also the owner of the House of Bacchus.[32] His depiction at the top of the mosaic would then mimic his position in real life, where he dined in the apse at the head of the grand dining hall. This interpretation of the hunt mosaic accords well with Blanchard-Lemée's theory that the construction of the seven-apsed dining hall during the middle of the fifth century was connected with an influx to Djemila of aristocrats dispossessed from Africa Proconsularis by the Vandal invasion. Blanchard-Lemée speculates that the new owner of the House of Bacchus, "deeming the large *oecus* insufficient for the receptions he expected to offer, added to his house a reception room of dimensions unparalleled in an urban residence."[33]

The hunt was one of the most common subjects in late antique domestic mosaics. The hunts shown have different degrees of formality or organization. The scene may be a "mock-hunt" within an amphitheater where the beasts shown are old favorites identified by names written below them, or where hunters resemble gladiators.[34] On other occasions the purpose of the hunt seems to have been to collect beasts from the wild for the amphitheater. These hunts were professional and highly organized, with emphasis placed on the size of the hunting party and the number of animals captured. Other scenes are more informal—a few friends out for amusement and a sporting chase.

At first glance, the House of Bacchus hunt could be taken as one of the informal occasions, but two emblems suggest that it is not. In the lower half of the mosaic a hunter kneels to oppose a large pouncing feline. On his right there is a palm leaf and on his left three ivy leaves. The palm leaf is a symbol of victory, and the three leaves may be a badge for one of the societies that collected animals for the amphitheater.[35] If so, the mosaic may commemorate a particular event in the arena, perhaps one sponsored by the owner of the villa. Thus, in a room designed for large dinner parties, whose location and separate entrance from the street mark it out as one of the main "public" rooms of the house, the *dominus* chose to represent himself, his country estate, and his munificence in providing games. Other hunt mosaics were probably intended to record and promote the achievements of the house owner, but I know of no other that represents the owner so prominently in such an important public room. For example, the famous Great Hunt mosaic at Piazza Armerina (fig. 6-5), which shows the owner or bailiff organizing a hunt for beasts to be sent to the games, is not placed inside the *triclinium* of the villa, but in the transverse corridor (room C in fig. 6-3) at its entrance.[36]

Other *domini* apparently chose to present their achievements in a less overt fashion, using myth and allusion. Although the mosaic floor in the grand dining hall of the "Palace of Theodoric" at Ravenna is very badly preserved (fig. 6-6), enough is left to reconstruct the main elements.[37] The square central area of the floor was divided into nine smaller panels. In the corner panels were busts of the Four Seasons, only one of which is well preserved. In the central panel was a depiction of Bellerophon and the Chimera. The Chimera is relatively complete, but it is only possible to see the rear quarters and one wing of Pegasus, while very little is left of Bellerophon himself. To the right and left of Bellerophon are panels in which two cupids carry inscriptions. The left hand panel is fragmentary, but the right hand panel is clear. The inscription reads:

Sum e quod autumnus, quod ver, quod bruma, quod estas alternis reparant.

[I am (he) through whom autumn, spring, winter, and summer are in turn restored.][38]

The motif of Bellerophon has been much discussed. A few examples suffice to show the range of opinion. Dunbabin is the most conservative.[39] She sees Bellerophon only as "a common type of the hunter [and] associated with the general theme of wealth and fertility." In contrast, Hanfmann sees the scene as Christ slaying the dragon of Revelations and talks of the astrological associations of the cycle of nature, or the seasons,[40] while Brilliant points out the moral lessons administered to Bellerophon and other heroes—pride comes before a fall.[41]

We have seen when considering the House of Bacchus mosaic that the hunt can reflect the munificence or the achievements of the owner, and the hunter can be the owner himself. In the same way, Bellerophon could represent the owner of the "Palace of Theodoric," as was first seen by Brandenburg.[42] Bellerophon has the same pose as the Djemila hunter—right arm thrown back, cloak flying behind him. His horse rears, and his spear, just released, has felled the beast. The association of munificence and the owner of the house is strengthened by the inscriptions on the mosaic at Ravenna. On the other hand, if the owner simply wished to demonstrate his liberality he could have used a typical hunt scene rather than the unusual motif of Bellerophon. There must be a further meaning behind the mosaic. Probably the most complete interpretation is that of Huskinson, who accepts the overall emphasis of the composition as relating to hunting and the seasons, and then explains the specific choice of the Bellerophon motif as a representation of the conflict of good and evil.[43] If we identify Bellerophon with the house-owner in the framework advocated by Huskinson, then the owner may be seen to be comparing himself with some benign god controlling the seasons and conquering evil. This interpretation might seem farfetched were it not for Ammianus's description of the flattering comparisons made to senators in Rome. At Ravenna we may have the benevolent aristocrat distributing the fruits of the season to his clients in a banquet, and the good patron fighting against the evils of officialdom and oppressive debt collectors on their behalf.

There seems to have been a revival of interest in the heroes of mythology in late antiquity.[44] One hero with a direct association to hunting was Meleager. A late antique mosaic from a villa at Halicarnassus, now in the British Museum,[45] depicts the Hunt of the Caledonian Boar in a realistic manner. If the heroic connotations had not been brought out by labeling the participants, no one would have been able to distinguish them from local sportsmen. A mosaic from Kos, described by Kondoleon, uses a mythological scene to record a particular real-life performance,[46] but the Halicarnassus mosaic reduces a mythological event to the level of an ordinary, everyday occurrence. Like the sycophants whom Ammianus scorns, and as in the Bellerophon motif of the Ravenna mosaic, the Halicarnassus mosaicist may be imputing heroic attributes to the owner of the villa and his aristocratic friends.

Thébert discusses a mosaic from a house in Uthina in which a nude hunter, most likely the *dominus*, is implicitly compared to Meleager. Thébert sees the mosaic not only as reflecting the courage of the owner in the hunt, but also as creating an analogy between the *dominus* and the Roman emperor, whose *virtus* ensured the prosperity of the realm.[47] Thébert might also have pointed to houses, such as those discussed in this paper, whose flamboyant architecture contributes to the heroic imagery of domestic art.

The large triconch (room G in fig. 6-3) of the grand dining hall at Piazza Armerina also has a well-preserved heroic mosaic (fig. 6-7). Not content with a mere hunting scene, or even the deeper allusions of Bellerophon, the owner of Piazza Armerina chose the Labors of Hercules! Although Piazza Armerina is no longer considered an imperial residence, H. P. L'Orange's interpretation of its mosaic decoration, whether that of Hercules or that of the owner organizing the Great Hunt, as an expression of semidivine power is still valid.[48] The owner may not have been an emperor, but in his villa he behaved as one. The mosaics and the architecture express the *auctoritas* of someone who felt he was born to rule.[49] Hercules had the preordained strength that allowed him to subdue many powerful beasts of the natural world. The owner or bailiff in the Great Hunt mosaic directs the hunting activity around him and also dominates the beasts of nature (see fig. 6-5).

On a purely aesthetic level, the mosaics of the triconch lend the grand dining hall an aura of baroque majesty. R. A. Wilson has characterized the style of the triconch mosaics as "strikingly different from the compositions elsewhere at Piazza Armerina: not only do huge masses of flesh and drapery heave and twist in great contortions with a bold use of foreshortening, but the scale of the figures is much vaster than elsewhere in the villa."[50] Can it be accidental that these pavements, the products of mosaicists "at the very top of their craft,"[51] were laid in the suite where the *dominus* hosted his most important banquets? The architecture of the triconch complex, moreover, is designed to focus attention on the interior of the room. As Wilson points out, the view from the triconch, "instead of commanding a pleasant tract of peaceful wooded valley, is blocked off by a high niche-relieved wall at the far end of the oval court."[52] The masterpieces of mosaic that pave the grand dining hall at Piazza Armerina introduce an element of sophisticated connoisseurship to the self-image that the *dominus* wished to present to his distinguished guests.

I have focused on a small group of particularly rich houses in which it is possible to relate the type of mosaic decor very closely to the function of a special type of room. The architectural development of multi-apsed grand dining halls, which themselves display an unusual degree of ostentation, can be associated with a decor that stressed the boastful power of the owner. The themes used for the decor of reception rooms might also be seen as a reflection of the ideals of the owner. A strong possibility for such an interpretation would be the series of fourth-century A.C. Orpheus mosaics from Roman Britain and elsewhere.[53] The British mosaics all come from the *triclinia* of villas, and there is a clear hunting association and a heroic content in each case.

In late antique houses, statues of gods and mythological heroes could also contribute to the glorification of the owner. Since Hercules has figured among identifications proposed for an over-life-size statue discovered in the apsidal *triclinium* (room *T* in fig. 6-3) at Piazza Armerina, it is tempting to think that the *dominus* wished to appear in the heroic company of Hercules in both major reception rooms of the villa. Moreover, statue bases found in the triconch, along with niches in the enclosure wall of the adjoining oval peristyle, suggest that sculpture was an important component of the decor of the grand dining hall at Piazza Armerina.[54]

Several sculpture collections are known from houses of the fourth to fifth centuries A.C. Unfortunately, in all but a few instances we do not know where the statues originally stood, since they had been hidden or disturbed before burial. Statues of Meleager have been found in collections from houses in Antioch in Syria, southern France,[55] and Ptolemais in Cyrenaica.[56] Four statues of Apollo have been found from three houses in these same areas of the Empire. Three statues of Diana come from three houses, including the *triclinium* of a house in Ostia, with others from the south of France and Ptolemais in Cyrenaica. The most popular divinity was Venus—seven examples from four houses (Antioch, Ostia, Ptolemais, and southern France).[57] A statue of Jupiter and Ganymede from a late fourth- or early fifth-century context most probably stood in or near a *triclinium* in the House of the Greek Charioteers in Carthage.[58]

One might expect to find in these sculpture collections a selection of historical heroes such as earlier emperors, but imperial personages are surprisingly rare. A bust of Antoninus Pius from the House of the Sculptures in Athens[59] is a suitable example of a good emperor, but the Antioch collection contained portraits of Pertinax, Gordian III, and Constantius Chlorus, none of whom had any obvious claim to heroic stature.[60]

Two pieces of evidence from the middle Byzantine period are important in that they tie in very closely to the late antique tradition of decorating dining halls as I have described it. The most important comes from the twelfth-century author Cedrenus,[61] who compiled a long history of Byzantium, drawing on earlier sources. He records that Lausus, the chamberlain of Theodosius II (who reigned 408–50 A.C.), had a large collection of sculptures. They seem to have been divided into two groups, one of gods and the other of animals. In the first category were Minerva, Juno, Venus, Eros, Jupiter, and perhaps Pan. In the second group were a centaur, rhinoceros, elephant, vulture (eagle?), tiger, and giraffe. The two groups were mediated by a statue of Kairos ("The Crucial Moment"), balancing the divine and the natural. In Christian conceptions, Kairos balances the pagan gods, an invention of man, and the animals who were created by God.[62]

The palace where Lausus is said to have kept the collection has been identified with the already mentioned seven-apsed hall uncovered in excavations close to the hippodrome in Constantinople.[63] This is the building I have cited as the closest parallel to the grand dining hall in the House of Bacchus in Djemila. The excavators confirmed a late fourth- to fifth-century A.C. foundation for the building, but they believed that the six apses along the sides of the hall were added in the sixth century. The precise stratigraphic and chronological reasons for this are hard to determine, and it is also difficult to tell whether this would preclude the possibility of earlier apses that were destroyed by the later ones. It is tempting nonetheless to restore the sculpture collection to the dining hall as another example of the hunting theme on a cosmic level, like Hercules in Piazza Armerina. Lausus could then be alluding to himself as Kairos. As the Djemila owner governs the hunt in his mosaic and the Ravenna owner claims to govern the seasons in his inscription, so Lausus as Kairos governs the opposition of the gods and nature. Indeed, as Kairos governs them, so Lausus balanced the rivalries of Theodosius's court. All the owners of these grand dining halls may be wryly alluding to the way they attempted to control political rivalries at the formal dinners held in these rooms.

The second Byzantine text is the famous legend of Digenis Akritas that probably dates from around the eighth or ninth century A.C. His dining hall was said to be decorated with scenes of the Trojan War, Alexander the Great, Bellerophon and the Chimera, David and Goliath, and Samson (Hercules?) and the lion.[64] These exploits were to be compared with those of the owner of the hall, Digenis himself. The scenes of the Trojan War and Alexander were probably individual combats as well—Hector and Achilles, Alexander and Darius. The text shows that the decoration of dining halls with heroic scenes that alluded to the owner continued into Byzantine times.

I have traced this iconography of power in dining halls from the fourth to the eighth century A.C. Now it is important to ask how it became acceptable to use such scenes in the houses of Roman provincial aristocrats. I have alluded to the growing importance of patronage as a reason for the architectural developments, and a growing number of clients obviously requires a bigger reception room, but these alone are not enough to explain the expression of power. The blatant expression of power is more likely to be rooted in the increasingly autocratic nature of society in late antiquity. This trend is said to have begun with the introduction of eastern monarchic ceremonies by third-century emperors and to have gained momentum with Diocletian's attempt to elevate the emperor to a transcendent plane. To illustrate the attitude in the fourth century there is Ammianus's well-known description of the *adventus*, or ceremonial arrival, of Constantius II at Rome.

> . . . he kept the gaze of his eyes straight ahead and turned his face neither to right nor to left but (as if he were a statue) neither did he nod when the wheel jolted nor was he ever seen to spit, or to wipe or rub his face, or move his hands about.[65]

If the Christian emperor on ceremonial occasions could be seen as the statue of a god, then an aristocrat who hosted lavish formal banquets could easily be compared with a mythological hero. As the general social changes of late antiquity influenced the public image of Rome emperors, so they determined how an aristocrat wished to appear before the clients and honored guests entertained in his home. In an apsidal grand dining hall, decorated with the iconography of power, a late Roman aristocrat could approximate before his guests the transcendent remoteness of Constantius II. The epic of Digenis Akritas demonstrates that the ideology of the heroic host survived the collapse of the western Roman Empire to affect the architecture and decor of private Byzantine dining rooms.

NOTES

1. See E. Dwyer, chap. 1 in this volume; see also B. Bergmann, chap. 2, in which the dramatic siting and luxurious decoration of Roman maritime villas emerge as emblems of the power and aesthetic sophistication of the owner. As Bergmann's reading of Statius makes clear, visitors were intended to make "a direct connection between the villa and the patrons."

2. On this development, see J. D'Arms, "Ville rustiche e ville di *otium*," in F. Zevi ed., *Pompei 79* (Naples 1984) 84–85; and H. Mielsch, *Die römische Villa: Architektur und Lebensform* (Munich 1987) 161–63.

3. See, for example, many of the Homilies of St. John Chrysostom, such as the *Tenth Homily on the Epistle to the Philippians*.

4. Amm. Marc. 28.4.12. Translation adapted from W. Hamilton, *Ammianus Marcellinus: The Later Roman Empire (A.D. 354–378)* (Harmondsworth 1986) 359–60.

5. See Dwyer (chap. 1 in this volume).

6. For the early history of the *stibadium* and the origin of the triconch, see I. Lavin, "The House of the Lord," *ArtB* 44 (1962) 1–27; comments by G. Becatti, *Case ostienses del tardo impero* (Rome 1948) 27; and S. Ellis, "The Palace of the Dux at Apollonia and Related Houses," in G. Barker, J. Lloyd, and J. Reynolds eds., *Cyrenaica in Antiquity* (Oxford 1985) 15–25. Several other houses with apsidal rooms are discussed by R. Wilson, *Piazza Armerina* (London and New York 1983) 78–85. See also E. Salza Prina Ricotti, "The Importance of Water in Roman Garden *Triclinia*," in E. MacDougall ed., *Ancient Roman Villa Gardens* (Washington, D.C. 1987) 135–84, on *stibadia* of the first and second centuries A.C. at Sperlonga, in the House of Loreius Tiburtinus at Pompeii, and in the author's reconstruction of the Laurentine villa of Pliny the Younger.

7. J. B. Ward-Perkins, *Roman Architecture* (New York 1977) 108 and 140, where he observes "the apse and semi-dome taking their place in Domitian's Palace as part of the religious-inspired ceremonials of the imperial court." See also W. MacDonald, *The Architecture of the Roman Empire: I. An Introductory Study* rev. ed. (New Haven and London 1982) 53–55 and 73–74, on the significance of apsidal rooms in Domitian's Palace. H. P. L'Orange, *Art Forms and Civic Life in the Late Roman Empire* (Princeton 1965) 74–78 detects an "emperor-axis" as the underlying architectural principle in the apsidal and domed audience halls in Diocletian's Palace at Split.

8. For example, there are several triconch *triclinia* at Thuburbo Maius. See A. Ben

Abed-Ben Khader, *Thuburbo Majus: Les mosaïques dans le région ouest* (M. Alexander and M. Ennaifer eds., *Corpus des mosaïques de la Tunisie* 2, 3, Tunis 1987).

9. On the political and social importance of dining, see J. D'Arms, "Control, Companionship, and *Clientela*: Some Social Functions of the Roman Communal Meal," *Studies in Roman Society* (*EchCl* 28, n.s. 3, 1984) 327–48; also, R. MacMullen, *Corruption and the Decline of Rome* (New Haven and London 1988) 64–65 and 84.

10. For this view, see Lavin (supra n. 6).

11. A similar argument for the development of the late antique reception room is given by N. Duval, "Les maisons d'Apamée et l'architecture 'palatiale' de l'antiquité tardive," in J. Balty ed., *Apamée de Syrie* 13 (Brussels 1984) 447–70.

12. A third type of room for special gatherings, the private chapel, begins to appear in wealthy late antique houses. See S. Ellis, "The End of the Roman House," *AJA* 92 (1988) 565–76, for a fuller discussion of this development.

13. I have discussed these houses and the role of the audience chamber in detail in Ellis (supra n. 6) 15–25.

14. See E. Wightman, *Roman Trier and the Treveri* (London 1970) 103–9; and, most recently, H. Heinen, *Trier und das Treverland in römischer Zeit* (Trier 1985) 274–76.

15. S. Drća et al., *Mediana* (Niš 1979); F. Berti, *Mosaici antichi in Italia: Aemilia-Ravenna* I (Rome 1976); J. Lassus, "La salle à sept absides de Djemila-Cuicul," *AntAfr* 5 (1971) 193–207; and M. Blanchard-Lemée, "La 'Maison de Bacchus' à Djemila: Architecture et décor d'une grande demeure provinciale à la fin de l'antiquité," *BAntF* 17 (1981) 131–42.

16. The fountain is found in the *triclinia* of three houses at Stobi: the House of Peristerias, the House of Psalms, and the "Casino." See J. Wiseman, *Stobi: A Guide to the Excavations* (Belgrade 1973).

17. These parallels are fully discussed by Lassus (supra n. 15); and by R. Krautheimer, "Die Decanneacubita," *RömQSchr* suppl. 30 (1966) 195–99; and id., *Early Christian and Byzantine Architecture* (Harmondsworth 1979) 74–75. See also Duval (supra n. 11).

18. N. Duval, "Comment reconnaître un palais impérial ou royal? Ravenne et Piazza Armerina," *FelRav* 115 (1978) 32–39.

19. Blanchard-Lemée (supra n. 15), which supersedes the Thedosian date proposed by P.-A. Février, "Remarques sur les mosaïques de basse époque à Djemila," *BAntFr* (1965) 85–92.

20. Wilson (supra n. 6) 73–78.

21. See A. Carandini, A. Ricci, and A. de Vos, *Filosofiana: The Villa of Piazza Armerina* (Palermo 1982) 311–25.

22. Wilson (supra n. 6) notes that the room was admirably suited to fulfill the functional role of a *triclinium*. "The hall was probably designed for receptions, parties and banquets; it may also have served as an audience-hall for hearing petitions from clients" (p. 25).

23. For a discussion of the niceties of status distinction inherent in Roman social relations (patron/client, patron/protégé, equal and unequal *amici*) see R. P. Saller, *Personal Patronage under the Early Empire* (Cambridge 1982) 7–39. For later developments in the exercise of power by private patrons, see R. MacMullen, "Personal Power in the Roman Empire," *AJP* 107 (1986) 512–24; and MacMullen (supra n. 9) 58–121.

24. Vitr. *De Arch.* 6.5.1–2, as quoted in full and interpreted by Dwyer (chap. 1 in this volume), elucidates the character of early Roman reception rooms. See Y. Thébert, "Pri-

vate Life and Domestic Architecture in Roman Africa," chap. 3 in P. Veyne ed., *A History of Private Life: I. From Pagan Rome to Byzantium* (Cambridge, Mass. and London 1987) 357–64, for a discussion of private versus public uses of the peristyle in the houses of Roman Africa.

25. A. Wallace-Hadrill, "The Social Structure of the Roman House," *BSR* 56 (1988) 43–97.

26. This derives from the concept of "asymmetry" expounded by B. Hillier and J. Hanson in *The Social Logic of Space* (Cambridge 1984) 143–75. "Asymmetry" is the degree to which a building is organized as a succession of spaces entered one from another. "Symmetry" is the degree to which all rooms are entered from a central space or court. Late Roman houses have a stronger asymmetry than earlier Roman houses.

27. Ellis (supra n. 12). See also P. Brown, "Late Antiquity," in P. Veyne ed. (supra n. 24) 371–74.

28. On the fragments of wall paintings from the Villa at Piazza Armerina, see Wilson (supra n. 6) 32–33. As Wilson points out, "A full publication of the frescoes at Piazza Armerina is highly desirable; they add an extra dimension, hitherto neglected, to the interior decoration of this sumptuous mansion" (p. 33).

29. For a relatively recent catalogue of marble tables, see G. Roux, "Tables chrétiennes en marbre découvertes à Salamine," *Salamine de Chypre* 4 (1973) 133–96.

30. For example, at Histria; see E. Condurachi, "Histria à l'époque du Bas-Empire d'après les dernières fouilles archéologiques," *Dacia* 1 (1957) 245–63.

31. For example, G. Akerström-Hougen, *The Calendar and Hunting Mosaics of the Villa of the Falconer in Argos* (Stockholm 1974), includes much discussion of the *stibadium* and the apsidal dining room.

32. Lassus (supra n. 15) 203–6; and Blanchard-Lemée (supra n. 15) 140.

33. Blanchard-Lemée (supra n. 15) 140.

34. K. Dunbabin, *The Roman Mosaics of North Africa* (Oxford 1978). Chapter 4 discusses the genre of hunting mosaics. The hunt mosaic from the House of the Laberii, Oudna (pl. 44 and p. 61), shows names under the animals. The hunt mosaic in the House of Isguntus, Hippo Regius (pl. 29), shows a very organized hunt as if in a makeshift amphitheater.

35. Lassus (supra n. 15) 203 sees the ivy leaves as an amphitheater badge, but Dunbabin (supra n. 34) 76 sees them as only a magical sign.

36. Carandini et al. (supra n. 21) 94–103.

37. Berti (supra n. 15) 73–78 discusses the mosaic of Bellerophon. Duval (supra n. 18) 32–39 reviews the chronological problems. The house has a very complex history that is imperfectly understood. The mosaic is said to date from the first quarter of the sixth century A.C., but it is very damaged and thus hard to judge on stylistic grounds. The excavations were conducted at the beginning of the twentieth century, and the structural sequence has only been pieced together with great difficulty in recent times by Berti.

38. My translation.

39. Dunbabin (supra n. 34) 216.

40. G. Hanfmann, "The Continuity of Classical Art: Culture, Myth, and Faith," in K. Weitzmann ed., *The Age of Spirituality: A Symposium* (Princeton 1980) 85–86.

41. R. Brilliant, "Mythology," in K. Weitzmann ed., *The Age of Spirituality: Late Antique and Early Christian Art, Third to Seventh Century* (Princeton 1979) 129.

42. H. Brandenburg, "Bellerophon Christianus," *RömQSch* 53 (1968) 49–84.

43. J. Huskinson, "Some Pagan Mythological Figures and Their Significance in Early Christian Art," *BSR* 42 (1974) 68–97, esp. 73–78 on Bellerophon. She also has a complete catalogue and bibliography of Bellerophon mosaics.

44. Brilliant (supra n. 41) 128–29.

45. British Museum 51A.

46. See C. Kondoleon, chapter 5 in this volume, on the Kos mosaic.

47. Thébert (supra n. 24) 388–89.

48. L'Orange (supra n. 7).

49. See Dwyer (chap. 1 in this volume) and especially n. 34 on the concept of *auctoritas* and its reflection in Roman domestic architecture and interior design.

50. Wilson (supra n. 6) 29.

51. Wilson (supra n. 6) 64. On the date of the mosaics of the triconch, see pp. 65–68, where Wilson finds no convincing reason to doubt that they are contemporary with the other pavements of the villa.

52. Wilson (supra n. 6) 38.

53. Most recently E. Black, "Christian and Pagan Hopes of Salvation in Romano-British Mosaics," in M. Henig and A. King eds., *Pagan Gods and Shrines of the Roman Empire* (Oxford 1986) 147–58. Huskinson (supra n. 43) also discusses Orpheus.

54. Wilson (supra n. 6) 33.

55. See Brilliant (supra n. 41) 129 on Meleager. Statues from Antioch and southern France are discussed in D. Brinkerhoff, *A Collection of Sculpture in Classical and Early Christian Antioch* (New York 1970).

56. G. Pesce, *Il "Palazzo delle Colonne" in Ptolemaide di Cirenaica* (*Monografie di archeologia libica* 2, Rome 1940) 80–89.

57. See E. Bartman, chapter 3 in this volume (especially citations in nn. 11–14, 31–32, and 67) for further discussion of sculptures from houses in Antioch, the Palazzo delle Colonne in Ptolemais, the late antique houses of Ostia, and villas in southern France. The sculptures from Antioch are discussed by Brinkerhoff (supra n. 55). For sculptures from Ptolemais, see Pesce (supra n. 56); C. Kraeling, *Ptolemais: City of the Libyan Pentapolis* (*University of Chicago Oriental Institute Publications* 90, Chicago 1962); and D. Nasgowitz, *Ptolemais Cyrenaica* (Chicago and London 1980). For those from Ostia, see G. Becatti (supra n. 6); R. Meiggs, *Roman Ostia* (Oxford 1973) 433–34; and R. Calza and M. Squarciapino, *Museo ostiense* (*Itinerari dei musei, gallerie e monumenti d'Italia* 79, Rome 1962). The most recent treatments of the sculptures from southern France are L. Valensi, "Deux sculptures romaines de la villa de St-Georges-de-Montagne," *RLouvre* 23 (1973) 7–12; and E. K. Gazda, "A Marble Group of Ganymede and the Eagle from the Age of Augustine," in J. H. Humphrey ed., *Excavations at Carthage, 1977, Conducted by the University of Michigan* 6 (Ann Arbor 1981) 150–66.

58. Gazda (supra n. 57) 125–78.

59. T. Shear, Jr., "The Athenian Agora: Excavations of 1971," *Hesperia* 62 (1973) 170.

60. Brinkerhoff (supra n. 55).

61. Cedrenus, *Historia Compendium* i. 564 Migne, *PG* 121.

62. This interpretation follows that of S. Bassett-Clucas, "The Collection of Statuary in the Palace of Lausos," in *The Seventeenth International Byzantine Congress: Abstracts of Short Papers* (Washington, D.C. 1986) 67–68.

63. R. Naummann, "Vorbericht über die Ausgrabungen zwischen Mese und Antiochus Palast 1964 in Istanbul," *IstMitt* 15 (1965) 135–48.

64. D. Hull, *Digenis Akritas* 7.60, as discussed in *Digenis Akritas: The Two-Blood Border Lord. The Grottaferrata Version* (Athens, Ohio 1972).

65. Amm. Marc. 16.10.9–10. Translation adapted from that of J. C. Rolfe, *Ammianus Marcellinus* 1 (*The Loeb Classical Library*, Cambridge, Mass. and London 1963) 246–47. Compare the comments of Thébert (supra n. 24) 401–4.

List of Illustrations

Sources of Illustrations

1-1.   K. Nelson after F. Brown, *Roman Architecture* (New York 1971) fig. 6.
1-2.   Photo by G. Sommer, neg. 1237. Courtesy of the Kelsey Museum of Archaeology, University of Michigan.
1-3.   Alinari photo 47031.
1-4.   K. Nelson after *Real Museo Borbonico* vol. 8 (1832) pl. A.
1-5.   Anderson photo 24528.
1-6.   K. Nelson after E. Falkener, *The Museum of Classical Antiquities* 2d ed. (London 1860)
1-7.   Photo by G. Sommer, neg. 1233. Courtesy of the Kelsey Museum of Archaeology, University of Michigan.
1-8.   After T. H. Dyer, *The Ruins of Pompeii (Pompeii Photographed): A Series of Eighteen Photographic Views* (London 1867).
2-1.   P. Mingazzini and F. Pfister, *Surrentum (Forma Italiae* 5, 1946) carta 5.
2-2.   Photo by B. Bergmann.
2-3.   Photo by B. Bergmann.
2-4.   Photo by B. Bergmann.
2-5.   Photo by B. Bergmann.
2-6.   Photo by B. Bergmann.
2-7.   Photo by B. Bergmann.
2-8.   Photo by B. Bergmann.
2-9.   Photo by B. Bergmann.
2-10. Photo by B. Bergmann.
2-11. Photo by B. Bergmann.
2-12. P. Mingazzini and F. Pfister, *Surrentum (Forma Italiae* 5, 1946) carta 6.
2-13. P. Mingazzini and F. Pfister, *Surrentum (Forma Italiae* 5, 1946) carta 4.
2-14. P. Mingazzini and F. Pfister, *Surrentum (Forma Italiae* 5, 1946) carta 3.
2-15. Photo by B. Bergmann.
2-16. Photo by B. Bergmann.
3-1.   Courtesy of the Deutsches Archäologisches Institut, Rome. Inst. neg. 70.936.
3-2.   Photo by E. Bartman; reproduced by permission of the Herakleion Archaeological Museum.
3-3.   Photo by E. Bartman; reproduced by permission of the Herakleion Archaeological Museum.
3-4.   Photo courtesy of Musée d'Aquitaine, Bordeaux, France; all rights reserved.

3-5.   Photo of the Musées Nationaux 65DN1254. Courtesy of the Musée du Louvre, Paris.

3-6.   Photo by E. Paribeni. Reproduced from E. Schwartzenberg, *Die Grazien* (Bonn 1966) pl. 9, by permission of Dr. Rudolf Habelt GMBH.

3-7.   Courtesy of the Deutsches Archäologisches Institut, Rome. Inst. neg. 58.2197.

3-8.   Courtesy of the Staatliche Kunstsammlungen, Dresden.

3-9.   Courtesy of the Staatliche Kunstsammlungen, Dresden.

3-10. Courtesy of Kenan Erim.

3-11. Courtesy of Kenan Erim.

3-12. Photo by E. Bartman.

3-13. Photo by E. Bartman.

3-14. Photo by B. Malter. Courtesy of the Musei Capitolini, Rome.

3-15. Photo by B. Malter. Courtesy of the Musei Capitolini, Rome.

3-16. Drawing by Shelly Smith Kellam.

3-17. After A. M. Mansel, *Ruinen von Side* (Berlin 1963) fig. 9, by permission of Walter de Gruyter and Co.

4-1.   After G. Calza, "Gli scavi recenti nell'abitato di Ostia," *MonAnt* 26 (1920) pl. 1.

4-2.   Courtesy of the Deutsches Archäologisches Institut, Rome. Inst. neg. 55.296.

4-3.   Courtesy of the Ashmolean Museum. Oxford.

4-4.   After G. Calza, "Gli scavi recenti nell'abitato di Ostia," *MonAnt* 26 (1920) fig. 13.

4-5.   Adapted from J. E. Stambaugh, *The Ancient Roman City* (Baltimore and London 1988) 181, fig. 20.

4-6.   Photo by Michael Larvey.

4-7.   Courtesy of the Istituto Centrale per il Catalogo e la Documentazione. Neg. E 7117.

4-8.   Drawing by J. R. Clarke.

4-9.   After E. Keuls, *The Reign of the Phallus* (New York 1985) fig. 247, by permission.

4-10. Drawing by J. R. Clarke.

4-11. Courtesy of the Deutsches Archäologisches Institut, Rome. Inst. neg. 75.2225.

4-12. Photo by Michael Larvey.

4-13. After S. Reinach, *Répertoire de reliefs grecs et romains* 2 (Paris 1912) 242, figs. 1–3.

4-14. After C. Robert, *Die antiken Sarkophagreliefs* 2, pl. 2,3.

4-15. After L. Guerrini, "*Las Incantadas* di Salonicco," *ArchCl* 13 (1961) pl. 19,2.

5-1.   Courtesy of Terry Allen.

5-2.   K. Nelson, after C. Polycarpou.

5-3.   Courtesy of the Department of Antiquities, Cyprus.

5-4.   Courtesy of the Department of Antiquities, Cyprus.

5-5.   After S. Aurigemma, *I mosaici di Zliten* (Rome 1926) 139, fig. 78.

5-6.   After S. Aurigemma, *I mosaici di Zliten* (Rome 1926) 137, table D.

5-7.   After T. Kraus and L. von Matt, *Pompeii and Herculaneum* (New York 1975) 52, no. 53, fig. 53.

5-8.   Photo by C. Kondoleon.

5-9.   Photo by C. Kondoleon.

5-10. Courtesy of the Deutsches Archäologisches Institut, Rome. Inst. neg. 64.323.

5-11. Courtesy of the Department of Antiquities, Cyprus.

5-12. Courtesy of the Department of Antiquities, Cyprus.

5-13.   Courtesy of the Department of Antiquities, Cyprus.

6-1.   (1) S. Ellis, after J. Keil, *ÖJh* 23 (1926) cols. 5–72, fig. 2; (2) S. Ellis, after K. Erim, *TürkArkDerg* 18.2 (1969) 87–110, fig. 21; (3) S. Ellis, after R. Goodchild, *Antiquity* 34 (1960) 246–58, fig. 1.

6-2.   (1) S. Ellis, after J. Lassus, *AntAfr* 5 (1971) 193–207, fig. 4; (2) S. Ellis, after F. Berti, *Mosaici antichi in Italia, Aemilia-Ravenna* 1 (Rome 1976); (3) S. Ellis, after S. Drća et al, *Mediana* (Niš 1979) fig. 13.

6-3.   S. Ellis, after A. Carandina, A. Ricci, and M. de Vos, *Filosofiana: The Villa of Piazza Armerina* (Palermo 1982) pl. 49, fig. 105.

6-4.   M. Francescon, after J. Lassus, *AntAfr* 5 (1971) 193–207, fig. 6.

6-5.   After G. V. Gentili, *La villa erculia di Piazza Armerina: I mosaici figurati* (Milan 1959) pl. 31.

6-6.   S. Ellis, after A. Berti, *Mosaici antichi in Italia, Aemilia-Ravenna* 1 (Rome 1976) pl. 48.

6-7.   After A. Carandini, A. Ricci, and M. de Vos, *Filosofiana: The Villa of Piazza Armerina* (Palermo 1982) pl. 49, fig. 17.

A Note on Abbreviations

The journal and series abbreviations used in this volume are those given in the *American Journal of Archaeology* 90 (1986) 384–94. Abbreviations of the names and works of classical authors follow N. G. L. Hammond and H. H. Scullard eds., *The Oxford Classical Dictionary*, 2d edition (Oxford 1970) ix–xxii.

Select Bibliography

The thesis of this book, that research on the decoration of Roman residences can contribute valuable new insights into the history of Roman art and society, has begun to gain acceptance. "Roman decor," however, is not a commonly acknowledged bibliographic category in the fields of Roman archaeology and the history of Roman art. With the exception of the section on ensembles, this select bibliography is therefore arranged according to traditional areas of specialization: architecture, sculpture, painting, stucco, mosaics, and social history. It is not intended to be exhaustive, but rather to collect representative examples of recent integrative and synthetic scholarship on the many-faceted subject of Roman interior decoration. This bibliography, like this book as a whole, is intended to serve as a sampler and resource for those interested in taking a contextually oriented approach to Roman art in the private sphere.

Hellenistic Background

Baldassare, I., "Pittura parietale e mosaico pavimentale dal IV al II sec. a.C.," *DialArch* n.s. 2 (1984) 65–76.

Bezerra de Meneses, U. T., "Essai de lecture sociologique de la décoration murale des maisons d'habitation héllenistiques de Delos," *DialArch* n.s. 2 (1984) 77–88.

Bruneau, P., *Les mosaïques (Exploration archéologique de Délos faite par l'École Française d'Athènes* 29, Paris 1972).

Fullerton, M. D., "Archaistic Statuary of the Hellenistic Period," *RM* 102 (1987) 259–78.

Harward, V. J., *Greek Domestic Sculpture and the Origins of Private Art Patronage* (Diss. Harvard 1982).

Jacob-Felsch, M., *Die Entwicklung griechischer Statuenbasen und die Aufstellung der Statuen* (Waldsassen/Bayern 1969).

Kreeb, M., *Figürliche Ausstattung späthellenistischer Häuser*. Teil I: *Interpretation*. Teil II: *Katalog* (Munich 1980).

———, "Zur statuarischen Ausstattung delischer Privathäuser," *Wohnungsbau im Altertum (Diskussionen zur archäologischen Bauforschung* 3, Berlin 1979) 145–46.

———, "Studien zur figürlichen Ausstattung delischer Privathäuser," *BCH* 108 (1984) 317–43.

Lauter, H., "Kunst und Landschaft: Ein Beitrag zum rhodischen Hellenismus," *AntK* 15 (1972) 49–59.

Ridgway, B. S., "Greek Antecedents of Garden Sculpture," in E. MacDougall and W.

Jashemski eds., *Ancient Roman Gardens* (*Dumbarton Oaks Colloquium on the History of Landscape Architecture* 7, Washington, D.C. 1981) 7–28.

———, "The Setting of Greek Sculpture," *Hesperia* 40 (1971) 336–56.

Tomlinson, R. A., "The ceiling of Anfushy II.2," *Alessandria e il mondo ellenistico-romano* (*Studi di onore di A. Adriani* 2, Rome 1984) 260–64.

Wartke, R. B., "Hellenistiche Stuckdekorationen aus Priene: Ein Beitrag zur Geschichte der hellenistischen Wanddekoration," *FuB* 18 (1977) 21–58.

The Architecture of the *Domus* and the *Insula*

Balty, J., ed., *Apamée de Syrie* 13 (Brussels 1984).

Boersma, J. S., et al., *Amoenissima Civitas: Block V.2 at Ostia. Description and Analysis of its Visible Remains* (Assen 1985).

Broise, H., and X. Lafon, "Un 'projet' dans l'architecture domestique romaine. L'exemple de la villa Prato à Sperlonga," *Le dessin d'architecture dans les sociétés antiques* (Strasbourg 1984) 199–211.

Coarelli, F., "La casa dell'aristocrazia romana secondo Vitruvio," in H. Geertman and J. J. de Jong eds., *Minus non ingratum, Proceedings of the International Symposium on Vitruvius' De Architectura and the Hellenistic and Republican Architecture, Leiden, 20–23 janvier 1987* (*BABesch Supplement* 2, Leiden 1989) 178–87.

Drerup, H., *Zum Ausstattungsluxus in der römischen Architektur: Ein formgeschichtlicher Versuch* (*Orbis Antiquus* 12, Münster 1981).

Duval, N., "Les maisons d'Apamée et l'architecture 'palatiale' de l'antiquité tardive," *Apamée de Syrie* 13 (Brussels 1984) 447–70.

Ellis, S., "The End of the Roman House," *AJA* 92 (1988) 565–76.

———, "The 'Palace of the Dux' at Apollonia, and Related Houses," *Cyrenaica in Antiquity* (*BAR International Series* 236, Oxford 1985) 15–25.

Eschebach, H., "Zur Entwicklung des pompejanischen Hauses," *Wohnungsbau im Altertum* (*Diskussionen zur archäologischen Bauforschung* 3, Berlin 1979) 152–61.

Etienne, R., *Le quarter nord-est de Volubilis* (Paris 1960).

Hallier, G., "Entre les règles de Vitruve et la réalité archéologique: *l'atrium toscan*," in H. Geertman and J. J. de Jong eds., *Minus non ingratum, Proceedings of the International Symposium on Vitruvius' De Architectura and the Hellenistic and Republican Architecture, Leiden, 20–23 janvier 1987* (*BABesch Supplement* 2, Leiden 1989) 194–211.

Hanoune, R., "La maison romaine: Nouveautés," *Apamée de Syrie* 13 (Brussels 1984) 431–46.

Hoffmann, A., "L'Architettura," in F. Zevi ed., *Pompei 79: Raccolta di studi per il decimonono centenario dell'eruzione vesuviana* (Naples 1984) 97–118.

Jashemski, W., "Giardini e vignetti in città," in F. Zevi ed., *Pompei 79: Raccolta di studi per il decimonono centenario dell'eruzione vesuviana* (Naples 1984) 119–29.

Lafon, X., "Vitruve et les 'villas de son temps,'" in H. Geertman and J. J. de Jong eds., *Minus non ingratum, Proceedings of the International Symposium on Vitruvius' De Architectura and the Hellenistic and Republican Architecture; Leiden, 20–23 janvier 1987* (*BABesch Supplement* 2, Leiden 1989) 188–93.

Lassus, J., "Sur le maison d'Antioche," *Apamée de Syrie* 13 (Brussels 1984) 361–72.

Leveau, P., "Les maisons nobles de Caesarea de Maurétanie," *AntAfr* 18 (1982) 109–65.

McKay, A. G., *Houses, Villas and Palaces in the Roman World* (Ithaca 1975).

Meiggs, R., *Roman Ostia* (Oxford 1973).

Packer, J., "Inns at Pompeii: A Short Survey," *CronPomp* 4 (1978) 5–51.

——, "The Insulae of Imperial Ostia," *MAAR* 31 (1971).

——, "Middle and Lower Class Housing in Pompeii: A Preliminary Survey," in B. Andreae and H. Kyrieleis eds., *Neue Forschungen in Pompeji* (Recklinghausen 1975) 133–46.

Pisani Sartorio, G., "Una domus sotto il giardino del Pio Istituto Rivaldi sulla Velia," *Città e architettura nella Roma imperiale* (Odense 1983) 147–68.

Rebuffat, R., *Thamusida II* (Rome 1977).

Richardson, L., Jr., "A Contribution to the Study of Pompeian Dining-Rooms," *Pompeii, Herculaneum, Stabiae: Bollettino dell'Associazione internazionale amici di Pompei* 1 (1983) 61–71.

——, *Pompeii: An Architectural History* (Baltimore and London 1988).

Sackett, L. H. and J. E. Jones, "Knossos: A Roman House Revisited," *Archaeology* 32 (1979) 18–27.

Salza Prina Ricotti, E., "Cucine e quartieri servili in epoca romana," *RendPontAcc* 51–52 (1978–80) 237–94.

——, "Forme speciali di triclini," *CronPomp* 5 (1979) 102–49.

Thébert, Y., "Private Life and Domestic Architecture in Roman Africa," in P. Veyne ed., *A History of Private Life: I. From Pagan Rome to Byzantium* (Cambridge, Mass. and London 1987) 313–410.

Van Aken, A. R. A., "Late Roman *Domus* Architecture," *Mnemosyne* (1949) 242–51.

Weiskittel, S. F., "Vitruvius and Domestic Architecture at Pompeii," *Pompeii and the Vesuvian Landscape (Papers of a Symposium Sponsored by the AIA Washington Society and the Smithsonian Institution*, Washington, D.C. 1979) 25–38.

The Architecture of the Villa

Bencivenga, C., L. Fergola, and L. Melillo, "Richerche sulla villa romana di Minori," *Annali del seminario di studi del mondo classico, sezione di archeologia e storia antica, Napoli* 1 (1979) 131–51.

Brockmeyer, N., "Die *villa rustica* als Wirtschaftsform und die Ideologisierung der Landwirtschaft," *Ancient Society* 6 (1975) 213–28.

Carandini, A., "Cosanum. La villa romana di Settefinestre (Orbetello). Un primo tentativo di interpretazione di insieme," *Scavi e ricerche archeologiche degli anni 1976–1979*, 2 (Rome 1985) 341–53.

Carandini, A., A. Ricci, and M. de Vos, *Filosofiana: La villa di Piazza Armerina* (Palermo 1982).

Carandini, A., et al., eds., *Settefinestre: Una villa schiavistica nell'etruria romana* 3 vols. (Modena 1985).

Cotton, M. A., *The Late Republican Villa at Posto, Francolise* (London 1979).

Cotton, M. A., and G. P. R. Métraux, *The San Rocco Villa at Francolise* (London 1985).

D'Arms, J., "Ville rustiche e ville di *otium*," in F. Zevi ed., *Pompei 79: Raccolta di studi per il decimonono centenario dell'eruzione vesuviana* (Naples 1984) 65–86.

Daszewski, W. A., "Researches at Nea Paphos, 1965–1984," *Archaeology in Cyprus, 1960– 1985* (Nicosia 1985) 277–91.

Dobbins, J. J., *The Excavation of the Roman Villa at La Befa, Italy* (*BAR International Series* 162, Oxford 1983).

Dyson, S. L., *The Roman Villas of Buccino. Wesleyan University Excavation in Buccino, Italy, 1969–1972* (*BAR International Series* 187, Oxford 1983).

Franciscis, A. de, "La villa romana di Oplontis," in B. Andreae and H. Kyrieleis eds., *Neue Forschungen in Pompeji* (Recklinghausen 1975) 9–38.

Ghini, G. and A. Danti, "La villa romana del Pigno presso Ceri," *IV convegno dei gruppi archeologici del Lazio* (Rome 1982) 79–86.

Hogg, A. H. A., "The Llantwit Major Villa: A Reconsideration of the Evidence," *Britannia* 5 (1974) 225–50.

Johannowsky, W., E. Laforgia, M. Romita, and V. Sampaolo, *Le ville romana di età imperiale* (Naples 1986).

Johnston, D. E., *Roman Villas* (Aylesbury 1979).

Lafon, X., "À propos des villas de la zone de Sperlonga: Les origines et le développement de la *villa maritima* sur le littoral tyrrhénien à l'époque républicaine," *MEFRA* 93 (1981) 297–353.

Lefèvre, E., "Plinius-Studien, I. Römische Baugesinnung und Landschaftsauffassung in den Villenbriefen (2,17; 5,6)," *Gymnasium* 84 (1977) 519–41.

Manganaro, G., "Die Villa von Piazza Armerina, Residenz der kaiserlichen Prokurators, und ein mit ihr verbundenes Emporium von Henna," in D. Papenfuss and V. M. Strocka eds., *Palast und Hütte* (*Alexander von Humboldt-Stiftung. Symposium* 6, Mainz 1982) 493–514.

Mansuelli, G. A., "La villa nelle *epistulae* di C. Plinio Cecilio Secondo," *Studi Romagnoli* 29 (1978) 65–71.

Mielsch, H., *"Die römische Villa: Architektur und Lebensform* (Munich 1987).

Mladenova, J., "Die römische Villa bei Ivajlovgrad (VR Bulgarien) und ihre Architektur-dekoration," *Altertum* 27 (1981) 38–48.

Painter, L., *Roman Villas in Italy: Recent Excavations and Research* (*British Museum Occasional Papers* 20, London 1980).

Rossiter, J. J., "Roman Villas of the Greek East and the Villa in Gregory of Nissa *Ep.* 20," *JRA* 2 (1989) 101–10.

Settis, S., "Neue Forschungen und Untersuchungen zur *villa* von Piazza Armerina," in D. Papenfuss and V. M. Strocka eds., *Palast und Hütte* (*Alexander von Humboldt-Stiftung. Symposium* 6, Mainz 1982) 515–34.

Todd, M., ed., *Studies in the Romano-British Villa* (Leicester 1978).

Tosi, G., "La villa romana nelle *epistulae ad Lucilium* di L. Anneo Seneca," *AquilNost* 45–46 (1974–75) 217–26.

La "Villa di Tigellio" Mostra degli scavi, Cagliari, Cittadella dei Musei, 24 Ottobre–14 Novembre 1981 (Cagliari 1981).

Wilson, R. J. A., *Piazza Armerina* (London 1983).

Wojcik, M. R., *La Villa dei Papiri ad Ercolano: Contributo alla ricostruzione dell'ideologia della nobilitas tardorepubblicana* (Ministero per i beni culturali ed ambientali, Soprintendenza archeologica di Pompei. *Monografia* 1, Rome 1986).

Sculpture in Houses and Villas

Bartman, E., *"Decor et Duplicatio:* Pendants in Roman Sculptural Display," *AJA* 92 (1988) 211–25.

Braemer, F., "La décoration en matériaux nobles (marbres, porphyres . . .) des édifices de la Gaule et des régions limitrophes durant le haut-empire et la basse antiquité," *Mosaïque: Recueil d'hommages à Henri Stern* (Paris 1983) 81–91.

Catling, W., and G. Waywell, "A Find of Roman Marble Statuettes at Knossos," *BSA* 72 (1977) 85–106.

Caro, S. de, "Sculture dalla 'villa di Poppea' in Oplontis," *CronPomp* 2 (1976) 184–225.

———, "The Sculptures of the Villa of Poppaea at Oplontis: A Preliminary Report," in E. MacDougall ed., *Ancient Roman Villa Gardens* (Dumbarton Oaks Colloquium on the History of Landscape Architecture 10, Washington, D.C. 1987) 77–133.

Döhl, H., and P. Zanker, "La scultura," in F. Zevi ed., *Pompei 79: Raccolta di studi per il decimonono centenario dell'eruzione vesuviana* (Naples 1984) 177–210.

Dwyer, E., *Pompeian Domestic Sculpture: A Study of Five Pompeian Houses and Their Contents* (Archaeologica 28, Rome 1982).

———, "Sculpture and Its Display in Private Houses of Pompeii," *Pompeii and the Vesuvian Landscape* (Papers of a Symposium Sponsored by the AIA Washington Society and the Smithsonian Institution, Washington, D.C. 1979) 59–77.

Froning, H., *Marmor-Schmuckreliefs mit griechischen Mythen im 1. Jh. v. Ch. Untersuchungen zu Chronologie und Funktion* (Mainz 1981).

Gazda, E. K., "A Marble Group of Ganymede and the Eagle from the Age of Augustine," in J. H. Humphrey ed., *Excavations at Carthage, 1977, conducted by the University of Michigan* 6 (Ann Arbor 1981) 125–78.

Hill, D. K., "Some Sculpture from Roman Domestic Gardens," in E. MacDougall and W. Jashemski eds., *Ancient Roman Gardens* (Dumbarton Oaks Colloquium on the History of Landscape Architecture 7, Washington, D.C. 1981) 81–94.

Jashemski, W. F., *The Gardens of Pompeii, Herculaneum, and the Villas Destroyed by Vesuvius* (New Rochelle 1979).

Larenz, T., *Galerien von griechischen Philosophen-und Dichterbildnisse bei den Römern* (Mainz 1965).

Marvin, M., "Copying in Roman Sculpture: The Replica Series," *Retaining the Original: Multiple Originals, Copies, and Reproductions* (Studies in the History of Art 20, Washington, D.C. 1989) 29–45.

Moretti, M., and A. M. Sgubini Moretti, *La villa dei Volusii a Lucus Feroniae* (Rome 1977).

Neudecker, R., *Die Skulpturenausstattung römischer Villen in Italien* (Beiträge zur Erschliessung hellenistischer und kaiserzeitlicher Skulptur und Architektur 9, Mainz am Rhein 1988).

Niemeier, J.-P., *Kopien und Nachahmungen im Hellenismus: Ein Beitrag zum Klassizismus des 2. und frühen 1. Jhs. v. Ch. (Habelts Dissertationsdrucke, Reihe klassische Archäologie 20, Bonn 1985).

Pandermalis, D., "Zum Programm der Statuenausstattung in der Villa dei Papiri," *AM* 86 (1971) 173–209.

Raeder, J., *Die statuarische Ausstattung der Villa Hadriana bei Tivoli* (Europäische Hochschulschriften 38, 4, Frankfurt am Main 1983).

Rawson, E., "Architecture and Sculpture: The Activities of the Cossutii," *BSR* 43 (1975) 36–47.

Robert, L., "Dans une maison d'Ephèse un serpent et un chiffre," *CRAI* (1982) 126–32.

Sauron, G., "*Templa serena.* À propos de la 'Villa des Papyri' d'Herculanum: Contribution à l'étude des comportements aristocratiques romains à la fin de la république," *MEFRA* 92 (1980) 277–301.

Stewart, A., "Sculpture in a Classical Landscape," in M. Del Chiaro ed., *Classical Art: Sculpture (Catalogue of the Santa Barbara Museum of Art,* Santa Barbara 1984) 86–94.

———, "To Entertain an Emperor: Sperlonga, Laocoon and Tiberius at the Dinner-Table," *JRS* 67 (1977) 76–90.

Torelli, M., "Una galleria della villa: Qualche nota sulla decorazione del complesso," in *I Volusii Saturnini: Una famiglia romana della prima età imperiale (Archeologia: Materiali e Problemi 6,* Bari 1982) 97–104.

Wojcik, M. R., "La 'Villa dei Papiri' di Ercolano. Programma decorativa e problemi della committenza," *AnnPerugia* 16–17 (1978–80) 357–68.

Zanker, P., "Zur Funktion und Bedeutung griechischer Skulptur in der Römerzeit," in *Le classicisme à Rome (Fondation Hardt, Entretiens 25,* Geneva 1978) 283–314.

———, *Klassizistische Statuen: Studien zur Veränderung des Kunstgeschmacks in der römischen Kaiserzeit* (Mainz 1974).

Painting in Houses and Villas

Allroggen-Bedel, A., "Herkunft und ursprünglicher Dekorationszusammenhang einiger in Essen ausgestellter Fragmente von Wandmalereien," in B. Andreae and H. Kyrieleis eds., *Neue Forschungen in Pompeji* (Recklinghausen 1975) 115–22.

Allroggen-Bedel, A., "La pittura," in F. Zevi ed., *Pompei 79: Raccolta di studi per il decimonono centenario dell'eruzione vesuviana* (Naples 1984) 130–44.

———, "Die Wanddekorationen der Villen am Golf von Neapel," *La regione sotterrata dal Vesuvio: Studi e prospettive. Atti del convegno internazionale 11–15 Novembre 1979* (Naples 1982) 519–30.

Andreae, B., "Rekonstruktion des großen Oecus der Villa des P. Fannius Synistor in Boscoreale," in B. Andreae and H. Kyrieleis eds., *Neue Forschungen in Pompeji* (Recklinghausen 1975) 71–83.

Andreae, B., and H. Kyrieleis, eds., *Neue Forschungen in Pompeji* (Recklinghausen 1975).

Aventicum V: Pictores per Provincias, Actes du 3e colloque internationale sur la peinture murale romaine, Avenches 1986 (Cahiers d'archéologie romaine 43, Avenches 1987).

Badoni, F., M. de Vos, and I. Bragantini, *Pompei, 1748–1980. I tempi della documentazione* (Rome 1981).

Baldassarre, I., "Pittura parietale e mosaico pavimentale dal IV al II sec. A.C.," *DialArch* n.s. 2 (1984) 65–76.

Barbet, A., *Bibliographie générale thematique de la peinture murale romaine (Centre d'étude des peintures murales romaines, Bulletin de liaison 5,* Paris n. d.)

———, *Bolsena V: La maison aux salles souterraines,* fasc. 2: *Décors picturaux (murs, plafonds, voûtes) (MélRom* suppl. 6, 2 vols., Rome 1985).

———, "The Diffusion of the Third Pompeian Style in Gaul," *Roman Provincial Wall Painting of the Western Empire (BAR International Series* 140, Oxford 1982) 75–84.

————, *Peinture murale en Gaule, Actes des séminaires 1982–1983* (*BAR International Series* 240, Oxford 1985).

————, *La peinture murale romaine: Les styles décoratifs pompéiens* (Paris 1985).

————, "Le quatrième style de Pompéi," *Peinture murale en Gaule* (*Actes des séminaires, 1979*, Dijon 1980) 65–76.

————, "Le troisième style de Pompéi: Perspectives nouvelles," *Peinture murale en Gaule* (*Actes des séminaires, 1979*, Dijon 1980) 29–40.

Bergmann, B., *Coast and Grove: Architectural Landscapes in Roman Painting* (Princeton, forthcoming).

Beyen, H., *Die pompejanische Wanddekoration von zweiten bis zum vierten Stil* 1–2, 1 (The Hague 1938; 1960).

Borbein, A., "Zur Deutung von Scherwand und Durchblick auf den Wandgemälden des zweiten pompejanische Stils," in B. Andreae and H. Kyrieleis eds., *Neue Forschungen in Pompeji* (Recklinghausen 1975) 61–70.

Bragantini, I., A. M. Dolciotti, L. Gigli, et al., *Museo Nazionale Romano, Le pitture: Le decorazioni della villa romana della Farnesina 2,1.* (Rome 1982).

Bruno, V. J., "Antecedents of the Pompeian First Style," *AJA* 73 (1969) 305–17.

Carettoni, G., "La decorazione pittorica della casa di Augusto," *RM* 90 (1983) 373–419.

Corlàita Scagliarini, D., "Spazio e decorazione nella pittura pompeiana," *Palladio* 24–25 (1974–76) 3–44.

Croisille, J. M., "La frise d'Héraklès de la Maison de Loreius Tiburtinus à Pompéi et la tradition épique," *Hommages à H. Bardon* (Brussels 1985) 89–99.

Dumasy, F., "Les peintures de la villa Liégeaud à la Croisille-sur-Briance (Haut-Vienne)," *Peinture murale en Gaule* (*Actes des séminaires 1980–1981*, Nancy 1984) 13–24.

Ehrhardt, W., *Stilgeschictliche Untersuchungen am römischen Wandmalereien* (Mainz am Rhein 1987).

Engemann, J., *Architekturdarstellungen des frühen zweiten Stils: Illusionistiche römische Wandmalerei der ersten Phase und ihre Vorbilden in der realen Architektur* (*RM-EH* 12, Heidelberg 1967).

Eristov, H., "Représentations architecturales du quatrième style en Campanie," *Peinture murale en Gaule* (*Actes des séminaires 1979*, Dijon 1980) 77–82.

Fittschen, K., "Zum Figurenfries der Villa von Boscoreale," in B. Andreae and H. Kyrieleis eds., *Neue Forschungen in Pompeji* (Recklinghausen 1975) 93–100.

————, "Zur Herkunft und Entstehung des 2. Stils: Probleme und Argumente," *Hellenismus in Mittelitalien: Kolloquium im Göttingen vom 5. bis 9. Juni 1974* (*Abhandlungen der Akademie der Wiss. in Göttingen. Philologisch-historische Klasse 3*, Folge 97, Göttingen 1976) 539–57.

Flécher, J. F., "Les peintures murales de la villa des Boueix-Cujasseix à Rougnat (Creuse)," *Peinture murale en Gaule* (*Actes des séminaires 1980–1981*, Nancy 1984) 25–37.

Franciscis, A. de, *The Pompeian Wall Paintings in the Roman Villa of Oplontis* (Recklinghausen 1975).

Frizot, M., "Peintures et stucs de Hongrie," *Peinture murale en Gaule* (*Actes des séminaires 1980–1981*, Nancy 1984) 39–46.

Fuchs, M., "Peintures murales romaines d'Avenches: Le décor d'un corridor de l'insula 7," *La peinture murale romaine dans les provinces de l'empire* (Oxford 1983) 27–75.

Gray, G. E., "Romano-British Wall Paintings from Tarrant Hinton, Dorset," *Roman Provincial Wall Painting of the Western Empire* (*BAR International Series* 140, Oxford 1982) 145–52.

Gury, F., "La forge du destin: À propos d'une série de peintures pompéiennes du IVe style," *MEFRA* 98 (1986) 427–89.

Heckenbenner, D., "Les peintures murales de la villa gallo-romaine de Saint-Ulrich (Moselle)," *Peinture murale en Gaule* (*Actes des séminaires 1980–1981*, Nancy 1984) 53–61.

Joyce, H., "The Ancient Frescoes from the Villa Negroni and Their Influence in the Eighteenth and Nineteenth Centuries," *ArtB* 65 (1983) 423–40.

Laidlaw, A., *The First Style in Pompeii: Painting and Architecture* (*Archaeologica* 57, Rome 1985).

———, "A Reconstruction of the First Style Decoration in the Alexander Exedra of the House of the Faun," in B. Andreae and H. Kyrieleis eds., *Neue Forschungen in Pompeji* (Recklinghausen 1975) 39–52.

Leach, E. W., "Landscape and the Prosperous Life. The Discrimination of Genre in Augustan Literature and Painting," in R. Winkes ed., *The Age of Augustus* (*Archaeologia Transatlantica* 5, *Publications d'histoire de l'art et d'archéologie de l'Université catholique de Louvain* 44, Providence 1985) 189–95.

———, "Patrons, Painters, and Patterns: The Anonymity of Roman-Campanian Painting and the Transition from the Second to the Third Style," in B. Gold ed., *Literary and Artistic Patronage in Ancient Rome* (Austin 1982) 135–73.

———, *The Rhetoric of Space: Literary and Artistic Representations of Landscape in Republican and Augustan Rome* (Princeton 1988).

———, "Sacral-Idyllic Landscape Painting and the Poems of Tibullus's First Book," *Latomus* 39 (1980) 47–69.

Ling, R., "The Kingscote Wall Paintings," in J. Liversidge ed., *Roman Provincial Wall Painting of the Western Empire* (*BAR International Series* 140, Oxford 1982) 124–25.

———, "Studius and the Beginnings of Roman Landscape Painting," *JRS* 67 (1977) 1–16.

Little, A. M. G., *Decor, Drama, and Design in Roman Painting* (Washington, D.C., 1977).

———, *Roman Perspective Painting and the Ancient Stage* (Kennebunk, Me., 1971).

Liversidge, J., ed., *Roman Provincial Wall Painting of the Western Empire* (*BAR International Series* 140, Oxford 1982).

Maiolo, M. G., "Gli intonaci dipinti della villa romana di Russi," *Studi Romagnoli* 29 (1978) 77–94.

Mellor, J. E., "New discoveries from the Norfolk Street Villa, Leicester," in J. Liversidge ed., *Roman Provincial Wall Painting of the Western Empire* (*BAR International Series* 140, Oxford 1982) 127–40.

Michel, D., "Bermerkungen über Zuschauerfiguren in pompejanischen sogenannten Tafelbildern," *La regione sotterrata dal Vesuvio: Studi e prospettive, Atti del convegno internazionale 11–15 Novembre 1979* (Naples 1982) 537–98.

———, "Pompejanische Gartenmalereien," *Tainia: Roland Hampe zum 70. Geburtstag am 2. Dezember 1978* (Mainz 1980) 373–404.

Mielsch, H., "Funde und Forschungen zur Wandmalerei der Prinzipätzeit von 1945 bis 1975, mit einem Nachtrag 1980," *ANRW* II 12, 2 (Berlin 1981) 157–264.

Peters, W. J. Th., "La composizione delle pareti dipinte nella Casa dei Vettii a Pompei," *MededRom* 39 (1977) 95–128.

——, "La composizione delle pitture parietali di IV stile a Roma e in Campania," *La regione sotterrata dal Vesuvio: Studi e prospettive, Atti del convegno internazionale 11–15 Novembre 1979* (Naples 1982) 635–60.

——, *Landscape in Romano-Campanian Mural Painting* (Assen 1963).

Picard, G.-C., "Les Grotesques: un système décoratif typique de l'art césarien et néronien," *L'Art décoratif à Rome à la fin de la republique et au debut du principat (Collection de l'École Française de Rome 55, Rome 1981) 143–49.

——, "Origine et signification des fresques architectoniques dites de Second Style," *RA* 1977, 231–52.

Schefold, K., "Der zweite Stil als Zeugnis alexandrinischer Architektur," in B. Andreae and H. Kyrieleis eds., *Neue Forschungen in Pompeji* (Recklinghausen 1975) 53–59.

——, "Römische Visionen und griechische Motive am Fuss des Vesuvs," *La regione sotterrata dal Vesuvio: Studi e prospettive, Atti del convegno internazionale 11–15 Novembre 1979* (Naples 1982) 1–40.

Sichtermann, H., "Zu den Malereien des Triclinium der Casa del Frutteto in Pompeji," in F. Krinzinger ed., *Forschungen und Funde: Festschrift Bernhard Neutsch* (Innsbruck 1980) 457–61.

Strocka, V. M., "Pompejanische Nebenzimmer," in B. Andreae and H. Kyrieleis eds., *Neue Forschungen in Pompeji* (Recklinghausen 1975) 101–6.

——, "Die Wandmalerei im römischen Ephesos (50–500 n. Chr.)," *Proceedings of the Tenth International Congress of Classical Archaeology, Ankara-Izmir, 1973* (Ankara 1978) 481–91.

Strocka, V. M., and H. Vetters, *Die Wandmalerei der Hanghäuser in Ephesos (Forschungen in Ephesos* 8, 1, Vienna 1977).

Thompson, D. L., "Painted Portraiture at Pompeii," in *Pompeii and the Vesuvian Landscape (Papers of a Symposium Sponsored by the AIA Washington Society and the Smithsonian Institution,* Washington, D.C. 1979) 78–92.

Thompson, M. L., "The Monumental and Literary Evidence for Programmatic Painting in Antiquity," *Marsyas* 9 (1961) 36–77.

——, *Programmatic Painting in Pompeii: The Meaningful Combination of Mythological Pictures in Roman Decoration* (Diss. New York Univ. 1960).

Vos, M. de, "Funzione e decorazione de 'Auditorium di Mecenate,'" in *Roma Capitale, 1870–1911: L'archeologia in Roma capitale tra sterro e scavo* (Venice 1983) 231–47.

Wesenberg, B., "Zur asymmetrischen Perspektiv in der Wanddekoration des zweiten pompejanischen Stils," *MarbWPr* (1968) 102–9.

——, "Römische Wandmalerei am Ausgang der Republik: Der zweite Pompejanische Stil," *Gymnasium* 92 (1985) 470–88.

Winkes, R., "'Natura Morta' and Cuisine," *Révues des archéologues et historiens d'art de Louvain* 16 (1983) 237–44.

Wirth, T., "Zum Bildprogramm der Räume n und p in der Casa dei Vettii," *RM* 90 (1983) 449–55.

Zevi, F., ed., *Pompei 79: Raccolta di studi per il decimonono centenario dell'eruzione vesuviana* (Naples 1984).

Stucco

Ling, R., "Gli stucchi," in F. Zevi ed., *Pompei 79: Raccolta di studi per il decimonono centenario dell'eruzione vesuviana* (Naples 1984) 145–60.
———, "Stucco Decoration in Pre-Augustan Italy," *BSR* 40 (1972) 11–57.
Martin, R., "Sur l'origine des décors en stuc dans l'architecture hellénistique," *Rayonnement grec: Hommages à C. Delvoye* (Brussels 1982) 247–62.
Mielsch, H., "Neronische und flavische Stuckreliefs in den Vesuvstädten," in B. Andreae and H. Kyrieleis eds., *Neue Forschungen in Pompeji* (Recklinghausen 1975) 125–28.

Mosaics in Houses and Villas

Balty, J., *Mosaïques antiques de Syrie* (Brussels 1977).
Bertacchi, L., "Architettura e mosaico," *Da Aquileia a Venezia: Una mediazione tra l'Europe e l'Oriente dal 2. secolo A.C. al 6. secolo A.C. (Antica madre: Collana di studi sull'Italia antica*, Milan 1980).
Blanchard-Lemée, M., *Maisons à mosaïques du quartier central de Djemila (Cuicul) (Études d'antiquités africaines*, Paris 1975).
Clarke, J. R., "Kinesthetic Address and the Influence of Architecture on Mosaic Composition in Three Hadrianic Bath Complexes at Ostia," *Architectura* 5 (1975) 1–17.
———, "The Origins of Black-and-White Figural Mosaics in the Region Destroyed by Vesuvius," *La regione sotterrata dal Vesuvio: Studi e prospettive, Atti del convegno internazionale 11–15 Novembre 1979* (Naples 1982) 661–88.
III Colloquio internazionale sul mosaico antico, Ravenna, 1980 (Ravenna 1983).
Daszewski, W. A., "Die Fußboden-Dekoration in Haüsern und Palästen des griechisch-römischen Ägypten," in *Palast und Hütte (Alexander von Humboldt-Stiftung. Symposium* 6, Mainz 1982) 395–402.
Dunbabin, K., *The Mosaics of Roman North Africa: Studies in Iconography and Patronage (Oxford Monographs on Classical Archaeology*, Oxford 1978).
Février, P.-A., "Images, imaginaire et symbolisme: À propos de deux maisons du Maghreb antique," in *Mosaïque: Recueil d'hommages à Henri Stern* (Paris 1983) 159–62.
Jobst, W., and H. Vetters, *Römische Mosaiken aus Ephesos: I. Die Hanghäuser des Ephesos (Forschungen in Ephesos* 8, 2, Vienna 1977).
Joyce, H., "Form, Function and Technique in the Pavements of Delos and Pompeii," *AJA* 83 (1979) 253–63.
Kondoleon, C., *The Mosaics of the House of Dionysos at Paphos* (Ithaca, forthcoming).
Lavagne, H., "*Luxuria inaudita*: Marcus Aemilius Scaurus et la naissance de la mosaïque murale," in *Mosaïque: Recueil d'hommages à Henri Stern* (Paris 1983) 259–64.
Mosaïque: Recueil d'hommages à Henri Stern (Paris 1983).
Parrish, D., "The Mosaic of Xenophon and the Seasons from Sbeitla (Tunisia)," in *Mosaïque: Recueil d'hommages à Henri Stern* (Paris 1983) 297–306.

Picard, G.-C., "Mosaïques reflétant des voûtes en Gaule," in *Mosaïque: Recueil d'hommages à Henri Stern* (Paris 1983) 307–10.

———, "La villa du Taureau à Silin (Tripolitaine)," *CRAI* (1985) 227–41.

Sarnowski, T., *Les représentations de villas sur les mosaïques africaines tardives (Archiwum filologiczne* 37, Wroclaw 1978).

Sear, F. B., *Roman Wall and Vault Mosaics (RM-EH* 23, Heidelberg 1977).

Stern, H., "La funzione del mosaico nella casa antica," *Mosaici in Aquileia e nell'alto adriatico, 1975 (Antichità altoadriatiche* 8, 1975) 39–57.

Ensembles

Barbet, A., "Quelques rapports entre mosaïques et peintures murales à l'époque romaine," in *Mosaïque: Recueil d'hommages à Henri Stern* (Paris 1983) 43–53.

Bek, L., *Towards Paradise on Earth: Modern Space Conception in Architecture, A Creation of Renaissance Humanism (AnalRom* suppl. 9, 1980).

Blanchard-Lemée, M., "La 'Maison de Bacchus' à Djemila: Architecture et décor d'une grande demeure provinciale à la fin de l'antiquité," *Bulletin archéologique du Comité des antiquaires de France* 17 (1981) 131–42.

Bragantini, I., and F. Parise Badoni, "Il quadro pompeiano nel suo contesto decorativo," *DialArch* n.s. 2 (1984) 119–28.

Clarke, J., "Notes on the Coordination of Wall, Floor, and Ceiling Decoration in the Houses of Roman Italy, 100 B.C.–A.D. 235," in M. Lavin ed., *IL60: Essays Honoring Irving Lavin on His Sixtieth Birthday* (New York, forthcoming).

———, "Relationships between Floor, Wall, and Ceiling Decoration at Rome and Ostia Antica: Some Case Studies," *Bulletin d'information de l'Association internationale pour l'étude de la mosaïque antique* 10 (1985) 93–103.

Joyce, H., *The Decoration of Walls, Ceilings and Floors in Italy in the Second and Third Centuries A.D. (Archaeologica* 17, Rome 1981).

Jung, F., "Gebaute Bilder," *AntK* 27 (1984) 71–122.

Lafon, X., "À propos des *villae* républicaines: Quelques notes sur les programmes décoratifs et les commanditaires," *L'Art décoratif à Rome à la fin de la république et au début du principat. Table ronde, Rome, 1979 (Collection de l'École Française de Rome* 55, Rome 1981) 151–72.

McKay, A. G., "Roman Interior Furnishing and Decoration," *Houses, Villas, and Palaces in the Roman World* (Ithaca 1975) 136–55.

Strocka, V. M., ed., *Casa del Principe di Napoli (VI 15, 7.8) (Deutsches archäologisches Institut. Häuser in Pompeji* 1, Tübingen 1984).

Tran Tam Tinh, *La Casa dei Cervi a Herculaneum (Archaeologica* 74, Rome 1989).

Vos, M. de, "Die Casa di Ganimede in Pompeji VII 13,4. Pavimenti e pitture: Terzo e quarto stile negli scarichi trovati sotto i pavimenti," *RM* 89 (1982) 315–52.

———, "Pittura e mosaico a Solunto," *BABesch* 50 (1975) 195–205.

———, "Scavi nuovi sconosciuti (I 9, 13.): Pitture e pavimenti della casa di Cerere a Pompei," *MededRom* 38 (1976) 37–75.

Zanker, P., *The Power of Images in the Age of Augustus* (Ann Arbor 1988).

———, "Die Villa als Vorbild des späten pompejanischen Wohngeschmacks," *JdI* 94 (1979) 460–523.

Zevi, F., *La Casa Reg. IX. 5, 18–21 a Pompei e le sue pitture (StMisc* 5, Rome 1964).

Social History

Andreau, J. P., "Remarques sur la société pompeienne," *DialArch* 7 (1973) 213–54.

Castrén, P., *Ordo Populusque Pompeianus: Polity and Society in Roman Pompeii* (*ActaInst-RomFin* 8, 1975).

D'Arms, J., *Commerce and Social Standing in Ancient Rome* (Cambridge, Mass. 1981).

———, "Control, Companionship, and *Clientela*: Some Social Functions of the Roman Communal Meal," *Studies in Roman Society* (*EchCl* 28, n.s. 3, 1984) 327–48.

———, *Romans on the Bay of Naples: A Social and Cultural Study of the Villas and Their Owners from 150 B.C. to A.D. 400* (Cambridge, Mass. 1970).

Friedlaender, L., *Roman Life and Manners under the Early Empire*, trans. C. A. Magnus (London 1908).

Garnsey, P., *Social Status and Legal Privilege in the Roman Empire* (Oxford 1970).

Garnsey, P., and R. P. Saller, *The Roman Empire: Economy, Society and Culture* (Berkeley and Los Angeles 1987).

MacMullen, R., "Personal Power in the Roman Empire," *AJP* 107 (1986) 512–24.

Marquardt, J., *Das Privatleben der Römer* (A. Mau ed., *Handbuch der römischen Alterthümer* 7, 1, 2d ed. Leipzig 1886).

Pavolini, C., *La vita quotidiana ad Ostia* (Rome and Bari 1986).

Saller, R. P., "*Familia, Domus,* and the Roman Conception of the Family," *Phoenix* 38 (1984) 336–55.

———, *Personal Patronage under the Early Empire* (Cambridge 1982).

Shaw, B., "The Family in Late Antiquity: The Experience of Augustine," *Past and Present* 115 (May 1987) 3–51.

Veyne, P., ed., *A History of Private Life: I. From Pagan Rome to Byzantium* (Cambridge, Mass. and London 1987).

Wallace-Hadrill, A., "The Social Structure of the Roman House," *BSR* 56 (1988) 43–97.

Wallace-Hadrill, A., ed., *Patronage in Ancient Society* (*Leicester-Nottingham Studies in Ancient Society* 1, London and New York 1989).

Zanker, P., *Pompeji: Stadtbilder als Spiegel von Gesellschaft und Herrschaftsform* (Mainz 1988).

Plates

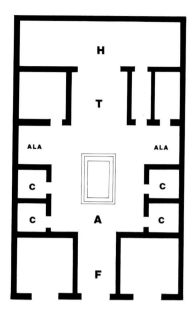

Fig. 1-1. Plan of the ideal
Pompeian house
A = atrium
C = cubiculum
F = fauces
H = hortus
T = tablinum

Fig. 1-2. Atrium and *tablinum* of the House of Cornelius Rufus with ancestor portrait, Pompeii

Fig. 1-3. Plaster model of the House of Diana at Ostia Antica, by I. Gismondi

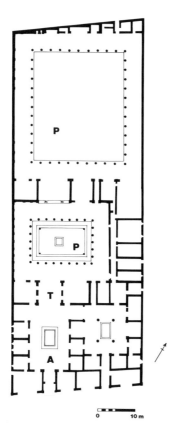

Fig. 1-4. Plan of the House of
the Faun, Pompeii
A = atrium
P = peristyle
T = *tablinum*

Fig. 1-5. View of the atrium and *tablinum* of the House of the Faun,
Pompeii

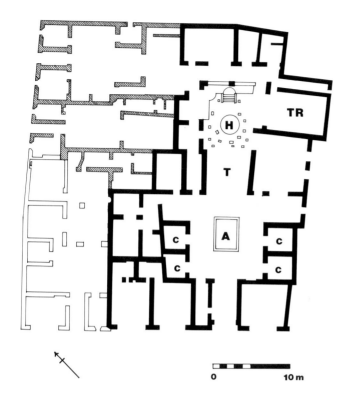

Fig. 1-6. Plan of the House of
Marcus Lucretius, Pompeii
A = atrium
C = cubiculum
H = hortus
T = tablinum
TR = triclinium

0   10 m

Fig. 1-7. Atrium, *tablinum,* and garden of the House of Marcus
Lucretius, Pompeii

Fig. 1-8. Fourth Style wall decoration in the House of Siricus, Pompeii, taken around 1865

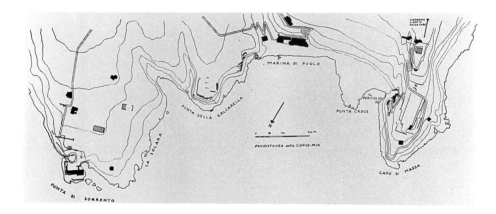

Fig. 2-1. Map of the capes of Sorrento, Calcarella, and Massa

Fig. 2-2. Detail of a wall painting, in situ, House of Lucretius Fronto, Pompeii (V iv a [or 11])

Fig. 2-3. Detail of a wall painting, Stabia Antiquarium 2518

Fig. 2-4. Detail of a wall painting, in situ, House of the Stags,
Herculaneum (IV 21)

Fig. 2-5. Detail of mosaic decoration, in situ, nymphaeum, Suburban Baths, Pompeii

Fig. 2-6. Upper half of a peristyle wall, in situ, House of the Little Fountain, Pompeii (Vi viii 23)

Fig. 2-7. Detail of a wall painting, in situ, House of the Menander, Pompeii (I x 4)

Fig. 2-8. Detail of a wall painting, Naples Archaeological Museum 949

Fig. 2-9. Detail of a wall painting, Naples Archaeological Museum
9511

Fig. 2-10. Detail of a wall painting, Stabia Antiquarium 4826

Fig. 2-11. Detail of a wall painting, Naples Archaeological Museum 9480

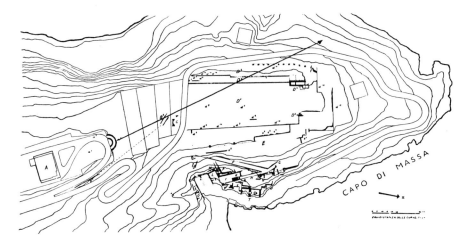

Fig. 2-12. Plan of Capo di Massa with author's indication of vista direction

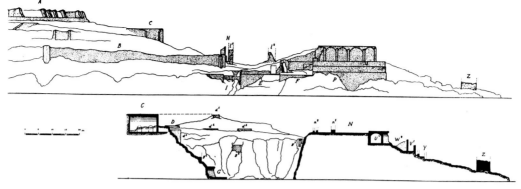

Fig. 2-13. Drawing of remains of substructures on Capo di Massa

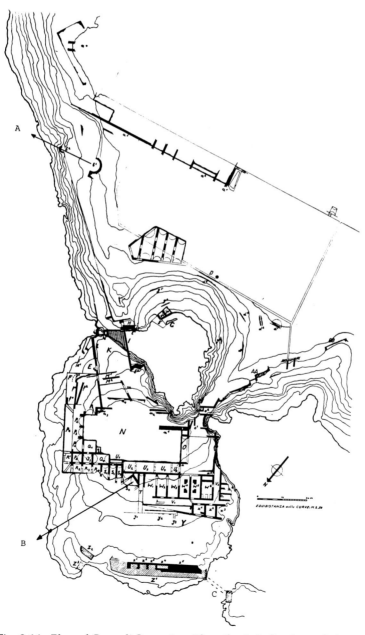

Fig. 2-14. Plan of Capo di Sorrento with author's indications of vista directions

Fig. 2-15. Detail of a wall
painting, Naples
Archaeological Museum 9414

Fig. 2-16. Yellow panels,
Villa at Oplontis, room 13

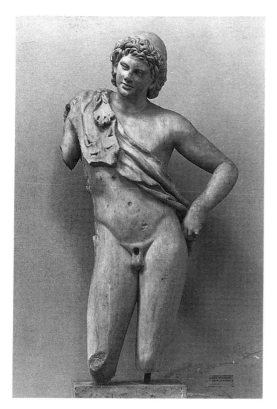

Fig. 3-1. Resting Satyr, Rome, Palazzo dei
Conservatori 2419

Fig. 3-2. Artemis, Herakleion Archaeological
Museum 265

Fig. 3-3. Niobe and her daughter, Herakleion
Archaeological Museum 266

Fig. 3-4. Artemis, Bordeaux,
Musée d'Aquitaine 71.16.1

Fig. 3-5. Aphrodite, Paris,
Musée du Louvre MA 3537

Fig. 3-6. Three Graces,
Cyrene Museum 14.348

Fig. 3-7. Three Graces,
Cyrene Museum 14.346

Fig. 3-8. Satyr and Hermaphrodite, Dresden, Staatliche
Kunstsammlungen, Skulpturensammlungen 155

Fig. 3-9. Satyr and Hermaphrodite, Dresden, Staatliche
Kunstsammlungen, Skulpturensammlungen 156

Fig. 3-10. Menelaos, torso fragment,
Aphrodisias Museum, Geyre

Fig. 3-11. Achilles and Penthesilea,
Aphrodisias Museum, Geyre

Fig. 3-12. Discobolus, Side Museum 93

Fig. 3-13. Discobolus, Side Museum 92

Fig. 3-14. Pothos, Rome,
Palazzo dei Conservatori 2416

Fig. 3-15. Pothos, Rome,
Palazzo dei Conservatori 2417

Fig. 3-16. Reconstruction drawing of the *domus* under the Via Cavour, Rome

Fig. 3-17. Restoration of an aedicular wall in the interior of building *M* at Side

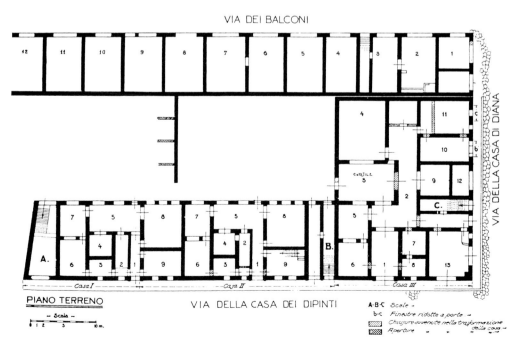

Fig. 4-1. The Insula dei Dipinti with the House of Jupiter and Ganymede, Ostia Antica (I iv 2)

Fig. 4-2. Red Figure Bell-Krater, London, British Museum

Fig. 4-3. Silver cup with homoerotic scene, private collection, on anonymous loan to the British Museum

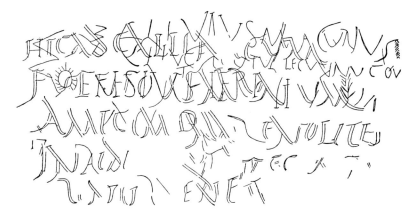

Fig. 4-4. Graffito in the "guest room" of the House of Jupiter and Ganymede

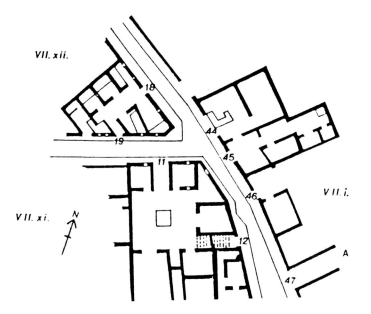

VII. xii.

18

19

44

45

46

11

12

47

A

VII. i.

VII. xi.

N

Fig. 4-5. Plan with Lupanar, Pompeii (VII xii 18–20)

Fig. 4-6. House of Jupiter and Ganymede, room 4, view of the east wall

Fig. 4-7. House of Jupiter and Ganymede, room 4, east wall, detail of the central picture

Fig. 4-8. House of Jupiter and Ganymede, room 4, author's tracing of the east wall, central picture

Fig. 4-9. Amphora by the Phrynos Painter, Würzburg HA 47

Fig 4-10. House of Jupiter and Ganymede, room 4, author's reconstruction of the east wall, central picture

Fig. 4-11. Leda and the
Swan, Rome, Capitoline
Museum 302

Fig. 4-12. Leda and the
Swan, Pompeii, House of the
Vettii, room *e*, south wall,
upper zone, center

Fig. 4-13. Drawing of a silver
cup from Cullera, Spain;
Paris, Musée Dutuit

Fig. 4-14. Drawing of a lost sarcophagus of Leda and Ganymede from Rome; Berlin, Codex Coburgensis

Fig. 4-15. Leda from *Las Incantadas*, Thessalonika; Paris, Musée du Louvre 1394a

Fig. 5-1. Orpheus mosaic from the House of Orpheus, Volubilis

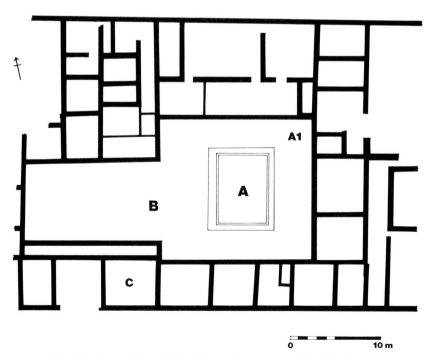

0   10 m

Fig. 5-2. Partial plan of the House of Dionysos, Nea Paphos

Fig. 5-3. Hunt mosaic, detail from the east portico of the atrium-peristyle, House of Dionysos, Nea Paphos

Fig. 5-4. Hunt mosaic, detail from the north portico of the atrium-peristyle, House of Dionysos, Nea Paphos

Fig. 5-5. Amphitheater mosaic from a villa at Zliten

Fig. 5-6. Amphitheater mosaic from a villa at Zliten, detail

Fig. 5-7. Relief sculpture of gladiators, Pompeii

Fig. 5-8. Mosaic from Kos, detail of hunters and acrobats

Fig. 5-9. Mosaic from Kos, detail of Judgment of Paris

Fig. 5-10. Ganymede mosaic, House of the Arsenal, Sousse

Fig. 5-11. Triumph of Dionysos mosaic from the *triclinium*, House of Dionysos, Nea Paphos

Fig. 5-12. Triumph of Dionysos mosaic from the *triclinium*, detail of Dioscuros, House of Dionysos, Nea Paphos

Fig. 5-13. Seasons mosaic, House of Dionysos, Nea Paphos

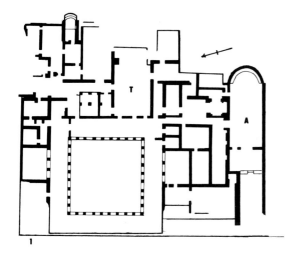

Fig. 6-1. Houses with audience chambers: (1) the villa above the theater, Ephesus; (2) the "Governor's Palace," Aphrodisias; (3) the "Palace of the Dux," Apollonia
A = audience hall
T = *triclinium*

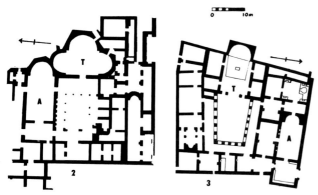

Fig. 6-2. Houses with multi-apsed grand dining halls: (1) House of Bacchus Djemila; (2) the "Palace of Theodoric," Ravenna; (3) Villa at Mediana, near Niš
G = grand dining hall
T = *triclinium*

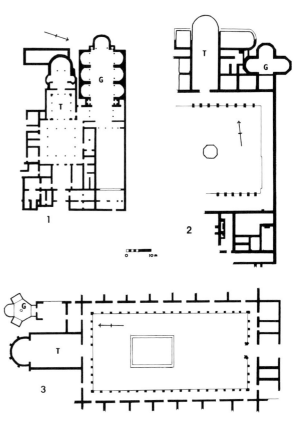

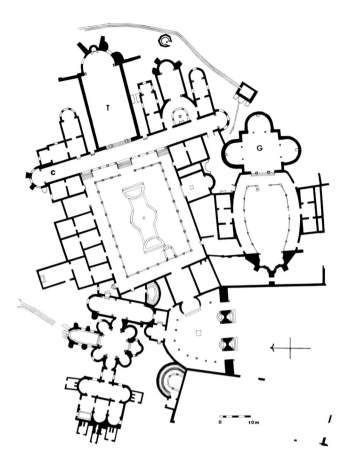

Fig. 6-3. Plan of Piazza
Armerina
C = corridor
G = grand dining hall
T = *triclinium*

Fig. 6-4. Drawing after the
mosaic from the seven-apsed
dining hall in the House of
Bacchus, Djemila

Fig. 6-5. The Great Hunt mosaic of Piazza Armerina, showing the owner or bailiff

Fig. 6-6. Drawing after the
central panel of the mosaic in
the grand dining hall of the
"Palace of Theodoric,"
Ravenna, showing
Bellerophon and the Chimera

Fig. 6-7. Drawing after the mosaic from the triconch, Piazza
Armerina